Law's Evolution and Human Understanding

Law's Evolution and Human Understanding

Laurence Claus

OXFORD
UNIVERSITY PRESS

OXFORD
UNIVERSITY PRESS

Oxford University Press is a department of the University of Oxford. It furthers the University's objective of excellence in research, scholarship, and education by publishing worldwide.

Oxford New York
Auckland Cape Town Dar es Salaam Hong Kong Karachi Kuala Lumpur Madrid
Melbourne Mexico City Nairobi New Delhi Shanghai Taipei Toronto

With offices in
Argentina Austria Brazil Chile Czech Republic France Greece Guatemala Hungary
Italy Japan Poland Portugal Singapore South Korea Switzerland Thailand
Turkey Ukraine Vietnam

Published in the United States of America by
Oxford University Press
198 Madison Avenue, New York, NY 10016

Library of Congress Cataloging-in-Publication Data
Claus, Laurence.
Law's evolution and human understanding / Laurence Claus.
p. cm.
Includes bibliographical references and index.
ISBN 978-0-19-973509-9 ((hardback) : alk. paper)
1. Law—Philosophy. I. Title.
K237.C53 2012
340.1—dc23
2012008784

Note to Readers
This publication is designed to provide accurate and authoritative information in regard to the subject matter covered. It is based upon sources believed to be accurate and reliable and is intended to be current as of the time it was written. It is sold with the understanding that the publisher is not engaged in rendering legal, accounting, or other professional services. If legal advice or other expert assistance is required, the services of a competent professional person should be sought. Also, to confirm that the information has not been affected or changed by recent developments, traditional legal research techniques should be used, including checking primary sources where appropriate.

(Based on the Declaration of Principles jointly adopted by a Committee of the American Bar Association and a Committee of Publishers and Associations.)

For Paul and Gloria

CONTENTS

Law's Evolution and Human Understanding

CHAPTER 1

What Makes Words Law?

This book is for anyone who has noticed that life cannot avoid encountering law. "It's the law," we hear people say to us, as if that news is supposed to affect how we live. What makes some sayings *law*? When a saying is the law, what difference should that make to us? This book is about the answers to those questions. What we understand law to *be* affects how we use it. What we understand law to be affects how we work out what law's words mean. What we understand law to be affects how law helps us when we are deciding what to do each day.

Law is words, only words—signs, sounds, symbols that people use to communicate with each other. Words in themselves cannot have purposes, goals, perspectives, rights, or duties. Only *people* can have those things. To claim that *law* has a purpose or goal is really to claim that people's attention to law has a purpose or goal. People attend to law in the same two ways that they attend to other communications—by giving and by receiving. People *contribute* to law's evolution, and people *consult* the law as it is from moment to moment. If people share a purpose in contributing to and consulting law, we might as shorthand say that the law has a purpose. This book suggests we can rightly say that, and learn a lot from that purpose about what law is, what it means, and what to do with it.

For what purpose do people consult the law? Why do we ever go to see lawyers? Not to learn the difference between right and wrong. Rarely would any of us think of lawyers as the best people to ask about moral truth. Neither the people who directly contribute to law's evolution, nor the people whom we pay to tell us about law, are necessarily better than anyone else at thinking about what is actually good, about what is actually the right thing to do. What lawyers distinctively offer us is *prediction*. In deciding what to do, we consult lawyers when we want to know what other people in law's community will likely do and expect in relation to what *we* might do. If I am thinking of promising to pay a lot of money in exchange for someone else's promise to sell me his business, I want to know how to act to make things most likely to happen the way I am hoping they will. Whether things happen that way depends on how the would-be seller acts, but if I do not know him well, my confidence about how he will act can be increased by knowing how other people will probably behave in relation to the two of us. If he breaks his promises at any point, will others within the community help me? What can I do to make it most likely that some of those whom my community calls government officials will back me up and force the seller to keep his promises, or to compensate me for having broken his word? With a lot of money at stake, it is worth consulting lawyers to give myself the best understanding I can get about how others will likely act in relation to an action I am contemplating. But law helps us understand what others are likely to do and to expect in many daily choices of action that must be made much faster, albeit not necessarily with lower stakes. When in driving toward an intersection I encounter a red traffic light, my life and the lives of others may depend on my ability to understand what that signal is telling me about the likely actions and expectations of others. That red light conveys the same message in my community as the English-language word "stop." It tells me not only what people whom my community calls police will likely do if I drive through it on their watch, but also what drivers coming toward the intersection from another direction will likely do and what they will likely expect of me, and therefore what I should do if I want to improve my chances of surviving the drive and not harming anyone.

If the purpose that people share when consulting the law is to find out what others will likely do and expect, that fact has to shape the purpose of those who contribute to law's evolution. What do law's contributors think they are accomplishing when they express themselves in words that lawyers will later tell clients about? If asked, they may say they are instructing; in substance, they are *informing*. In any human community, an opportunity to contribute to the law of that community is an opportunity to communicate a kind of information that those who consult that law want to know. What kind of information is that? It is information about what people in that community will likely do and expect. That is the common denominator that explains our shared attention to law. When people do things for the purpose of contributing to law and when people do things for the purpose of finding out what law is, they all share a core purpose of prediction. We have always seen that law helps us predict the behavior of others. This book will explain why we should see law as all about prediction. When a lawgiver "decides" what people will do and tells them so, she really just predicts what they will do and expect. This fact lets us say as shorthand that prediction is the irreducible, essential *purpose* of law.

Both those who contribute to law and those who consult law may think that their actions will have good consequences or are for some other reason the right thing to do, but that need not be true, and in fact, in our human experience, it sometimes isn't. Moralizing about choices to contribute to or consult law is commonplace, but not always honest. Sometimes it just covers for drives to dominate or to possess. Morality talk is no good guide to the full range of people's real motivations for contributing to or consulting law. People can be wonderful. People can be awful. Their reasons for contributing to or consulting law may often accurately be characterized in one of those ways or the other. But among those reasons, motives, purposes, what is always shared by those who seek to contribute to or learn about the law of a human community is the purpose of contributing to or learning about what people in that community will likely do and expect.

Law is, as Oliver Wendell Holmes famously phrased it, "systematized prediction."[1] Every human community has evolved its own unique prediction source, its own signaling system[2] for what people in that community are likely to do and to expect. Community comes through communication. We have law anywhere humans have talked to each other enough to form a group identity.[3] As community identity evolves, that evolution is expressed through a cross-referenced system of communications that both insiders and outsiders understand to be the *law* of that community. What do they understand the expressions of community we call law to achieve? They may have all sorts of hopes for what those expressions will achieve, which is just to say, they may have all sorts of hopes for the character of life in that community. But the common denominator of achievement, the essence of what makes those expressions of community always seem worth contributing and consulting, is *understanding each other better*—understanding what distinctively follows from the fact of community for what those in it are likely to do and to expect.

A theory of law that sees this is not limited to communities that we might call nation states. It is not limited to community institutions that we often call government. It applies to systems of communications that signal the character of life in even the most simple communities, such as the expressed customs of people who live together in small numbers as hunter-gatherers, and in even the most savage communities, such as the rules of a Manhattan co-op.

Law is not a morality meter. What law signals and what people *ought* to do are not always the same thing. In some human communities at some moments in history, they are *often* not the same thing. Historic claims that they *are* the same thing have often been immoral, manipulative efforts by some humans to control others. Once we understand our community's legal system to be a purely predictive signaling system, we can see that its value to us does not depend on claims that those who contribute to law have a "because I said so" right to be obeyed. And our human history affords strong reason to suspect that those claims were never true. Even coming from the lips of exasperated parents, "because I said so" draws whatever moral force it seems to have from an altogether different reason for attention, namely, expertise at living. Parents sometimes say "because I said so" when they are just too impatient to explain why what they say is truly the right thing to do; right not merely because the parent says it, but right all things considered. Parents rightly tell young children that parents know better. During teenage years, as the plausibility of that claim begins to recede and nascent adults begin to contest it, parents tend to shift rhetoric away from "because I said so" and toward a totally different basis for attention, namely, "while you're under my roof." Now the assertion is no longer that the parent knows best. Maybe the teenager's musical tastes are superior, but those whom the legal system signals to have what that system calls property rights can make a moral argument for those rights, including the right to decide what music is played (and at what volume) on premises called theirs.

Why am I raising the specter of recent parenting problems or unhappy childhood memories by going on about "because I said so"?

Because the philosophers who over our history have most busied themselves with talking about what counts as law have mostly argued or assumed that words can be law only if those words come from people who imitate exasperated parents—people who claim that they can rightly say: "because I said so." The claim of *authority* in the historic sense of a "because I said so" right to be obeyed has been very widely treated as a defining ingredient of law and government. But it is not, and this book is meant to help make that clearer, by suggesting how law's evolution likely happened with no thanks to any such thing. The *claim* of authority has often been present when law appeared, but that correlation was not necessarily causation. The claim of authority seems especially unlikely to be part of what makes words law if authority actually never exists. Most of us would now acknowledge that the arguments used to support ancient authority claims were bad, and that the motives of many who historically claimed authority were worse. To the tale of authority, we shall return.

Being predictive is not enough to distinguish the words we call law from many other things that we say to each other. To separate law from all the rest, we need at least one more essential feature. Fortunately, we can readily recognize a feature of law that really is unique, freeing us to forsake and ignore false claims of right to be obeyed. We find what truly distinguishes law in Holmes's key phrase. Law is *systematized* prediction. Holmes just threw those words out in a public speech, revealing only a fraction of their explanatory power. Modern systems theory[4] helps us comprehend the concept more fully. Law's signals of what people are likely to do and to expect emerge within a system that grows itself.[5] Law's signals can predict the potential for further predictions, signaling who in law's community is likely to succeed in adding effective signals to the system. In this way, a system evolves sequences of signals, which we may visualize as emanating from a core or descending in a hierarchy. Those branching sequences of signals credential potential signalers with signaled scope for likely success at starting new branches, adding to the system through further effective signals of likely behavior and expectation.

Instead of seeing the legal system as a pyramid down which is delegated a right to be obeyed, we can take law's *systemic* nature more seriously and find a more accurate way to think about how legal systems work. Law signals who in law's community is likely to be effective at issuing self-fulfilling predictions that shape the actions and expectations of people in that community. Law evolves because to live in community is ever to be looking to the left and to the right, seeking to understand the likely attitudes, actions, and expectations of the people with whom we live. Law evolves in tandem with the life of a human community, so that law's signals form a self-perpetuating system, ever expanding like the universe from the community's earliest beginnings. In human relations, there is never "law" without an "of" immediately following, and that "of" always turns our gaze to a human community.

The law of a community is the *expression* of its *customs*. As we will discuss in chapters 2 and 7, when our group grows beyond people we personally know, one mode of conveying to others those behavioral regularities we call group customs takes center stage—the mode of using *words*. The signs, sounds, and symbols of a group language let us communicate even beyond those with whom we interact personally. The moment when we expand beyond those personally known is the moment when linguistic description of custom becomes critical. It is also the moment when we need a way to have many more customs that will let us live with people we do not know by letting us understand much more about those unknown people—what they are likely to do, what they are likely to expect. That is the moment when our customs of following leaders come into their own. Our leaders supply self-fulfilling expressions of many more customs. And those expressions, along with our existing descriptions of group customs, are what we come to call . . . laws.

We have always known that law helps us predict what others in our community will likely do and expect, but too often when consulting law for this purpose we have mistakenly seen ourselves as mere observers of a separate, active reality called the exercise of authority. In truth, the reality is just us. Prediction is not passive when it converges with the predictions of others and is about our life together in community. Systematized prediction is active, it self-fulfills its predictions, it is human community listening and talking to itself.[6] We experience law authentically as a conversation about who we together are and who we together are becoming. To be law is to be predictive, to be systemic, and to belong uniquely to a human community. The law of a human community is dedicated and devoted to telling truths about the character of life in that community, the community which that law defines and to which that law belongs.

CHAPTER 2

How Law Grows Up in a Group

In any human community, there are just people doing actions, forming attitudes, and nursing expectations. What we say to each other can help us do all three things better. The sayings that are law in our community join the rest of our life experience in helping us decide from moment to moment what to do and what to think.

Law lets us live with people we do not know. In a small group, we can hope to know each other through personal interaction, at least enough to live together. Our direct communications with each other, including our uses of a group language to talk, help us discover truths about each other, and so understand each other in the ways we need to do if our lives in community are to flourish. But how do we live together in a big group? Law is our answer to that question. Law is the way our growing group uses our group language to fulfill our need to understand those in the group whom we do not know, to learn about people we may never have met. Law tells us what those people are likely to do and to expect, just because they are in our group. And like many other communications among us, law has a self-fulfilling effect—law helps make true what law expresses. Law lets us *expect* of people we do not know.

Have you ever tried to work with someone from whom you could *not* expect anything much, someone who proved to be unpredictable? How was it for you? In our lives together, spontaneity has a precious place. But it is a small place. If our relations with each other are to grow in depth and duration, we must be able to *expect* of each other. That, after all, is what lets us look forward to good things in life. As Niklas Luhmann observed of our deepest human relations, of love: "One finds oneself expected in the worldview of the other as the person one endeavours to be. . . . Accompanying this . . . is . . . a reciprocal expecting of expectations and of all that this implies: joyfulness of steps coming through the door, and the certainty of thinking the same thing at the same moment."[1]

As sane people, we cannot nurture and sustain the expectations that grow relationships, whether in business or pleasure, if the buds of expectation are too often savaged by disappointment. Instead, we rationally give up and move on to other, more predictable people. Within ourselves we may feel a certain tension between the benefits of belonging in real relationships, with all of the expectations that they allow and introduce, and the allure of adventure, of acting unpredictably. But we know that relationships mostly make reliability worthwhile. Even when tempted to do differently, most of us would readily concede the great value of all the reciprocal expecting that shapes most of our work and play.

What has any of this to do with law? Law expresses the expectation that comes from community.[2] The law of any community gives us a heads-up on what others in that group will likely do and expect just because they are *in the group*. This lets us relate to them without the kind of individualized, personalized knowledge that might otherwise be essential for any kind of trust. We are willing to risk driving on the same roads as strangers without actually knowing what they are thinking. Likewise, we willingly transact all sorts of business with them. Our lives would be much less interesting and much less productive if the risks in doing those things were too high to tolerate. What makes risk tolerable is the expectation of others' behavior that the law of our communities helps us have.

How did we get law? How did we humans find a way to express what our lives in community would be like? Imagine the beginnings of a new community, perhaps one emerging from an accident, like the group of children marooned together on a desert island in William Golding's staple from high school English class, *Lord of the Flies.*[3] Living together is unavoidable—the accident has deposited quite a number of us here, and the island is just not that large. That seems a fair metaphor for the lives of our human billions, who mostly must cluster in large numbers in the habitable spaces of this little planet.

The first thing to notice when we are looking for law in a group is talk about "what we do" or "what is done" in the group. When actions work well, when we see consequences that seem good to us or we otherwise sense goodness in what happened, our intelligent minds tend to return to those actions. Successful repetition reinforces our sense of actions' rightness *for us*. In a small group whose life together works through direct communication with each other, we may start to see support added for some of the things we say to each other through expressions such as "our practice has been to do that," or "that is our way." For example, if in early days on the island some of the children managed to get a fire going or to catch some food by working together in a particular way, that record of success may become part of the reason that some of them express for trying the same action again. Notice that while perceptions of goodness may help turn behaviors into customs, once they are customs, that fact is worth knowing even when we think that some other behavior might be better. The behavior that is custom is what others in the group will likely do and expect, and anyone in the group who is contemplating doing differently needs to weigh the likely consequences of disappointing expectations against whatever good might come from doing differently. Elman Service observed:

> Very powerful forces of social control inhere in small face-to-face societies; this is especially so in primitive societies where the individual normally spends his whole life among his kinsmen. Since escape is impossible he cannot recover by moving to some new group the esteem he might have lost by a social mistake in his own group. Cooperation, alliance, love, reciprocities of all kinds are totally important to the survival of any individual in primitive society. This must be why such people seem so extraordinarily sensitive to the reactions of the group to any social action. Praise and blame, affection and withdrawal, and other such socio-psychological sanctions are extremely powerful reinforcers in small societies of stable membership, and it has been noted over and over by many observers of egalitarian societies how carefully social customs, especially in etiquette, are observed. . . .[4]

The distinction between sayings that express customs and all the other expectant things we say to each other may not be sharply drawn when our numbers are small. Only when we grow in numbers do we really need a way to learn about people we do not know well, a way to understand what strangers are likely to do and to expect. That is when the sayings that express our community customs need to become clear and distinct from all the other expressive and expectant chatter that fills our days. Not only do our customs need to become clearer, but we need more of them. The more that our lives involve relating to people we do not know, the more information about them we need to be able to get from the fact of their membership in our community. How can the evolution of our customs, of who we communally are, be sped up? Through *leadership*, or as we come to call it, *government*.

Leadership may exist among us long before we are conscious of really needing it. We see it in even the smallest groups of chimpanzees.[5] Natural selection supplies an obvious explanation for this prevalence. Groups that are effectively led compete successfully against groups that are not,[6] so we should be unsurprised that the groups of humans who have survived and thrived have had gene pools that reliably produced persons who liked to lead and persons who liked to follow, and that those desires in at least some instances tracked abilities—qualities of body and mind, personality and character, that made some persons "born leaders" and others, instinctive followers.[7] Max Weber described this psychological dynamic within a group as the experience of "charismatic authority."[8] The ancient Romans called it *auctoritas*.

An emerging leadership co-opts custom. We could say that through leadership, custom converts itself into a more nimble, more dextrous, more comprehensive way for us to understand each other in a group.[9] We have leadership when a group evolves a custom of treating the sayings of particular people as expressions of new customs or . . . laws. The mechanism of evolution is human nature, the fact that some people assert themselves within groups and relate to others within groups in such a way that those others are drawn to treating particular assertive persons as leaders. Treating people as leaders means treating them as people whose words succeed self-fulfillingly in signaling what others will likely do and expect.

We have leadership, we have government, whenever someone has succeeded in situating herself as the signaler of what is likely to happen in a group. We say that she has *power*. Power in a group is effectiveness at signaling what people in the group are likely to do and to expect. To lead a group is to succeed in lawgiving, to be able through one's words not merely to repeat long-known group customs, but to predict anew and successfully what will be done and expected within the group. Only actual success at self-fulfillingly signaling what those in the group will likely do and expect makes someone a lawgiver for the group. The lawgiver may have come to power in a way we might call good, such as by a majority vote of everyone in the group, or in a way we might call evil, such as by killing a previous leader and threatening everyone in the group with violence. The lawgiver may be issuing laws that we might call good, or laws that we might call evil. Whether she got the role in a good way, whether she fulfills the role in a good way, are equally irrelevant to whether she really is a lawgiver for the group. She is lawgiver so long as the actual customs that constitute the group's identity include a custom of treating what she says as signaling what those in the group are likely to do and to expect. Notice that someone who succeeds in leading others, whose words succeed in becoming law, will not necessarily claim a *right* to be followed—the following may just happen. In some, there may be genuine desire to follow. But in all there is a common denominator of understanding that *this* is the person who is likely to be followed by everyone else, and whom everyone else will expect everyone to follow.

John Austin, who wrote influentially in the nineteenth century about the nature of law, said that people follow the leader out of a habit of obedience.[10] In fact, our following is *reasoned*, it is not just habitual, and our reasons for following at least include our valuing what the legal system tells us about the likely actions and expectations of others. Our choices to follow the law are not focused on a "sovereign," they are focused on *each other*. We mostly look and listen to leaders because they are channeling through their say-so what everyone is likely to do and to expect, and as that ceases to be true, we tend to stop paying attention to them, which cascades their loss of leadership. Look at how one Tunisian fruit vendor's suicidal response to oppression[11] set off protests that crescendoed into the Arab Spring uprisings that brought down not only the Tunisian government, but those of the neighbors too. Lawgivers risk becoming "so last season" as surely as some clothes designers do, but may endure for decades, much as other trendsetters sometimes do. Our judgments about whose words are law, like our judgments about the condition of the economy or about today's fashions, are all about what we expect others' judgments about those things to be. The rise and fall of leaders, like the booms and busts of the economic cycle and the changes in what is fashionable, happen because our decisions to follow, like our decisions to invest and to consume, are in large part rationally driven by what we expect others to do and to expect. Elections, where they occur, provide a formal outlet for displaying this group dynamic. They usually reflect what Max Weber called a "routinization"[12] of government, an advanced stage in communal evolution. If we were to seek out what H. L. A. Hart called the internal point of view[13] of law inside a human community, we could say that an understanding about the likely actions and expectations of others is not just the central case of that point of view, it is the universally shared aspect of that point of view. Some community members may harbor additional reasons for following, such as love of the leader, but they are optional extras. What makes him the leader is not universal love but universal understanding that everyone is likely to treat him as the leader, that is, as the one whose words will be the best evidence of what everyone will end up doing and expecting.

Imagine that the children on our desert island are never rescued. They grow to become adults, and, if we include young women in our variant of the story, another generation is born under the leadership of the belligerent character who at the end of Golding's novel was seeing off his hapless predecessor. Over time, as the group grows and leading requires more and more lawgiving, our leader might signal that particular other people could speak for him in certain ways, for example, in resolving disputes among members of the group. Then what those people signaled within the scope indicated by the leader would likewise enjoy the status of law of the group—the leader's existing laws would signal scope for other persons to issue additional laws. When those other persons spoke within the scope for speaking that the ultimate leader had signaled, their words would be comparably good evidence of what people in the group were likely to do and to expect, and so would have the same relevance as the ultimate leader's words to everyone's choices each day about what to do. The words both of the ultimate leader and of his officials signaling what people are likely to do and to expect might include signals of what various people are likely to do in reaction to a range of things that others might do. These may include signals of how particular people are likely to react to instances of nonconformity to the predictions of the system. Law often signals punishments for nonconformity by signaling what other persons will likely do to the nonconformist, and in turn signaling adverse consequences for those other persons if they do not follow through and punish as predicted. The highway patrol officer who never issues speeding tickets will likely not keep his job for long.[14]

Suppose that within the group we begin recording the sayings of the ultimate leader and of his officials, so that we more readily remember what people are likely to do and to expect. Suppose that the officials themselves review these recorded messages when deciding what to say next, conscious that to contradict themselves and each other comes at a price, that the community's conformity with what the leadership says will be done and expected depends on everyone understanding from day to day what the leadership is saying. Steadily the legal system grows itself through this expanding network of recorded sayings about what people are likely to do and to expect. The recorded sayings become a consultable guide to life in our community. No one ever had a *right* to dictate the character of that life in community, but a way of living evolved, and it evolved under leadership that itself grew up and outward through evolutionary processes, having at their core the variations in human genetics and genealogy that situate some to lead and most to follow. This is the mechanism of law's evolution.[15] We see it in our records of ancient civilizations, and we see it under only a thin veneer of obfuscating authority rhetoric within our communities now.

Law *evolves* rather than being *created*. What lets people contribute to law is their being credentialed as lawgivers *by existing law,* not by some outside source of right to be obeyed. Even when law appears in a community's beginnings through an initial display of *auctoritas,* of Weberian "charismatic authority," or later through a revolution that breaks with much of a preexisting system, these are still not creationist occurrences. The reality of leadership, even revolutionary leadership, depends upon the evolution of community customs, upon community *response* to the assertions of assertive individuals. So-called "charismatic authority" is not a personal possession, it is a psychological dynamic *among* people in a group. A community's expressed customs of treating persons as leaders are instances of deep, constitutive community law. Words become law by being recognized inside an existing legal system, not from any exercise of rights to be obeyed.[16]

Niklas Luhmann gave us a pioneering vision of law as a self-evolving social system. He recognized that law has a predictive function, one of stabilizing expectations.[17] He saw that law lets us "live in a more complex society, in which personal or interaction mechanisms to secure trust no longer suffice."[18] And he recognized that "there never have been societies without law."[19] But Luhmann argued that law as a system of communication is a subsystem of society that is coordinate (and implicitly, coequal) with, and systemic in the same sense as, other identifiable categories of social communication, including politics, economy, science, and art. And that is where Luhmann and this book part company. Law is more than just another conversation we are having in community. Law is the conversation that is *distinctively* about the character of our life in community. Once we acknowledge, as Luhmann did, that law's function is expectation-shaping for *its society*, that makes law *the* system of communication distinctively about what is likely to be true of human behavior in the group, including human behavior that we may call political or economic or, as with so much of what we do, hopelessly mixed in motivation, purpose, and effect. When people contribute to or consult law, they are doing something specific to one society in a way that no other aspect of human behavior need be. And law, uniquely among Luhmann's candidates for social systems, has a communicative *corpus*—a body of consultable words that *are* the law of the society at any given moment in time, that acknowledge and pedigree each other as such, and that are consulted for what they convey about what people *in the group* are likely to do and to expect across every dimension of social life.[20] The boundary between legal communication and everything else we say expectantly to each other is drawn not, as Luhmann supposed, by whether our words deploy a legal/illegal binary code,[21] but by predictive sequencing that tells the self-fulfilling story of our life together as community in a far more comprehensive and nuanced way than any mere permission-versus-prohibition distinction ever could. Citing the "variety of laws" was one of H. L. A. Hart's most devastating blows against the old Austinian command theory of law.[22] Having a custom of letting a particular person *add to custom,* including by adding customs of letting *additional people* add to custom, is like the old fairy-tale trick of using the promise that one wish will be granted to wish for more wishes to be granted.[23] And as the history of law's evolution in our communities reveals, the trick can work. It can evolve for us a signaling tree, a *system,* that supplies us with intricate detail about what all sorts of people we have never met will likely do and expect in all sorts of situations. If you want to know how to run for office or to start a business in some community, you will likely talk to all sorts of people there and glean valuable information from a wide variety of sources. But the one *system* of information that will be worth consulting just because you are dealing with life in a human *community* is the law of that community. As we humans can be idiosyncratic, and our legal systems are neither exhaustive accounts of our predilections nor necessarily altogether accurate, all those other conversations may well be worth having. Consulting more than law may tell you not only of personal predilections that law does not address but also of likely behaviors and expectations so widespread within a community as to deserve the label *culture,* perhaps even to be considered custom on the same foundational plane as the custom of paying attention to leaders, of recognizing constitutive lawgivers. But if those other conversations flatly contradicted much of what the law told you, then you might start to suspect either that you had been looking in the wrong database and the current law is to be found elsewhere, or that life in that community is too unstable and unpredictable to be worth choosing and change your plans accordingly. That second possibility is a very real one. Achieving a legal system's purpose is a matter of degree, and many human communities at various stages of their evolution have legal systems that fulfill law's function poorly. Life in those communities *is* less predictable, and most people in those communities are literally poorer as a consequence.

HART'S "FUNDAMENTAL OBJECTION"

Let us return to the children's first day on the desert island and suppose that their early exploring does not reveal any source of food or fresh water. Fortunately, a small supply has washed ashore with them, enough to keep them all alive for long enough to look around the island more thoroughly, so long as it is carefully rationed. Imagine that as the day wears on, and their searching in the hot sun leaves them tired, thirsty, and hungry, one child snaps, grabs the little reserve of food and water, and begins devouring it well beyond what he needs to survive.

What should everyone else do? No one *owns* the food and water that is disappearing down the one child's throat. There is no law, no government. Life together is just beginning, and community identity has yet to emerge. Of course we know very well what we *would* do. We would stop him, by whatever means necessary. If we already shared a language, we might first tell him to stop. But what if the water is disappearing very fast? Then the right thing to do might be to move straight to force without forewarning, and physically separate him from whatever is left. In our human relations, force came first, long before language. Notice that the right thing to do would not necessarily track majority opinion. If more than half the children were irrationally consuming more than necessary on that first day, forcibly stopping them might be the right thing for the rational minority to do.

What difference would it make if this incident occurred after we had law and government? Suppose that one assertive child's words had already become the best evidence of what everyone in the group was likely to do and to expect. Never mind how that happened. Maybe the child gave a splendid speech and was elected leader by acclamation. Maybe the child viciously attacked and injured the first person who failed to do as the child said, Tiananmen Square style, and now everyone acts out of fear in precisely the way the child's words predict they will. However the child became leader, let us assume his words now achieve law's function of, as Luhmann put it, "stabilizing expectations" in the group. How then would the leadership, the government, of this evolving community react to someone overconsuming the available food and water? Surely in just the same way as we would act in the pre-law, pre-government "state of nature."[24] With force. Would it make a moral difference whether the leadership had earlier issued a *law* about how much food and water each person would consume per day? Like telling someone to stop in the state of nature, *forewarning* of force would help to justify subsequently using force, by first exhausting communication's potential to prevent bad behavior and achieve the good consequence of stretching the supplies. But using force might sometimes be morally justified even without forewarning, such as when the supplies are disappearing fast. That may be true even of force used by people who are outside government, without any support of law, simply because they happen to be nearby and can stop the harmful behavior. On the other hand, some uses of force might *not* be morally justified, even if the law forewarned of them. If the leader had earlier issued a law saying that anyone who consumed more than a specified share of food and water would be *killed* by specified other people, that would not necessarily justify those other people in killing.

Ultimately, we humans each think through for ourselves the rightness of what we do, including the rightness of individual uses of force against others, regardless of what the law predicts. Notice, however, that in weighing reasons for acting one way or another and deciding what is best to do, the fact that particular action is signaled by our community's legal system adds a *distinctive* reason to do the action. That added reason for action is the good of *having* the legal system—of having a community identity that comes through an effective signaling system to tell us what people in our community are likely to do and to expect. The system's predictive effectiveness depends on our mostly doing what it predicts we will do. That reason for doing what the system predicts we will do varies in weight from one instance of action-choosing to another, depending on how much danger to the system's predictive effectiveness is posed by the particular instance of potential nonconformity *and* depending on how valuable the legal system really is. If a judge disregards existing law when deciding disputes, that obviously hurts law's predictive effectiveness more than if a late night pedestrian jaywalks, so the good of having the legal system deserves more weight in the judge's decision making about what to do than in the pedestrian's. Preserving and promoting the lawgiving effectiveness of a liberal democracy obviously deserves greater weight in anyone's mind than preserving and promoting the lawgiving effectiveness of a kleptocratic dictator. The good of having the legal system may well not outweigh moral reasons that count against doing a signaled action, but the good of having the legal system is obviously a morally *relevant* consideration, something we should and do take into account when deciding whether to do what law predicts we will do.[25]

This little story helps us answer H. L. A. Hart's "fundamental objection" to treating law as all about prediction. Hart observed that "where rules exist, deviations from them are not merely grounds for a prediction that hostile reactions will follow or that a court will apply sanctions to those who break them, but are also a reason or justification for such reaction and for applying the sanctions."[26] Being able to predict what others in our community will likely do and expect is a *good* thing, and a *reason* in itself to reinforce law's predictive effectiveness by ourselves doing what law predicts we will do unless we have morally weightier reasons to do differently. When a community's law signals adverse consequences for those who act contrary to some of law's other signals, law does indeed help to justify doing actions that inflict the predicted adverse consequences. Law provides moral support to those whom law predicts will impose punishments by supplying them with at least one reason they would not otherwise have for doing the action that law predicts: the fact that the predictive effectiveness of the legal system has been staked on the punishment happening. Usually the prediction of punishment will apply to some instance of nonconformity with other predictions of the system, so that the good of preserving and promoting the system's predictive effectiveness both *was* a moral reason for the nonconformist to have done differently and *is* a moral reason for the predicted punisher to punish. Law often also affords other reasons for punishing as predicted, such as by predicting punishments for failing to punish and by warning the person who is in prospect of being punished not to behave in the punishable way. Forewarning morally supports punishing by first exhausting communication's potential for deterrence, partly by helping make the person who is in prospect of being punished more aware of reasons he has *anyway* not to behave in the punishable way. As we will consider further in chapter 6, law often predicts behavior that tracks what we would morally owe each other regardless of what the law said, such as the duty not to overconsume limited supplies in the story just told. And some of what we would morally owe each other anyway is shaped in its concrete detail by expectations of each other's behavior to which various parts of the law contribute. We would have a moral duty not to drive dangerously regardless of what the law said, but that duty owed to other highway users concretely requires that we drive on the side of the road that law signals, because that is what others will expect and therefore is what will in fact minimize the risk of harming them. Forewarnings of punishment may add to awareness of all of these reasons for behavior and morally support punishment by first exhausting mere communication's potential to prevent bad behavior.

All of the reasons for punishment that law contributes deserve some weight in a prospective punisher's thinking about what to do. But none of these reasons preempt or exclude thinking about all the *other* reasons that might exist for *and against* using force as law predicts. Maybe, for example, the predicted punishment is disproportionate and should not be inflicted. Maybe, on the other hand, using force to deter bad behavior or otherwise to prevent harm is morally justified even in some circumstances where the law does *not* predict it. Think back to our overeater on the island. If we rightly judged that the only way to put him off further attempts at hogging the supplies was to tie him up or to thump him, we might be morally justified in doing that whether or not a law predicted our doing so. And that is just as true after we have formed a group identity and have law and government as it is beforehand. Support of sayings from something we hear people tremulously call "the State" is neither always necessary, nor always sufficient, to justify using force. Ultimately, each member of a human community decides for herself what is right to do, weighing the various reasons her conscience tells her she has for and against doing the various actions that life (including law) presents for her contemplation. Legal rules do not exist to relieve us from moral reasoning; legal rules exist to inform us about each other, about what is likely to be done and expected in our community. Rules are vehicles for understanding each other, and therein lies their moral contribution to our own, necessarily personal choices of what to do each day. What law predicts about the character of life in our community is something we have reason to take seriously, but not to the exclusion of everything else that morally matters. Law valuably contributes to our moral reasoning about what to do without any need or basis for us to believe that lawgivers have, or even claim, a "because I said so" right to be obeyed.

CHAPTER 3

The Invention of "Because I Said So"

Sometimes, reality responds to what we say about it. As self-fulfilling predictions, law's words tell us how those around us will likely act and think. Our understanding that law self-fulfillingly predicts how life will be in our community lets law fulfill its potential to tell us about each other. We learn from law both of opportunities that life in community opens up and of constraints that life in community imposes. That knowledge helps us individually choose actions that raise our own prospects of fulfilling our life's potential for flourishing. But why is our history so full of claims that law works in a different way? Why do we so often read and hear that law has something to do with obeying people who have a right to be obeyed?

In search of answers, let us go back to the island and to a time when our leader's leadership, his government, has been around for a while. Everyone has adapted to life on the island. They have found ways to build houses, to grow and to catch food, and to use the island's resources to make other things that enhance their lives. The leader has helped make all of this possible by saying that he will ensure people get to keep what they create, so long as they share a slice of it with him. To make that prediction effective, to ensure that both the keeping and the sharing happen, the leader has appointed people whom he knows well and trusts to help him manage the community in various ways. Through them he collects a share of the community's growing wealth, and to them he pays portions of the take, allowing them to live well too.

Another generation is born, and the leader grows old. Individuals emerge who display the qualities of mind and body that had distinguished the leader among the original group back in those early days on the island. The ultimate leader sees something of himself in them. They restlessly stand out as potential leaders. They are not necessarily children of the current leadership. They begin to question why everyone is paying attention to what the current leadership says. Pointing out that good consequences have come from leadership does not satisfy them—they concede the truth that law and government have achieved good things, but they continue to ask why *they* should not have a chance to lead and to govern.

Well, why not let them? We now know that the law and government of a community can evolve enough to accommodate peaceful sharing and transfers of power among those with talent for leadership. Legal systems that we recognize as advanced can so co-opt the talented and invest them with incentives to work within the system that risks of revolutionary change are reduced, continuity of the system is safeguarded, and substantial predictability of life in the community is preserved. Law and government in a community can become universally recognized to be a way of understanding each other and living together that is bigger and beyond any one person. That is where we are now in many modern societies, but it is not where we were then, back in early communities led by cult of personality. It is not where Libya was in 2010. How would the leader of our island community, and those who share in his leadership, likely respond to reasoning that challenges his leadership? By finding ways to fight it.

Leaders mostly *like* being leaders. An awful lot of what leaders do is clearly driven by desire to keep leading. In even the most sophisticated systems of law and government, we can see that this is true of many who govern. The proportion of their mental energy that politicians spend on trying to stay in office is visibly huge. Those calculations of how to keep leading, how to perpetuate incumbency, are motivators not only for an ultimate leader, but also for everyone who enjoys office thanks to him and who might lose office if he does. The psychological and material rewards of leadership are so often so great, and the prospects for life after leadership so often so poor or unclear, that those who lead tend to clutch leadership as reflexively as we clutch our wallets and purses. We humans hate giving up privileges. At my law school, faculty offices are allocated strictly on the basis of seniority, but once allocated, more senior people cannot change their choices if doing so involves an eviction. It somehow hurts much more to lose than never to have had, a phenomenon that we all know well, and rarely dispute except when on the roller-coaster of romance. When we get to lead, we often come to conceive of our leadership as a *possession,* just as deserving of that description as the personal qualities that helped us get it. We may become addicted to having it, disconsolate without it. J. R. R. Tolkien metaphorically captured power's corrosive effect on character through his depiction of Gollum's emotional enslavement to his Precious, the One Ring to rule them all.[1]

In some other species, and sometimes in our own, leadership is settled by contests of physical strength. But even Lucky Luciano and his fellow mobsters, in choosing to create a crime boss "commission,"[2] could see that a group's law and government cannot fulfill their function of making life more predictable if what will be law next week and who will govern next week are not themselves predictable. And everyone who gets to participate in giving law and governing through a community's experience of "charismatic authority" yearns, as Max Weber memorably put it, to "routinize" their law and government.[3] They want to help it endure by giving it a basis they can talk about other than the transient qualities of a particular person. They want a way to keep calling it their *possession*.[4]

Law and government have helped us humans to evolve concrete ideas of property, of particular people having exclusive *right* to use particular things. Throughout the ancient world, a pattern of argument about leadership that draws on the property idea regularly appears in such historical records as we have. In seeking to say in words why someone should stay leader, those with strong reason to want that, with strong stakes in the existing system, were drawn to arguing that the leader had a *right* to lead, a right to be obeyed—that leadership was his possession, his property. Where did that right come from? From the *source* of the qualities that first made people want to follow the leader. If the qualities *themselves* were the source of right, that would not explain why leadership should last longer than others' feelings of desire to follow. No, the community's experience of charismatic authority had to be cast as a sign of something greater and more enduring—a sign of the leader having been given a right to be obeyed by some source *above and beyond* the group itself. Who could give such a right to someone in a group? Only the creator of the group.

We naturally enough think that what we create, we should get to use as we please, that what we create, we "own." We can easily understand the idea that the creator of humans should be obeyed by humans. That property right to be obeyed might be delegated to human leaders for its more effective use. When giving law and governing, the divinely chosen human leader would be speaking for the divine as surely as the leader's deputies would be speaking for the leader.[5] Law and government could, by this reasoning, be put on a surer footing, by being conceived as a hierarchy of delegated "because I said so" rights to be obeyed. Principles for transferring power that served the interests of incumbents, such as letting the leader choose his successors or calling the leader's children his successors, were consistent with thinking about leadership as like a property right. And that is what we see, almost everywhere we turn, among the records of ancient civilizations.[6] We see it still in the residual rhetoric of the world's most visible formally surviving monarchy. The British queen, whose personal traits of dignity and diligence have deservedly afforded her immense, status-securing respect, nonetheless speaks of "her" subjects under a royal coat of arms whose motto reads **Dieu Et Mon Droit**—God And My Right.

Authority, a "because I said so" right to be obeyed, was a transitional argument that helped us through a phase in our communal evolution.[7] Authority helped us through the time when we humans were moving from experiences of highly personalized leadership in small groups to what we often have now—stable and intricate systems of law and government that shape our lives across space and time far more than the say-so of any one person could ever do. There were moments in our communal histories when the "because I said so" claim may have helped law and government achieve their predictive function, by helping law and government last longer.[8] But once our law and government have grown their own supports, by involving many people and achieving predictable changeovers in personnel through principles distanced from the self-interest of incumbents, we can frankly say that our communities have outgrown the idea of authority. That old idea that once supplied our training wheels for communal continuity is now for us, in Holmes's phrase, "a fifth wheel."[9]

John Locke lived too soon to see this. What he could see was that the idea of authority as a *property* right was wrong and was having bad consequences by supporting badly behaved leaders. But he thought that the idea of authority was still needed for law and government to work. So he recast that idea as one not of *property*, but of *contract*. If people promised to obey someone, then that person had a contractual right to be obeyed and those who had promised put themselves under a corresponding duty to obey.[10]

Locke published his contract argument to support a revolution. He had just returned to England from exile in Holland on the coat-tails of the invading Prince William of Orange. Locke argued that William was morally justified in taking the throne, and the English people were morally justified in treating William as king, because rightful leadership was based on a bargain between a leader and those who were led. The ousted monarch, James II, Locke accused of not having kept the leader's side of the leadership deal. James had been a lousy leader, and his breaches of the leadership contract freed the English people from their contractual obligation to obey him. William had arrived in England at the invitation of some prominent people and had been greeted by sufficient local enthusiasm to count, Locke argued, as the tacit consent of the English people to William's kingship.[11]

Locke was not the first person to think of contract as an alternative reason to obey leaders. We can trace the idea back to Socrates, who mentioned it as one of his reasons for obeying the laws of ancient Athens. But as David Hume was quick to point out, keeping a promise is not what most people think they are doing when they follow the law, and this for the very good reason that most people never actually promise to obey their leaders.[12] Hume's way of putting it was that we are "born to such an obedience."[13] We are mostly born into communities that already have systems of law and government, and we see strong reasons for doing most of the things that law and government say we will do, strong reasons that have nothing to do with keeping a promise to obey. Locke shared with Socrates the idea that we tacitly promise by not leaving our communities—that staying around is an implicit commitment to our communities that includes promising to obey community leaders. That may have been a viable understanding of Locke's and Socrates' own life choices as bohemian gadflies with highly portable, widely appreciated, authentically unique talents. But of course it is a totally unrealistic way to talk about the options that have faced most humans in most communities over the history of this planet.[14] Most of us never choose and really cannot. We are stuck with the community into which we were born and with whatever its law and government is and becomes. Promise keeping does not explain the role that law and government play in our lives. The idea of contract does not help us understand law's contribution to our choices of what to do each day.

The idea of contract does not even help us understand law's contribution to our choices of what *we contribute* to law's evolution. Even when we are acting within institutions that we call government, our choices about whether to do actions that lead people do not turn on whether we think that those people have promised to obey us. We can see that some ways of choosing law and government are better than others, that some laws signal better behavior than do others, and that some of the people who get to govern behave better than do others. But in all of our moral theorizing about how our legal systems should evolve and how best through those systems we should identify particular people to contribute to law from seats in palaces and oval offices and parliaments and congresses and courts and bureaucracies, *nothing turns* on whether we all *consent* to living together in community. Most of us most of the time *must* live in our communities. We have no choice. And we want law and government both to fulfill their predictive function and to predict good things so that we can live together well. The idea that we choose our communities adds nothing to our thinking about how law and government affect what we should do, even how we should use any opportunities we have to affect what law and government become. To borrow from the comedian Eddie Izzard, for most of us most of the time, choosing whether to belong to our communities would be like answering the query "cake or death?"[15]

Facing the fact that we mostly do not promise to obey our leaders, some theorists have followed up on Locke's ambiguous idea of *tacit* consent and argued that even if nothing people do expresses or even implies an actual promise to obey leaders, some leadership might be so good that people *should* be willing to promise to obey.[16] An appropriate response to this argument would be: "whatever for?" How *good* a government is, whether in its constitution or its operation or both, does not help explain why anyone in it should, let alone would, have a "because I said so" right to be obeyed. How good a government is *does* help explain why that government does *not need* a "because I said so" right to be obeyed in order for what that government says mostly to be what we should do. If you had a horrible parent who was forever saying "because I said so" when telling you not to eat your greens and not to brush your teeth and not to do your homework, the *right* thing to do on many days might have been different from what the parent said. If you had a wise friend who of course never uttered the words "because I said so," that wise friend's advice nonetheless might well have often been the *right* thing to do. A good government is like a wise friend. It does not need to claim authority, and if ever its leaders say "because I said so," those words are redundant, superfluous to every real reason you have for paying attention. Once we see that law's purpose is essentially predictive, essentially about helping us understand *each other,* then lawgivers lose any good reason to claim "because I said so" rights to be obeyed. Our right responses to law are not focused on lawgivers, they are focused on each other. Being obeyed is just not what lawgiving is *about*.

Even when we actually do make promises, that fact only adds one reason among many that we may need to weigh when we are deciding what to do each day. If you promised to obey someone who then told you to do bad things, the good of promise keeping would no more justify doing the bad things if the promise had been made to someone in government than if the promise had been made to a stranger on the street.[17] Promising to obey adds no more to our relations with the people whom our community's law calls government than it would add to our relations with anyone else. As soon as we distinguish the people in government based on the goodness of *having* a system of law and government, we are onto a totally different reason for taking what they say seriously, a reason that has nothing to do with promise keeping and everything to do with prediction, with understanding what people in our community are likely to do and to expect. And notice that a big part of what makes promise keeping good at all is predictability—promises are *one* way to build expectations about what we will do, and if others rely on those expectations when choosing what to do themselves, that may be a big part of the moral case for keeping the promises. But law and government in fact exist among us and build expectations about what we will do and expect *without* having or needing the support of promises to obey. Promises are one way to build expectations among those around us about what we will do and expect. Belonging to communities that have law and government is *another* way to build expectations among those around us about what we will do and expect. And that belonging to communities for most humans over most of human history has not been a matter of choice. Consent is not what brings law and government into our lives. Consent is not what keeps law and government in our lives. Consent does not help explain what law and government do in our lives.

Why did Locke not see any of this? Maybe he did, but thought that his seventeenth-century audience could not be mentally moved far enough fast enough to welcome William's rule without believing in William's right to be obeyed. But probably Locke just did not see how law and government could ever achieve all of the good that they distinctively do without widespread belief that community leaders have a "because I said so" right to be obeyed.[18] Locke lived before Charles Darwin. Noncreationist ways to think about the emergence and effectiveness of law and government in human communities[19] were likely no more within his reach than noncreationist ways to think about the emergence and energy of humans.[20]

What about *wise* words? Have we skipped through the "wise friend" analogy too swiftly? Might lawgivers have a "because I said so" right to be obeyed when they know better than we do? Does authority genuinely exist when we are more likely to do the right thing by uncritically doing what someone says than by fully thinking through for ourselves each choice of action that life offers us? That is the reasoning that lies behind most occasions when parents use the phrase "because I said so" and the only occasions on which parents can morally defend doing so—no one thinks children are under a moral duty to comply when a parent instructs them to submit to molestation or to shoplift. Knowing better was also part of the "divine right" idea of authority that we see in the writings of ancient communities. The divine had a right to be obeyed by humans not only because being creator gave the divine a property right but also because being creator meant that the divine knew what was best for the creation. If human minds thought otherwise, then those minds were necessarily mistaken. Even in ancient religious traditions that depicted the divine as not altogether loving, the deities' boundless ability to affect human lives adversely made doing what the divine demanded necessarily the right thing for humans to do. If a human sacrifice was the only way to avoid the destruction of the whole community, then the moral case for doing it had some juice.[21] Joseph Raz has made an argument for lawgivers' authority along a parallel line. His "normal justification" of authority is "that the subject would better conform to reasons that apply to him anyway (that is, to reasons other than the directives of the authority) if he intends to be guided by the authority's directives than if he does not."[22]

These "father knows best"–style arguments for authority mix up two totally different dictionary meanings of the word. We sometimes use the word "authority" to mean expertise, as in "she is an authority on Shakespeare." When we say that, we do not mean that she has a right to boss Shakespeare around or to make us study Shakespeare, we mean that she knows a lot about Shakespeare. Someone's apparent expertise may give us good reason to do as she says, because of what she *knows*. Authority as expertise shares with authority as right to be obeyed a linguistic origin in the ancient Roman concept of *auctoritas*, which sought to express the psychological dynamic through which some humans see reason and feel desire to follow others. Max Weber spoke similarly of "charismatic authority."[23] But the reason seen by the charismatically led need not be a leader's *right* to be obeyed. Authority as an argument for taking expert advice is about mastery of *knowledge*. Authority as an argument for obeying leaders is about mastery of *people*. Mastery of knowledge implies mastery of people not at all. For example, if my doctor tells me to stay home from work because I am contagious, my duty to stay home is owed not to my doctor, but to my coworkers. My doctor has no right to be obeyed any more than would the anonymous authors of a *Wikipedia* article that might equally have been the source of expert advice about my condition. But my coworkers do have a moral right not to be needlessly put at risk of harm, and I have a moral duty to do what I can, based on what I know, to avoid needlessly putting them at risk. Rights to be obeyed form no part of that moral picture.[24]

Shifting to the lawgivers' perspective, neither expertise nor consent let the leaders of any of our actual communities honestly *claim* a right to be obeyed. Can you think of any human leader who today can honestly claim that everyone in her community is consenting to the system that lets her lead? Even if everyone did implicitly promise to obey her, could she honestly claim that their promises *morally* gave her a "blank check" right to be obeyed? Relatedly, can you think of any human leader who today can honestly claim that everyone will likely do better by following all of the laws she issues than by thinking for themselves? Issuing a law might definitely be the right thing for the leader to do, and yet behaving differently from what the law signals might also be the right thing for some people to do on some occasions. Having a speed limit on a road is an obvious example. Just because the limit was rightly imposed does not mean you should do as it signals when you are rushing someone to the hospital. Even if the law expressed no exception for your circumstances, your own moral compass might tell you that the right thing to do on that occasion is different from what the law predicts you will do. As applied to you on that day, the lawgiver who posted the road sign could not honestly claim even to have guided you to the right action, let alone claim to have a right to be obeyed. But that does not make the separate human action of imposing the speed limit pointless or wrong. Once we see that lawgiving is essentially predictive, we can see why attempts to issue rules are not necessarily either "redundant or unjustified."[25] Even if the road rule tells few road users anything they did not already know about safe driving speeds, issuing the rule still self-fulfillingly shares information with every road user about what other road users and enforcement officers are likely to do and to expect. That may help people move around more safely and successfully. Assuming that their safe and successful movement is on balance a good thing, then helping them move by issuing the rule may be a good thing to do. That can be true without anyone having a right to be obeyed by anyone else.

How, then, can we keep talking as if the idea of authority is relevant to what counts as law and who counts as government? How can we keep talking about law as if it comes from a hierarchy of people who have been delegated a right to be obeyed from higher-ups? If there is such a hierarchy, who sits at the summit?

CHAPTER 4

The Empty Idea of Authority

Have you ever been in a room, perhaps a gym, where wall mirrors were both in front and behind you? Did you happen to notice that at a certain angle, if you raised and lowered your arms, copies of you could be seen behind doing the same thing, stretching back beyond sight? You looked like a less grim version of the actor Hugo Weaving on set in the *Matrix* movies.[1] Or maybe you have seen a similar sight in a painting that contains an identical painting, that therefore contains an identical painting, that contains. . . . We call that infinite regress. It is just fine, and somewhat amusing, in mirrors and paintings. But it can give us a headache when we see it in concepts that we think we need to have do work for us. The petulantly brilliant Ludwig Wittgenstein pointed to such a problem with the idea of *interpretation*. Interpreting cannot of itself give us *understanding*, he complained, because if interpretation were the key, then every interpretation would itself need to be interpreted, ad infinitum.[2] A language dictionary is in itself a closed loop that presupposes an existing vocabulary in the mind of anyone who consults it, and even then cannot fully capture and convey quite how word meanings shade into each other through degrees of synonymity. A child somehow enters the language and uses it to communicate without an initial reservoir of words with which to construct synonymous, expository expressions in her head for the new words and phrases she is hearing and picking up from life among the community of humans who surround her.[3] As the story of Helen Keller reveals,[4] this can be achieved even without sight and hearing, and the symbol-object association games that help it happen can no more explain the wonder of our understanding than chicken soup can explain the wonder of our immune systems. Understanding each other, or anything else in the world, is an experienced reality for us that we cannot adequately explain in words, though our experience persuades us that words can help understanding happen. After all our chattering, we come to a great silence in which there is understanding, or there is not.[5]

If the history of human talk about authority as a "because I said so" right to be obeyed were not off-putting enough to make us doubt the idea's value for thinking about law and government, the idea of authority, like that of interpretation, also leaves us with an infinite regress headache. Suppose you are driving along merrily one day when you see in your rearview mirror that you are being tailgated by a black car with multicolored roof lights that are flashing. You pull over to the side of the road, and someone in a severe uniform with a gun on one hip and a flashlight on the other walks to your window. Suppose that he asks you to step out of your car. One reason to do what he says is that if you don't, he may arrest you and take you to a building full of people who look like him, and if you fuss further, you may end up with all sorts of people whom the legal system calls government officials piling on to give you more problems. But suppose you enjoy squabbling and feel indignant at being asked to get out of your car for no reason that seems good to you. So you stay in the driver's seat and say: "What gives you a right to tell me what to do?" Now, he may not take that well, but let us imagine that he is enrolled in night classes in political science and is feeling chatty, so he decides to humor you with an answer. "I have a right to tell you what to do in some ways, such as telling you to step out of your car when you have been driving on a California highway, because that right is given to me in some words that we call a government regulation." That response does not seem altogether satisfying, so you ask further: "What gives the people who issued the government regulation a right to give *you* a right to tell me what to do?" He responds: "Well, they have a right to tell you what to do, and they shared that right—the fancy word is, they *delegated* that right—to me." That seems a little mystifying, and invites an obvious rejoinder. "What gave *them* a right to tell me what to do?"

Now the man in uniform is losing patience, but he decides that this is good practice for dealing with his kids, so he replies: "A right to be obeyed is delegated to the issuers of the regulation by some words we call a statute of the State of California." He knows what's coming next from you, so he just continues. "And those words succeeded in delegating to my department a right to be obeyed because the statute was agreed upon by a majority of members of each chamber of the California Legislature and by the State Governor, and *they* have a right to be obeyed because some words called the Constitution of the State of California give them that right, and those constitutional words succeeded in delegating to the Legislature and Governor a right to be obeyed because the words were agreed upon by a gathering called a constitutional convention or by one of the ways that the constitution's existing words say more words can be added, and they are fully compatible with the words of the Constitution of the United States and . . ."

Now it is your turn to be impatient, and you butt in: "How can any of these words, from any of the people who helped contribute them, create a right to be obeyed and delegate it down a chain that ends with *you*? What gives the people who issue the highest words, the words of constitutions, a right to be obeyed by *me* that they can delegate to *you*?" This is the moment when an arrest is most likely to happen.

What is the answer? That the issuers of constitutional words and statutory words were chosen in a good way? Maybe the way was good in that it let many people participate in choosing the lawgivers. Maybe the way was good in that it was likely to select wise lawgivers. Maybe, whatever way the lawgivers were chosen, their words do express ways of behaving that look likely to produce good consequences. Maybe lots of people in times past have agreed that it is better to call these words the law than not to call these words the law. But what does any of that have to do with giving anyone a right to be obeyed by *you*? If, like a mischievous child, you keep asking "says who?," don't we end up running out of higher authorities? The laws of California do not come from anyone who owns you and probably have not come from anyone you have promised to obey. So the ideas of property and contract do not help us identify an ultimate source of right to be obeyed by you. There are good reasons to do what the man in uniform asks you to do, just as there are often good reasons in life to do what others ask us to do. But the idea of authority, of a right to be obeyed, turns out not to be the best, most truthful, way of understanding what those reasons are.

The idea of authority relies on a creation-delegation way of thinking about how law comes to *be*. If someone truly has a right to be obeyed by you, then she can delegate that right to someone else, and then that other person also has a right to be obeyed by you. But if the first person has no such right, then she cannot help anyone else have that right. As twentieth-century philosophers wrestled with how to think about the *ultimate* source of law's reality, they found themselves tiptoeing away from the idea of authority and toward something quite different.[6] H. L. A. Hart explained that any legal system will have at its core what Hart called a rule of recognition that signals what counts as law.[7] Hans Kelsen comparably influenced continental European thinking about law with the idea of a *Grundnorm*.[8] If lawgiving involved drawing on some ultimate source of right to be obeyed, then the rule of recognition, or *Grundnorm*, would come from that source. But what if there is no such source? What if, as Kelsen eventually put it, the higher authority that delegates its right to be obeyed through the *Grundnorm* "is merely figmentary?"[9] What really makes some of our sayings the law and others not? People in any community say lots of things to each other. What distinguishes an eccentric in fancy dress who is shouting on a street corner from the man in uniform who told you to step out of your car?

Inside every legal system, said Hart, there is a shared understanding of ways that words can become law—of ways that words can become "pedigreed" as part of the legal system.[10] That understanding is shared by the most strategically situated people, whom we can circularly call officials. Of course, their status as officials depends on the very system of signals that they together recognize.[11] Their shared understanding of ways that words can become law we could call a core "law." What makes a legal system's core law work? What makes it effective? Simply the fact that its community's key players are all treating it as effective. They have a custom of treating the core law, the rule of recognition, as effective to signal what counts as law. What keeps that custom alive? Why does each person treat the core law in a legal system as effective to say what counts as laws of the system? Only one answer suggests itself from the story so far.[12] Each person treats the core law as effective because she expects *everyone else* to treat that rule as effective.[13] The custom is what scholars in more recent years have called a *convention*.[14] In other words, when we peel away the rhetoric surrounding law's reality in our lives and focus on what actually makes law real to us, we converge on the idea that at their core, legal systems grow from a shared understanding among the most significantly active participants in a community about what others are likely to treat as law.

A legal system's rule of recognition is effective because it is treated by people as accurately signaling what other people in their community are likely to do and to expect. But if that is true for the core "law" that we may call the rule of recognition, then it must be true for all the laws in the system. Law *works* purely because it successfully signals what others are likely to do and to expect. Branching sequences of signals emanate from the core of the system, as existing effective signals of likely behavior and expectation signal the likely scope for success in issuing further effective signals of likely behavior and expectation. Existing effective signalers issue signals that predict who else is likely to be an effective signaler and within what scope. We can think of the signals and their signalers as forming hierarchies, much as we previously conceived of authority rippling down through a legal system, if that helps us visualize what is going on. Someone who is being treated as a leader can tell everyone to treat others she identifies as leaders too. She can signal the extent of that sharing in leadership. And her signals can be understood as effective predictions rather than as delegations of a right to be obeyed. Predictions can predict further predictions from further predictors as readily as any right to be obeyed can be delegated. From the common core and cross-referencing of the predictive signals we call law, there emerges a self-sustaining *system*. All the signals of the system are supported, are made effective, in the same way as those that were expressed at the system's beginnings, and that support, that effectiveness, *is* their self-fulfilling success at signaling, at predicting, what people in their community are likely to do and to expect. If our legal systems did not work in this way, they would not exist at all. That is a truth we have not seen and said enough. As there is no right to be obeyed at a legal system's core, the idea of right to be obeyed is completely irrelevant to the nature of law.

If the core of the legal system is just shared expectations, then everything in the system owes its life and effectiveness to shared expectations. To reposition David Hume's words, we have law "because every one thinks so."[15] What everyone thinks is *not* enough to let us say that someone has a moral right to be obeyed, as Hume of all people must have quietly realized. We have him to thank, after all, for the observation that no "ought" follows merely from an "is."[16] What everyone thinks does not in itself determine whether someone *ought* to be obeyed. But what everyone thinks *does* in itself determine whether there is a community custom, and the expression of *custom* is what law is. A rule of recognition that does not come from someone who has a right to be obeyed cannot itself create and delegate to anyone else a right to be obeyed. The idea of authority depends on a creation-delegation basis for being.[17] Law's basis for being is altogether different. Law *evolves* into being in tandem with the human community to which it belongs, and its basis is the basis of community—a shared understanding of what those in community are likely to do and to expect.

CHAPTER 5

Ideas that Endure

LAW, GOVERNMENT, AUTHORITY

So far we have painted a picture of what law and government are,[1] and seen that a clear-eyed vision of those things has no use for the historic idea of authority as a "because I said so" right to be obeyed. But does authority's irrelevance to the nature of law and government dissociate the *word* from law and government completely? Certainly not. We have already noticed that we use the word "authority" in more than one sense. Sometimes we speak of "authorities" when we mean "experts," as in "she is an authority on the law of torts." And sometimes we speak of "authorities" in a third way that does not necessarily imply expertise and does not address what *makes* words law and what *makes* people lawgivers. Sometimes we speak of "authorities" when we *mean* laws or lawgivers. For example, consider occasions when a judge asks counsel: "Do you have any authority for that proposition?" or when we complain: "The local authority just raised our taxes." These uses of the word are distinct and of ongoing value to us.

When the judge asks her question of counsel and when we complain about our taxes going up, she and we are using the word "authority" as a *synonym* respectively for law and for government, not as one of their defining ingredients. Those are related but wholly distinguishable uses of the English-language word, with their own separate entries in the dictionary. What all of these usages have in common, from rights to be obeyed to expertise to *being* law and government, is descent from the Latin *auctoritas*,[2] which expressed for the ancient Romans the psychological phenomenon that Max Weber called "charismatic authority."[3]

What of attempts to salvage relevance for the old idea of right to be obeyed by arguing that the law *itself* has authority, even if the people who are lawgivers do not?[4] Those attempts wash away when we see that law is just words. We never obey *words*; if ever we obey, we obey communicating persons. We never owe moral duties to words; whenever we owe duties, we owe them to persons. Words never have rights to be obeyed; unless persons do, then nothing does. To say that the words of the law have "authority" independent of lawgivers is either to talk tautologically, because we are really using "authority" as a synonym for "legality," or to attribute to law's words some unidentified moral value in guiding us, that is, to speak of authority in the sense of *expertise*, including coordinative expertise.

There is only one kind of valuable guidance that *all* law provides, and that is news of what other people in law's community are likely to do and to expect. And supplying *that* news in a uniquely *systemic* way for its community is the one kind of valuable guidance that *only* law can provide, exclusively among human communications. Nothing but the law of a human community can, for example, give us confidence about what counts as *property* there, about what we need to do to know that a vacation home we want to buy in that neighborhood will likely be treated by other people there, including strangers, as *ours*. That circles us back to an understanding of law that has no use for the old idea of right to be obeyed, and sees law's true value in what it tells us about each other. When we call a law an "authority," we use a synonym for law that adds nothing to our understanding of what law is.

Once we see that authority's valuable connection to the ideas of law and government is not as a defining ingredient but merely as a synonym, we are ready to tackle two other words that are often heard in association with authority, law, and government: legitimacy and sovereignty.

LEGITIMACY

The word *legitimacy* comes from the Latin *legitimus*, which means lawful.[5] Legitimacy of someone's leadership conveys the idea that a community's existing legal system supports the person's leadership of that community. We see the word used to express ideas of proper selection, particularly of a proper coming into being. Going back to the records of ancient human communities, we see an idea that there was a correct, divinely ordained way to obtain leaders, just as there was a correct, divinely ordained way to obtain children. The instrumental idea of bloodline succession drew moral support from a thought that divine selection was on display in divinely created nature.[6]

Legitimacy of leadership was a companion concept to the old idea of authority. Designation by the divine was both what identified the correct choice of leader and what delegated a right to be obeyed. As the two sides of the leadership coin, legitimacy hailed the divinely ordained leader as rightly chosen, and authority hailed the divinely ordained leader as rightly obeyed. Legitimacy was about the constitution of government. Authority was about the operation of government. Legitimacy meant that someone was morally justified in claiming a right to call himself leader, and everyone else was obliged to forsake all other candidates for leadership. Authority meant that someone was morally justified in claiming a right to be obeyed, and everyone else was obliged to obey. Legitimacy was about getting the job of governing; authority was about doing the job of governing.

When we stop thinking of leadership as a property right, we can focus our attention fully on what good it actually does us. That lets us swiftly see plenty of work for the idea of legitimacy still to do. If someone claims to be leader even though he just lost an election, if someone claims her words are law even though no existing law calls her a lawgiver, we will quite quickly hear others in our community call those actions illegitimate. We have a moral reason for caring whether someone who is trying to be a lawgiver has the support of the existing legal system. The overall predictive effectiveness of the system, its value to us as a source of information about what others in our community will likely do and expect, depends on lawgiving itself following predictable patterns. The system needs to succeed in telling us who is a lawgiver and within what scope, or it ceases to be a system.

As we will discuss further in chapter 8, communities do indeed experience moments of major transition from time to time in which large parts of their legal systems lose predictive effectiveness and eventually are replaced by more successful substitutes. We often call those transitional moments revolutions. But on *any* occasion when someone acts contrary to the existing system's predictions and yet succeeds in issuing effective signals that take the community and its legal system in a new direction, we witness a successful revolution, albeit often only in a very small segment of the system.

Revolution is any unpredicted turn in a legal system's evolution. Sometimes these mini revolutions are dressed up as conforming to the existing system through an accompanying claim that the words of the existing system *mean* something that supports the revolutionary action. Revolutionary action may in this way be difficult to distinguish from conforming actions that add to the system through words that resolve vagueness or ambiguities in existing law.[7] But when arguably revolutionary events occur, we will be unsurprised to hear the rhetoric of illegitimacy raised in criticism. That rhetoric points to a moral reason we have for acting as our existing legal system predicts we will do, namely, the good of having the system work effectively. As the frequent failure of that rhetoric to prevent revolutionary change reflects, the good of having an existing legal system is just one moral consideration we each have when deciding what to do. That reason for action may be outweighed by others, as it has often been throughout human history when tyrannical leaders who could accurately claim the support of existing law were overthrown.

The language of legitimacy has a worthwhile role to play even in a sophisticated society where no one is overtly thinking about full-scale revolution. Suppose the U.S. Constitution says that someone can be convicted of treason on the testimony of two witnesses to the same action.[8] Suppose that someone is accused of treason, and in support of the charge, the prosecution produces one live witness, and the signed statement of another person, who is now deceased. A third person is available to testify that he witnessed the deceased write and sign the statement. There are questions whether this counts as the testimony of two witnesses, and whether prosecuting and convicting on this basis would violate a constitutional amendment that guarantees the right of an accused "to be confronted with the witnesses against him."[9] Suppose the accused is convicted and appeals his conviction to the Supreme Court at a time in American history when no existing law directly addresses the questions whether the witnessed statement of a deceased person can meet the requirement of a second witness and whether the confrontation clause excludes testimony about the statements of dead people from being admitted into evidence to help prove the truth of their content. However the Court answers those questions, we can see that more than one possible answer to each could honestly be reached by reasonable readers of the English language. Does someone have to be alive and in court to be a witness? Can someone who is alive and in court ever count as a witness to what he did not personally experience? Is being "confronted" with adverse witnesses about seeing and hearing them live in a courtroom, or about your lawyer having a chance to cross-examine them, or about your being personally told who they are so that your defense can adequately address any reasons they might have to lie, or some combination of these things and maybe more? Suppose that historical evidence available to the Court yields no consensus on the answers to these questions. The questions must nonetheless be answered. If we disagree with the Court's answers, we might call them wrong, but we would nonetheless likely call them a legitimate exercise of the Court's jurisdiction, signaled by Article III of the Constitution, to decide disputes arising under the Constitution. We would say this because the American community's legal system signals that the Court is likely to be effective in resolving doubts within the American community about what the Constitution tells us. The words of the Constitution predict that role for the Court.

Now suppose that the conviction were made with only one witness and nothing more. Now there is no doubt among reasonable readers of American English that the conviction falls outside the scope signaled by the Constitution for convicting people of treason.

If the Court were to hold that one witness is enough, it would not be elaborating on the words of the Constitution, it would be ignoring the words of the Constitution and substituting a different and incompatible signal of what is likely to happen in America when people are accused of treason. That decision would not be a predicted evolution of the law of treason, it would be a revolution in the law of treason, because it is not within the range of possibilities predicted by the existing system. Now we are more likely to hear people call the decision illegitimate. They will do that because they notice that there is a good reason to do what existing law predicts, namely the good of having a predictively effective legal system. If the Supreme Court starts saying that black means white, what's to stop other people from treating the *Court's* words in a similar fashion, undermining the predictive value of American law? If we think that reasons for revolution do not outweigh the good of predictability in law and government, we are likely to accuse people who behave in a revolutionary way of illegitimacy. Using the language of illegitimacy to target departures from predicted behavior is a useful way to commentate on law and government, valuably more subtle than simply saying that actions are wrong. Illegitimacy points to a particular reason for calling actions wrong. Choice to act in a revolutionary fashion will not always in fact be wrong, as we will discuss further in chapters 6 and 8. Sometimes the reasons for departing from predicted action outweigh the good of promoting the predictability of the system. But those who disagree can highlight their reason by calling the action illegitimate, rather than simply wrong. The value of using the word "legitimacy" in this way depends not at all on anyone having "because I said so" rights to be obeyed by anyone else.

Beyond the narrow sense of conformity to existing law, we do sometimes hear the word legitimacy used to bless behavior in the broad sense that the action is authentically *good,* that the action is morally justified, all things considered. This less precise usage is most frequently heard of actions through which someone becomes a leader or in debate about whether someone should stay a leader. Using legitimacy to mean overall goodness of becoming or staying leader can be associated with the word's core concept of enjoying support of the existing legal system, because our legal systems' deepest constitutive elements include those expressed customs of community response that treat particular persons as leaders. An unabashed revolutionary may call himself a legitimate leader on the basis that, all things considered, his rising to leadership was the right thing for him to do and others' treating him as leader is the right thing for them to do. Reasons to support those conclusions might include the goodness of the way he became leader, such as an election in which most people in his community had an opportunity to participate, the goodness of what he is doing and promising to do as leader, and the absence of others who could do better. These reasons might outweigh the social costs of instability, of diminished predictability, that revolutionary change inflicts on a community. Such a co-opting of morally elevating language is understandable, though hardly indispensable. Used in its narrow and precise sense of conformity with existing law, "legitimacy" has sometimes been actively deployed on only the opposing side of a society's debate about the goodness of revolutionary change, with those on the revolutionary side at least initially content to say that legitimacy in the narrow sense of conformity with existing law did not matter as much as the good things achieved through the change. This position was made easier to occupy when, as occurred in France, the "legitimist" side claimed that legitimacy called for a full return to the past even after the costs of revolutionary change had been absorbed, citing an old divine-delegation, property right notion of leadership that the revolutionaries frankly rejected.[10]

SOVEREIGNTY

Sovereignty is a characteristic of community, sometimes present, sometimes not, and like community and law themselves, a matter of *degree*.[11] As we will discuss further in chapters 7 and 8, communities' legal systems vary in how comprehensively they address the character of life for their community members and in how successfully they predict the aspects of life that they do address. *Sovereignty* speaks to how independent a community is from other communities.[12] Sovereignty recognizes that a community's independence from other communities means that community members will likely have reason to give the predictions of the community's legal system priority in their thinking about what to do over incompatible predictions from other legal systems. When we call a community sovereign, we are noticing the limited nature of any downlinks to that community's legal system from other legal systems. For community members, the community's legal system is, to the extent of the community's independence, supreme, or *sovereign*. When we notice a community's dependent relation to another community, we may speak of the dependent community and its legal system as being subject to the sovereignty of the other.

Sovereignty is likely to affect the *weight* that the sovereign community's laws will have relative to those of other legal systems in the decisions of community members about what to do each day. If your town council issues laws signaling that you will do one thing, and your national government issues laws signaling that you will do the opposite, the *sovereignty* of the nation over the town predicts priority for the national law in your thinking about what to do. That prediction may prove inaccurate—local pressures and other reasons may push you to do what local law says, but that is just an instance of your nation's laws falling short in fulfilling their predictive function.

A comparable predictive failure may occur if you are a dual national and laws of the two national communities to which you belong address your behavior in incompatible ways. If you were a national of both the United States and Israel in 1967, and received draft notices from both governments predicting your simultaneous participation in the Vietnam and Six-Day wars, obviously your decision about what to do would necessarily have gone against at least one legal system's prediction. The lack of any dependent relation between your two national communities would have forced you to discount the fact of sovereignty and to focus on other reasons when deciding what to do, such as your life's greater actual integration into one community than into the other.

Suppose that you have the misfortune to be on the board of your condominium association, and you receive a letter from your association's lawyer advising that the association's rules are incompatible with a recent change in state law. Your rules prohibit residents from putting satellite dishes on their balconies—the rule was made because the board at some time past thought that the devices would make the building look like a tenement. Now you know that the state legislature, after intense lobbying from satellite television providers, has changed state law to require that residents of condominium towers be free to deploy dishes on their balconies. Your board's reasons for not wanting dishes on your balconies are unchanged, but as a board member you can now see a strong reason to vote for change to your rules, the strength of the reason perhaps varying with the consequences that state law signals for disregard of the new state law. As a resident, if you want to put a dish on your balcony, the association's prohibitory rule now has less weight, because you know that if you disregard it, the association will not be able to obtain the support of state government courts or agencies to stop you, and if the association's employees take matters into their own hands, *you* will be able to secure the support of state officials to stop *them* from removing your dish. You are still a member of a community for which the association rules are community law, but you and the other members of that community are also part of a larger community, with which your condominium community has a derivative relationship.

Each of us belongs to multiple communities, including multiple geographic communities—towns, counties, states, nations—and maybe a range of institutional and other interactive communities.[13] The geographic communities to which we belong each has a dedicated legal system that is linked vertically and horizontally to the legal systems of other geographic communities. Our institutional and other interactive communities, from government bureaucracies to corporate bureaucracies to churches to schools to Internet-based (virtual) groups, may have uplinks to and downlinks from the legal systems of one or more geographic communities, so that the nongeographic communities' own legal systems are subsystems with a derivative, dependent relation to larger legal systems. The configurations of people we call government institutions contribute to the words we call law even as they derive their internal arrangements and contributory capacity from existing law that comes in part from a system or systems larger than their own. Institutions of government are like organs evolving within a developing species, and help promote the growth of the legal systems to which they belong. Some of the rules that run a police department come from within, some from other lawgivers in the larger, geographic legal system or systems within which that police department operates. Likewise for a court, and a court's words may return the favor, by adding to the words that count as part of a larger, geographic legal system from which the court derives. And geographic legal systems' shaping of nongeographic communities goes well beyond shaping the internal life of groups that law typically calls governmental. The members of a motorcycle gang may not be as conscious of their rules' derivative, dependent relation to state law as are, say, the members of a condominium association, let alone the members of a police department. But the state's sovereignty over *what* the gang can be and become will likely assert itself soon enough should the gang's rules shift gang behavior in directions outside the potential scope that state law predicts for such communities.

Our largest geographic community embraces everywhere that humans are, and we call it the international community of nation states. *Being* a nation state is a status that the international community's legal system expresses. International law addresses the relative independence of nation states from each other by calling them sovereign. Inside a nation state, we may see the same word used by the nation state's legal system to express the relative independence, usually the independence in some identified respects, of internal geographic communities, subsets of national society.

We are particularly prone to calling a nation state's legal system *federal* when that system calls some geographic communities within it sovereign states. That usage alludes to the old idea that federal government existed where nation states agreed to act in concert for certain purposes through an international law that we call a *treaty*, the Latin *foedus*. Even where a nation state's legal system no longer resembles a treaty among smaller nation states, even where a nation state's legal system *never* resembled a treaty among smaller nation states, we still sometimes see the language of sovereignty used by the nation's legal system. That use signals the relative independence of internal geographic communities, from each other and from the institutions of the nation, in shaping through their laws some aspects of their citizens' lives.

Ideas expressed through our enduringly valuable uses of the words authority, legitimacy, and sovereignty all help us think and talk about the three inseparable realities of our lives together on which this book is focused: *law, government,* and the experience of human *community* that law and government express and enable. In the next chapter we return to thinking more about how these three great realities affect our choices of what to do each day.

CHAPTER 6

When *Should* We Do What Law Signals?

Enlightenment is man's emergence from his self-imposed immaturity. Immaturity is the inability to use one's understanding without guidance from another.

Immanuel Kant, *An Answer to the Question: What is Enlightenment?* (1784).

Man has continued to evolve by acts of disobedience. Not only was his spiritual development possible only because there were men who dared to say no to the powers that be in the name of their conscience or their faith, but also his intellectual development was dependent on the capacity for being disobedient—disobedient to authorities who tried to muzzle new thoughts and to the authority of long-established opinions which declared a change to be nonsense.

Erich Fromm, *Disobedience as a Psychological and Moral Problem* (1963).[1]

> Up to a certain point it is better that the law and its interpretation be settled than that it be settled rightly. Therefore it may be protested that the preceding account does not determine who is to say when circumstances are such as to justify civil disobedience. It invites anarchy by encouraging everyone to decide for himself, and to abandon the public rendering of political principles. The reply to this is that each person must indeed make his own decision. Even though men normally seek advice and counsel, and accept the injunctions of those in authority when these seem reasonable to them, they are always accountable for their deeds. We cannot divest ourselves of our responsibility and transfer the burden of blame to others.
>
> John Rawls, *A Theory of Justice* (1971).[2]

Explosions pierced the air from inside the valley, and their fierce reverberating reached the ears of U.S. Marine Corporal Dakota Meyer, about a mile away. He was following an order to protect the rear of the column, but the attack had come from everywhere else. Trapped in a narrow space, with mortar shells, rocket-propelled grenades, and bullets raining down from hillsides to their left and right and from the Afghan village that had been their destination, his comrades faced massacre by the ambushing Taliban. From his place of safety, Meyer radioed for permission to go in and help the others. He was ordered to stay put. But he could hear from the radio traffic that no one else was coming to the rescue any time soon, so he asked again, and again, and again. Each of those four times he was ordered not to move. He decided to disobey. Five times he disobeyed, manned the guns on a Humvee, and attacked his comrades' attackers. His disobedient actions over six hours rescued three dozen men. And for those actions, a grateful nation awarded him the Congressional Medal of Honor.

The story told at Dakota Meyer's White House investiture by the President of the United States on September 15, 2011, celebrated the vivid virtue, the luminous *rightness,* of Meyer's actions, while frankly acknowledging that in choosing those actions, he disobeyed his lawful superiors.[3] This tells us something important about the role that law rightly plays in our daily choices of what to do. Three features of this uplifting story are especially illuminating. First, if sufficiently good, "legitimate" governments had a "because I said so" right to be obeyed by their people, then that right clearly would have applied here, and imposed a duty on Corporal Meyer to obey his lawful superiors. If a theory of authority is so highfalutin that the constitutional government of the United States does not qualify, then that theory is utterly irrelevant to what real people should do in the real world and therefore is of no value to us in deciding what to do each day. Second, the lawful instructions that Corporal Meyer disobeyed were issued directly to him in the context where the moral case for not second-guessing government seems strongest. They were issued on a battlefield, as part of the communications system that coordinates those on whom we depend to defend us from enemies. And Corporal Meyer had voluntarily signed up to be a soldier. He had made *actual promises* to obey his superiors' lawful instructions. Third, the order that Meyer disobeyed was *not* an order to do some affirmatively *evil* action, of a kind that might fall into some categorical exception to a government's right to be obeyed. No, the action that was ordered—just staying put until the cavalry arrived—was precisely what most of us would probably have done anyway, without any need for prompting from anyone.

Corporal Meyer instantaneously judged that the best thing to do was something different from what he had been ordered to do. If he had been wrong about that, and his disobedient actions had made matters worse, such as by rescuing no one and getting his driver killed, he might have faced a court martial rather than a beer with the President beside the Rose Garden. He knew from military law that he was taking that risk, so he first asked *four times* for permission before disobeying. But he was not wrong. Having decided that the best thing he could do was different from his superiors' instructions, he knew that the *right* thing to do was to act contrary to those instructions. And we acknowledged his sound and virtuous judgment with the United States' highest honor. In doing so, we acknowledged that no idea of authority, no "because I said so" right to be obeyed, should ever preempt or exclude our own independent thinking about what is actually the right thing to do each day. To our daily thinking we bring all of the information that life gives us. Corporal Meyer received from his lawful superiors news of what they expected of him. That was relevant information. But it did not exclude taking into account what was unfolding in front of him. And the information supplied by his own eyes and ears on the battlefield pointed to a different and better choice of action.

In headlong retreat from the claim that law *preempts* our own thinking about what to do, we might wonder whether law's moral contribution to our choices of action is nonetheless still the old idea of a "because I said so" right to be obeyed, but with the duty to obey lawgivers downsized to being very weighty, not preemptive. If that were true, how would we work out the weight that the duty to obey deserves from one life choice to the next? If you were in Corporal Meyer's boots, how would you have *reasoned* about the relevance of your superiors' orders to what you should do? If you recognized that their words did not shut down your own thinking, so that in deciding what to do you had to compare the weight of their words with the weight of what you could see in front of you, how could you have discovered what weight each thing deserved? To figure that out, you would have had to ask yourself, what *information* is each of these sensory experiences giving me? The sights and sounds of the battlefield are telling you that *you* are your comrades' only hope of survival. Corporal Meyer reportedly said as much. Your superiors' orders are telling you . . . what? That they *expect* you to stay put. What is the relevance of their expectation? That relevance was well explained to you in basic training. Achieving the good things that the U.S. Marines can potentially achieve for the nation depends upon each member of the group behaving in ways that are highly predictable to everyone else in the group, so that coordinated actions involving many people can be swiftly chosen and achieved. Military discipline matters, and is all about predictability. The predictive effectiveness of the Marines' signaling system depends on everyone almost always doing what the system signals they will do. To reinforce the likelihood that this will occur, the system signals very adverse consequences for any soldier who acts contrary to what the system signals he will do. In defying an order to stay put, Corporal Meyer was risking real punishment, and he knew it. Those were the competing reasons that Meyer had to weigh in those desperate moments in the Afghan desert. He weighed them, and decided that doing what he could to save his mates mattered most.

When we reflect on Corporal Meyer's reasoning, we can see that weighing reasons is all about reaching behind what is said to us and letting our minds touch the likely consequences of alternative actions, as well as what life so far tells us about what is good and what is not, who we are and who we aspire to be. When we reach behind the words that are law in our community, we may find various consequences of our possible paths made clearer by the information that law's words supply. As we will discuss further in this chapter, law's words may supply valuable information of various kinds that could equally have been forthcoming from other sources. But there is one kind of valuable information that law distinctively supplies, and that is news of what others in law's *community* will likely do and expect. News of what others will likely do and expect may contribute to knowing what we should do in various ways, but the one way that law always contributes is by putting a thumb on the scale for behaving as law predicts, simply to help law stay predictive, because having a system of signals that helps us understand each other and live and work together is *good*.

As Joseph Raz has explained, the whole point of a "because I said so" right to be obeyed is to short-circuit the reasoning process, the moral weighing, by which we reach behind what is said to us and compare the consequences of, and our other understandings about, alternative actions.[4] The old idea of authority works like a moral circuit-breaker. When the authority switch is tripped, we shut down our thinking about what to do, stay in the dark, and blindly do what we are told. Reports from Tiananmen Square in 1989 said that the troops who attacked their own protesting people seemed drugged.[5] The idea of authority is binary—a right to be obeyed either exists and deserves to preempt our thinking, or it doesn't exist at all. If someone has it within defined scope, we have to do whatever she says within that scope. Leaders cannot *half have* authority. It's just not that kind of thing. We cannot work out what *good* there is in conforming to orders, and therefore what weight conformity deserves in our thinking, without considering the *consequences* for the world and for who we are that "because I said so" tells us not to consider. If Abraham had tried to assign a *weight* to the divine command to sacrifice his son Isaac, how would he have gone about that?[6] The exercise of a divine right to be obeyed was preemptive in that its weight as a reason for action was *infinitely great*. It wiped out all reason to think further, because the divine was the master, the divine was sure to know better, and the divine had boundless ability to affect human life adversely. The idea of authority cannot accommodate the truth that law really but merely deserves a *relative weight* in our thinking, a weight always to be compared with the weight of our reasons for doing differently, and a weight which varies in *degree*, depending at least on how good having the legal system is and how much risk to the system's predictive effectiveness our nonconformity would pose. The idea of a "because I said so" right to be obeyed cannot be salvaged when we sever and discard the ancient claim that it came from the divine. If you are talking about authority as something other than preempting your own thinking on the say-so of someone else, then you are not really talking about the historic idea of a "because I said so" right to be obeyed; you are just talking about some other reason or reasons to take some sayings seriously when deciding what to do, such as that you promised to do so or that you expect good things will happen if you do. In this chapter we are going to consider the range of reasons that you might actually have in mind. To keep using the word "authority" for the contribution that lawful orders rightly made to Corporal Meyer's reasoning process is to ditch the old idea of a "because I said so" right to be obeyed and to use "authority" as a mere synonym for law and government, not as a distinctive ingredient in what makes words law and what makes people lawgivers. What makes words law and what makes people lawgivers is, as Holmes said, "systematized prediction,"[7] not rights to be obeyed. We can keep using the word "authority" for the reality of systematized prediction, but doing so adds nothing to our understanding of law and government.

In this chapter, we will explore various kinds of information that may come to us through law and that may help to persuade us that we *should* do what law predicts we will do. Even if none of us ever believed that lawgivers had a moral right to be obeyed, we might still often rightly criticize each other for "not following the law." Our reasons for that criticism need not have anything to do with failure to fulfill a moral duty to obey lawgivers. Our reasons for criticism might have everything to do with other moral reasons for behavior that law often helps us have or better appreciate. When the weight of reasons we have for acting one way or another tips our moral scales in favor of doing what law predicts we will do, then of course that is what we should do. And the weight of reasons we have usually will tip our moral scales in favor of doing what law predicts in any community where those in government are not complete monsters or morons.

WHAT USE *DO* WE MAKE OF LAW WHEN DECIDING WHAT TO DO?

Before we think more about what use we *should* make of law when deciding what to do, let us reflect a little on what use we already actually *do* make of law when deciding what to do. When people decide whether to do as law signals, is their thinking actually affected by belief in the old idea of authority? Do people really believe that those in government have a moral right to be obeyed and that we have a corresponding moral duty to obey lawgivers by following the law? Does such a belief *explain* the law observance that we actually do see? Or is the fact that we mostly do what law signals really down to other reasons we have for our actions?

Asking whether the idea of authority actually affects people's thinking about what to do is important even after we have satisfied ourselves that authority is an illusion. If that illusion is as widespread in people's *minds* as it is in what people *say*, then we might worry that dispelling the illusion from their minds could do more harm than good, by luring people into not following the law on occasions when for other reasons they really should.

In *Why People Obey the Law*, Tom Tyler set forth survey results of Chicago residents' attitudes to law and to government that suggest some reason to worry. When put to them as interview questions, the residents overwhelmingly said that they accepted the old idea of authority in its full preemptive force—that people *should* obey the law even when they think doing otherwise is the right thing to do. Respondents overwhelmingly affirmed that "[p]eople should obey the law even if it goes against what they think is right" and "I always try to follow the law even if I think that it is wrong."[8]

Tyler's study relied on self-reporting.[9] To test their claim of belief in authority, can we find evidence of what the interviewed people actually *do*? As it happens, we can. Illinois, like most American states, has among its laws a use tax. This is a tax on goods that state residents have bought outside the state for use inside the state. The use tax is designed to compensate for the loss of sales tax revenue that would otherwise result from state residents buying goods outside the state from retailers who are beyond the reach of the Illinois sales tax law. In contrast to the story when the state levies income, property, and sales taxes, for the use tax the state has no easy way to track whether its residents are paying the amounts of tax that conforming with the law would involve. The use tax, therefore, supplies us with a splendid little empirical study in what role the mere fact that words are law really plays in people's reasoning about what to do. Indeed, it tests actual attitudes to law, displayed in what people do, not what they merely say, for the very same community that answered Tyler's survey so emphatically in favor of treating law as preempting all other reasoning about what to do. If we were to find that lots of use tax was being paid, this would not establish that people view law as morally preemptive in the way that Tyler's respondents reported—the payments might reflect residents' all-things-considered judgments that paying the tax is the right thing to do. But if we were to find that very little use tax is being paid, nowhere near the most conservative estimates of what would be paid if Chicagoans really were conforming their behavior to the law, then we may confidently conclude that people's claims that they treat law as preempting their reasoning about what to do are false.

When I moved to Chicago to clerk at the federal court of appeals, I was told a possibly apocryphal story that at one time Illinois stopped printing forms for its use tax because the cost of printing the forms was exceeding the revenue raised through the tax. In an endeavor to raise some real revenue through its use tax, Illinois, like some other cash-strapped states, has recently been trying to force online retailers such as Amazon.com to collect the use tax on behalf of their customers.[10] There are constitutional obstacles to imposing state laws on out-of-state businesses,[11] so why has Illinois taken this turn? Precisely because Illinois residents, the very people who in Tyler's study spoke up for a preemptive right of lawgivers to be obeyed, are mostly not conforming their behavior to the state's use tax law. They are mostly not paying the tax directly, as the law signals they will do. Part of the story for some periods in the past may have been ignorance of the tax, but there is no excuse for that now that it is a line item on residents' state income tax returns.[12] Yet Illinois continues its quest to have out-of-state sellers pay on residents' behalf.

The story of the Illinois use tax suggests that people do not treat the fact that behavior is signaled by law as their *automatic* answer when thinking about what to do. And the overall findings of Tyler's study, as distinct from the answers to specific questions about authority, support this. Tyler found that, overall, people are more likely to comply with what they perceive to be good law and government than with what they perceive to be bad law and government. And this, of course, reflects the reality that in deciding what to do, we exercise independent moral judgment.[13]

Some years ago, the State of California adopted a law that allowed Californians to possess and to use marijuana for physician-certified medicinal purposes. The national government of the United States has an existing law that signals serious adverse consequences for marijuana possession. The national Supreme Court has by majority upheld the validity of the national law.[14] People who belong both to the community of the United States and to the community of California and who would like to smoke pot have had to decide what weight to give to the news supplied by each of these laws. What the Supreme Court has said about the Constitution of the United States predicts that the national law is more likely to signal accurately what people in California will do and expect. That has proven to be an inaccurate prediction. Prospective pot smokers have assessed the actual behavior of state and national officials over time and judged that the state law is actually a better predictor of life in California. If California's pot smokers were believers in the idea of authority, in the notion that law is a hierarchy of delegated rights to be obeyed, then after the Court's decision upholding the national law, their moral answer to the question whether to smoke pot in California would clearly have been a big *no*. In fact, Californians in numbers sufficient to create a booming industry are taking their cue from the lack of current enforcement of the national law, and continuing to inhale.[15]

Even where the Supreme Court has held that state laws are unconstitutional, not merely trumped in operation by national laws, state lawgivers have not always rushed to repeal the unconstitutional laws. Sometimes state lawgivers have simply sulked and left their unconstitutional words on the statute books, unenforced but unrepealed. Had those lawgivers really believed in the idea of authority, of a duty to *obey* higher lawgivers, then those illegal words would have had to go.[16]

Looking beyond American borders and further back into our history, we see support for a sense that the overall effectiveness of our legal systems at making our lives more predictable does not depend on whether we emphasize *authority* as a reason to conform. Contesting authority claims was at the core of the European religious controversy that we call the Reformation. When the dust settled and the killing stopped, northern Europe had mostly broken away from the Mother Church, mostly rejecting the authority claims of the Pope in Rome. If despite its unique story of historic continuity, the papacy had *no* divinely delegated right to be obeyed, then who did? Though Protestant theologians were careful not to rub their princely patrons' noses in it, the Protestant critique of papal authority implicitly cast doubt on any claim by any human leader to have a divinely delegated property right to be obeyed. And as we have seen, only the divine delegation theory offered any real support for the essential character of authority as a *preemptive* right to say "because I said so" and shut down independent thinking. Only the exercise of a divinely delegated right could wipe out all reason to think further, because only the divine was sure to know better and only a divine right was backed by the divine's boundless ability to affect human life adversely. The attempts of various Protestant scholars, John Milton and John Locke among them,[17] to substitute contractual promising for divine delegation just did not succeed in creating a way to *preempt* people's own moral thinking. Promising, even where it really occurs, just adds a reason for action—the good of promise keeping—to be weighed against other reasons that might point to doing differently. While the Reformation Protestants could not quite see their way clear to discard the whole idea of authority, their approach to thinking about how we humans find truth and goodness put people on a path to skepticism about *any* human's claims of a right to be obeyed by other humans.[18] Has centuries of authority-skeptical thinking in northern Europe made the law of Germany, of Sweden, of the Netherlands, or of England, Scotland, and Wales a *less* predictively effective guide to life in those places? Is the law of southern European communities that never overtly rejected the authority claims of Roman Catholicism a *more* predictively effective guide to what will be done and expected? Clearly we see, both in Europe and in the Americas, that law is *not* more effective at predicting life in the south than it is in the north. As Alexis de Tocqueville observed, quite the contrary.[19] Of course myriad cultural factors contribute to the relative effectiveness of any community's signaling system. People in some communities seem to enjoy leading highly organized lives in intricately predictable patterns more than do people in other communities. It just matters more to get your act together every day when the climate is cold, because if you don't, you might freeze.[20] The point of the north-south observation is simply that our history does not reveal reason to fear that law's success depends on continuing to talk loudly about the right of some humans to be obeyed by others.

WHY DO PEOPLE SO OFTEN *SAY* THAT LAW PREEMPTS THEIR THINKING?

How do we reconcile the obviously widespread exercise of independent judgment in disregard of authority claims with the answers that Tyler's respondents gave? Were they being deliberately untruthful when they reported trying to follow the law even when they thought it was wrong? The responses to the survey, so overwhelmingly in one direction, came from such a representative cross-section of population that it is difficult to view the respondents as other than us. They are unlikely to have been uniquely habitual liars and hypocrites. What lured them into saying that they defer to law more than they really do?

Part of the answer may be suggested by the series of studies that followed Stanley Milgram's groundbreaking tests of people's willingness to administer electric shocks of increasing severity under orders from a domineering experimenter. The experimenter had explained at the outset that "[a]lthough the shocks can be extremely painful, they cause no permanent tissue damage."[21] When participants questioned what they were doing, they were told directly by the experimenter, in successive responses to their questioning:

> Prod 1: Please continue, *or*, Please go on.
> Prod 2: The experiment requires that you continue.
> Prod 3: It is absolutely essential that you continue.
> Prod 4: You have no other choice, you *must* go on.[22]

When they could only hear but not see evidence of the victim's suffering, a majority of people went as far as they were told to do, ultimately showing willingness to deliver a massive electric shock to another person merely for getting an answer wrong. A substantial minority did so even when the victim was in the room.[23]

What reality did this reveal? Not that some humans have duties to obey other humans, or even believe in the abstract that they do, but that what we do, and what we *say* we do, are influenced by the psychological effects of our interpersonal relations. Humans sometimes slip psychologically under the thumb of another human. The psychological hold of one person over others that Max Weber called "charismatic authority" and that the ancient Romans called *auctoritas* really can exist, and cause those charismatically led to do things that they would not otherwise do. The potential for evil consequences that this entails was what got Milgram interested in running his experiments. Reflecting on the mass complicity of so many in the horrors of the Holocaust, Milgram wanted to explore how readily our moral compasses may be thrown off by being told that we must obey.[24] And he found that people can be browbeaten into doing bad things.

People who mostly exercise independent moral judgment may have their judgment compromised when they are in the grip of an intense interpersonal relationship. When a dominant person is barking orders, independent judgment is much more likely to be distorted or even shut down. There is a *reason* that drill sergeants adopt the tone that they do. Just as the lyrics of a song may move us and stay in our minds more than the same message spoken in monotone would do, so the idea of authority may take hold in our psyches when conveyed charismatically, whether that charisma is experienced as inspiration or domination. And so we see that through some of our interactions with each other, people *may* come to practice extreme deference to leaders, with charismatic assurance that those in government have a preemptive moral right to be obeyed playing a corrupting part in producing that outcome. In Milgram's words: "The most common adjustment of thought in the obedient subject is for him to see himself as not responsible for his own actions. He divests himself of responsibility by attributing all initiative to the experimenter, a legitimate authority. He sees himself not as a person acting in a morally accountable way but as the agent of external authority."[25] Discussing later studies, Tyler observed that "because people authorize another to make judgments for them about what is appropriate conduct, they no longer feel that their own moral values are relevant to their conduct. As a consequence, when directed by that legitimate authority to engage in immoral actions, people are found to be strikingly willing to do so."[26] In contrast, when presented dull-professor style as an abstract idea *away* from intense interpersonal relations, away from the psychological *experience* of charismatic authority, we see plenty of evidence that the moral claim of a "because I said so" right to be obeyed mostly does *not* succeed in preempting people's independent reasoning about what to do. If Milgram's experimenter had been in the room at tax time, Illinois' use tax receipts would doubtless have gone up.

Our reasoning about what to do is naturally affected by emotions that well up as we relate to each other. That is true not only when our relations involve extreme dominance of the kind that Milgram documented but also in gentler settings where we encounter lesser levels of judgment-shaping influence. And emotions such as feelings of trust need not be devoid of rational basis. One critique of Milgram's conclusions is that many of the participants in the experiment may have relied on a reasonable perception of the experimenter's *expertise*. They may have thought to themselves that the experimenter must have known what he was doing and couldn't be doing anything all that bad. After all, they were at Yale.[27] That form of psychological dependence on another person need include no shred of belief in that person having a "because I said so" right to be obeyed, even though, as we have seen, expertise is another context where we use the word "authority." Apparent expertise shares with the idea of right to be obeyed a presence within the ancient concept of *auctoritas*, of "charismatic authority." And the perceived expertise of Tyler's team in presenting the idea of a "because I said so" right to be obeyed as *the way* for the Chicago survey respondents to say that they were *law abiding* may have helped produce respondents' massive vote for lawgivers' "because I said so" right to be obeyed. Just as the influence of others can in some circumstances distort our judgment about what to do, so it can distort our judgment about what to *say* that we do. Just being *asked* authority questions by Tyler's team, without also being offered plausible alternative accounts of law's moral contribution to their reasoning, may well have channeled many of Tyler's respondents into affirming extreme deference to lawgivers. That was the only behavioral option they were offered that let them present themselves to the questioners as right-thinking, decent members of their community. As social animals, we may be affected by what we think those around us will likely do and expect even beyond what our moral reasoning supports, and we may come out with authority rhetoric when we think that doing so is expected of us. Tyler's respondents were not offered a way to say that they were law *abiding* in the deep sense of conscientiously giving law the weight it morally deserves, other than by saying that they were lawgiver *obeying*.

Lacking an alternative account of law's contribution to right thinking, people who want to think of themselves as right thinking, and who want others to think well of them, may naturally gravitate to saying that they are careful to obey the law. They may see that answer as a hallmark of overall virtue. This migrates us to a second strand of explanation for the contradiction between people's actual exercise of independent judgment and their telling a scholarly questioner that they defer to lawgivers. Maybe the respondents were mixing together a whole range of reasons for doing what law happens to signal, and treating the idea of obeying lawgivers as shorthand for all of those reasons that may variously apply to our daily choices of what to do. It is easy to muddle up and mush together our reasons for doing things when asked to explain what those reasons are, especially when prompted with one candidate answer, as the survey respondents were. We have lacked a way to talk about valuing law's moral contribution rightly *other than* as obedience. This is why it is so important that we recognize the range of reasons for conforming to law that have nothing to do with authority but were likely mixed up in the minds of Tyler's respondents when they said that they defer to law. Their lack of another way to express their constructive integrating of attention to law into their moral reasoning left them with huge overstatements of their own deference.

WHAT USE *SHOULD* WE MAKE OF LAW WHEN DECIDING WHAT TO DO?

All of us can see that our lives need law. All of us can see that living together in community is the only way we humans can flourish on this little planet. All of us can see that having a legal system that *works* is what lets us live together in community. What we have not asked enough is *how* the working of the system helps us live together. When we focus on that question, we find that our answer is all about *understanding each other*. It is all about finding out how people we do not directly know will probably behave and what they will probably expect of us. We need that information if we are to do much with our lives. We have to know what people around us are likely to do and to expect of us if we are to have any hope of navigating our way fulfillingly through our lives together. We need to be able to *expect* of others in ways that our community's legal system lets us do far more than we otherwise could. We need to be able to predict how our lives will go, depending on what we do. We need our legal systems to be good at predicting how our lives will go, depending on what we do. That is a big moral reason to do what we can to help our legal systems be good at predicting. That is a big moral reason to reinforce law's predictive effectiveness, by doing what law predicts we will do. People in the past have described the good of *having* the legal system as giving us a "fair play"[28] or justice-promoting[29] reason to do as our community's law signals, or an "associative" reason[30] to do as our community's law signals. These accounts point to benefits of living in community that law may indeed help accomplish for us, but the *way* law helps accomplish those things for us, when it does, and to whatever degree it does, is by being an effective guide to what people in our community will likely do and expect. The range of good consequences that we can see sometimes coming from having legal systems all come to us through our being able to predict what others will likely do and expect.

Helping to keep law effective at predicting for us is a reason for behavior, but it does not shut down the rest of our moral thinking and has nothing to do with obeying lawgivers. Helping to keep law effective at predicting for us is just one of the things we need to think about when deciding what to do each day. It does not preempt or exclude our thinking about reasons that might point to doing differently and might sometimes outweigh the good of supporting the system, reasons like those that rightly led Corporal Meyer to act contrary to the system's predictions of his conduct. Supporting the system is not about what we owe *lawgivers,* it is about what we owe *ourselves and each other* as people who are living together in community. If a lawgiver were to say that the benefits of belonging in community impose upon us a duty to *obey him,* we could rightly respond: "we have reason to help ourselves have the legal system, but that's not about *you,* it's about *us;* it's about having law's way of understanding each other." Sometimes we can do more good for ourselves and each other by acting contrary to law than by following it, and in those circumstances, we may judge that the right thing to do is different from what law predicts. But often this will not be so. Often the good of having a legal system that works will be reason enough to do what law signals, because we have no better reason for doing differently. The actual behavior of Tyler's respondents showed that they understood this, they were just not offered a way to say it.

What weight does the good of having the legal system deserve in our thinking about what to do each day? That is a question of degree that will vary, depending on what we are thinking of doing and what good the system is doing us. If the action we are thinking of doing is one that in itself has a big effect on how well the system works, then the good of having a predictively effective system deserves greater weight in our thinking about what to do. The actions that most obviously have big effects on whether the system predicts well are actions that themselves try to add to the system—actions that try to be lawgiving. Think back to the Korean War, when the Supreme Court held that the President of the United States could not constitutionally issue a decree seizing the nation's steel mills to ensure continuity of supply.[31] Suppose that the President had announced that he was disregarding the Court's decision and ordering the Army to seize the mills anyway. Jump forward to 2011. Suppose that the U.S. Congress had not voted to raise the statutory limit on what the United States could borrow and the President had ordered the Treasury to go ahead and borrow more anyway. In each case, the President could have given real, weighty reasons for doing those actions. But in each case, we can see that preserving the legal system would have been a *very* strong, *very* weighty reason not to do those actions, because those actions really might have reduced the effectiveness of law at predicting what people in America will do. If existing law becomes less effective at predicting what our *lawgivers* will do, then what will make effective whatever words our lawgivers issue next? Why would the Army, the Treasury, or anyone else do what the President said? The only reason the President is *the President* is because existing law signals so. Otherwise he is just a guy who is popular in some circles and was once even more so. Without the support of existing law, his ability to shape the behavior of others through his actions extends no further than whatever ephemeral sheen of Weberian "charismatic authority" he has left. Leadership with nothing more than that to rest on is a recipe for social instability, for a community that is much *less community*, because life in it is much *less predictable*.

Now let us think about an altogether different kind of action about which law nonetheless makes predictions. Suppose you are driving home on a well-lit and almost empty freeway late at night. There is a large divide between the lanes that run in one direction and those that run in the other, and on each side there are five lanes, all now wide open. You have great night vision and an excellent car. The next morning is set to be a busy one for you, so you want to get home and to bed as soon as you can. The official signs placed beside the road by the government of California signal a maximum speed of 65 miles per hour. You decide that all things considered, it is best to go 80.

Doesn't preserving and promoting the predictive effectiveness of California law deserve some weight in your thinking about what to do? Sure it does. But not as much as preserving and promoting the predictive effectiveness of U.S. law deserves in the thinking of the President. What you choose to do on that freeway just won't affect the usefulness of the legal system very much. Indeed, the only reason you really need to consider it at all is that you *do* need to think about the potential cumulative effect of everyone behaving as you do, of your possible contribution to concerted nonconformity. In the case of late night speeding on deserted freeways, you are probably just fine with the thought of concerted nonconformity. The legal system's overall effectiveness can easily survive concerted disregard of some signals in some settings. Laws that long predicted punishment for various sexual behaviors even when done in private by consenting adults were notoriously ignored in private by consenting adults with no loss in the overall predictive effectiveness of the systems to which those laws belonged. If concerted disregard of *particular* laws worries us, that is likely to be not so much because it is undermining the whole legal system as because we think that those particular laws actually achieve particularly good things for us. As we will discuss more in a moment, one of law's biggest contributions to our lives is to coordinate large numbers of us for good purposes, by letting us predict what others will do in situations where our paths cross. If toward the end of your high speed drive home you turn off the freeway into an empty street and encounter a red traffic light, you will probably stop, even if you can see that the intersection is *empty*. Being able to count on drivers stopping at red lights matters a *lot* to us. It frees us from the need to slow to a crawl when our lights are green. The predictive effectiveness of red lights is just too precious to mess with. But of course not limitlessly so. If the light did not change for five minutes, you might conclude that it was broken and creep through. For drivers in Johannesburg during the carjacking epidemic, the good of reducing collision risk was outweighed by the good of avoiding attack, and drivers stopped stopping.[32]

Our noticing that law can coordinate us for good purposes brings up a less happy thought—law can also coordinate us for *bad* purposes. Without the predictive effectiveness of Nazi Germany's legal system, the Nazis could never have killed so many people. How much weight to give the good of having the legal system in our thinking about what to do also depends on *how good* having the legal system really is. If you were a judge in Nazi Germany, with real ability to affect how effectively the Nazi laws predicted the way people's lives would go in Germany, there might have been many days on which the right thing to do when you went to work was to issue decisions that threw a wrench into the system and undermined its effectiveness. Notice how much more useful thinking about law this way is than thinking about authority. Your question in deciding how to decide the disputes on your docket should *not* have been whether the government had become so bad as to have lost a preemptive "because I said so" right to be obeyed. No government ever has that right. All that the good of having the system would ever have rightly contributed to your thinking was a thumb on the scale in favor of doing as predicted, a thumb that would proportionally have reduced its moral pressure as the system got worse and less worth preserving. Where law and government are turning rotten, a decent official stuck in the binary "on/off" mindset of authority is like a frog in slow-heating water who thinks he cannot jump up until he has to jump out, and ends up cooked.

The good of *having* the legal system is the *one* reason for conforming to the words we call law that applies *because those words are law.* On various occasions, we may well have other good reasons for doing what law's words happen to predict we will do, but those other reasons do not come distinctively from the fact that the words are law. To see this, we just need to recognize that the other reasons sometimes apply when law is nowhere in sight. Where law is part of the picture, failing to act on those other reasons may be criticized as "not following the law," even though the real reasons for criticism are not distinctively *about law*.

Think about all the ways that living together involves what we hear technical types call *coordination*. If I promised to meet you under the clock at Grand Central Station at noon and then failed to show up, you might well send me a cranky text message that reads: "Why weren't you under the clock at Grand Central Station at noon?" Your real reasons for being justifiably cross with me are that I broke a promise to you and, assuming that our meeting was set to have good consequences, such as a fabulous lunch, that I failed to *coordinate* with you in a way that would have achieved those good consequences. The clock at Grand Central Station gets mentioned because it figured in the promise and in our coordination plan, not for any reason distinctive to being the clock at Grand Central Station. If we had picked a different landmark, our good reasons for action would have applied just as much, and you would be just as critical of me for messing things up. Likewise, if you saw me driving past you in the wrong direction down a one-way street and you called out to me "why aren't you following the rules?," your reason for criticism might just be that I am disregarding words that coordinate our behavior in a good way. You might be equally upset about that if "the rules" were merely words we agreed upon between ourselves for driving on our own land, as you would be if "the rules" were the law of a larger human community that covered a public road on which we were both driving.

Coordination can come from law or it can come from other sources. Where it comes from law, failing to act in a way that coordinates our behavior for good purposes can be criticized as not following the law, but the real reason for criticism may simply be failure to achieve the good of coordination. Doing what words signal because that coordinates for good purposes is a *different reason* from doing what words signal because they are law. Agreeing on plans and promising among ourselves is *one* way to coordinate our behavior for good purposes. Belonging to communities defined by legal systems that predict what we will all likely do and expect is *another* way to coordinate our behavior for good purposes. Having law is like having a message from a mutual friend. If we are both friends with someone, then I can count on seeing you at her birthday party without having to talk directly with you about making a plan to meet up. Being part of law's community is like being on a mutual friend's guest list. Law helps us achieve the good consequences of coordination by being a partial *substitute* for direct conversations that produce planning and promising. Because law helps us understand each other, helps us predict what each other will likely do and expect, law often lets us coordinate our actions for good purposes *without* being parties to actual plans. We do not need to negotiate about which side of the highway to drive on. Law already lets us know what each of us will do, and that is just as true if the law is our direct expression of communal *custom* as it is if the law was issued by some person whom we have a communal custom of treating as a lawgiver. If the Lockean social contract theory of authority were accurate, we could conceive of our legal system as one big plan in which we have all promised to participate. But as we have noticed, that theory of authority, like all others advanced so far, does not tell a truthful story of our lives together. Because law may achieve coordinative consequences comparable to what plans do, we may see some analogy between lawgiving and planning.[33] Having legal systems and making plans are really just alternative and often complementary ways of working out how to live together well, and we make much use of both of them.

Coordination as a reason to do things is never better than the consequences it is likely to achieve. As a way to shape expectations of others, law shares with planning and promising a big moral question mark. The same conformity to expectations that keeps to lunch plans and forms the British bus queue also drives the getaway car and synchronizes the North Korean goose step. Nazism would have hurt far fewer people if the Germans had been disorganized.

Law sometimes lets us know information that helps us live well in ways beyond coordinating our actions to achieve good things. Law, like a wise friend, sometimes gives us very good advice about what to do all by ourselves, conveying an understanding of what is good that we might not otherwise have. Even when a road is clear of other cars, we have reason to value learning from a roadside sign that it is dangerous to turn a yet-unseen upcoming corner at more than a specified speed. Law can convey information that adds concrete detail to moral duties we owe ourselves and others anyway, helping us know what doing the right thing requires. But other sources of information can of course do that too. My moral duty to care for my child involves a duty not to give him a harmful drug just as surely when information that the drug is harmful comes through a credible news report as when the information comes through a legal ban on use of the drug. If the way I found out that the drug is harmful was a government announcement that the drug has been banned, I might say that I am following the law when I avoid giving my child the drug, but my real reason might just be having received expert information that the drug is harmful. Caring for children is a context in which we may also be particularly concerned to set a good example, because we owe them moral education, including education about the value of law's contribution to our choices of what to do each day. That may cause us to do as law signals more than we otherwise would, so that impressionable observers are not misled into undervaluing the information law supplies when they are themselves deciding what to do. On the late night freeway drive home, you might keep closer to speed limits when children are in the car, not so much because doing so makes your driving safer, as because your example might help make *their* future driving safer.

Some of the harms that law helps us avoid are actions of others that we call *punishments*. Punishments showcase law's self-fulfilling character. Someone who does not give his other good reasons, including the good of *having* the legal system, the weight that those reasons deserve in his thinking about what to do may nonetheless be pushed into "following the law" because law predicts that he will be punished if he does not. His grudging conformity helps law achieve its predictive purpose. The good of securing that conformity helps to justify the actions of those who use force to punish others as law predicts. Deciding whether to do punishing actions that law predicts we will do is an occasion for all-things-considered judgment as surely as the rest of our life choices.

The forewarnings of force supplied by laws that predict punishments morally mirror many other instances in life where we may encounter warnings of force, beginning with the words of parents to naughty children. Our warnings to each other, and the uses of force of which they warn, each may or may not be justified, and whether those warnings appear in law does not conclusively answer the moral question. Support of law is neither always sufficient, nor always necessary, to justify our uses of force in our relations with each other. All things considered, some predicted punishments may be the wrong thing to do, however much good is being accomplished through the legal system that they support. And some legal systems may be so morally bankrupt and evildoing that inflicting *almost any* of their predicted punishments for nonconformity may be the wrong thing to do. But from the perspective of any person weighing reasons for doing one thing or another, the fact that he may be harmed if he acts in a particular way is always a reason not to act that way. Among the reasons to be weighed in deciding whether to punish as predicted will be whether the system predicts punishments for not punishing. Avoiding harm always deserves some weight in our thinking about what to do, though weightier reasons sometimes call for taking that risk of harm. Corporal Meyer risked multiple harms when he rode to the rescue of his comrades. His action risked both death or injury from the enemy for coming within range and court martial from the system for not conforming to its predictions of his conduct.

Last and least, though commonly enough, law may tell us what we already know, repeating moral truths already well understood and adding that our neighbors think much as we do about those things. In any community where lawgivers are not altogether awful people, a lot of law will predict for or against behavior that we already know we ought do or not do anyway, regardless of what the law says. We do not need the criminal law to know that most of the things that it predicts we *will not* do are things that we *should not* do. Criminal law's contribution to the life choices of good people mostly arises where it predicts punishments for evildoers, and good people who are predicted to punish have to decide whether the predicted punishments are the right things to do. A prison official who decides that a death sentence is morally unjustified may have to quit his job if the law predicts that whoever is in that job will carry out the sentence.

When telling off others who have morally strayed, we may lecture them for "not following the law" when our real reason for condemning them is their doing actions we would consider wrong regardless of what law said. "It's the law," we sometimes say, without necessarily meaning that law stops us reasoning for ourselves about what is good. Sometimes we may merely be expressing concern about potential punitive consequences of doing differently. And sometimes, with a distinctly different tone of voice, we say "it's the law" as a sort of tiebreaker in moral debate, a way to point to widely shared or expert opinion supporting our own moral understanding. We may say such a thing without at all thinking that law *preempts* our own moral reasoning, or even re-weights it very much.

That lawbreakers will often be harshly condemned by everyone else is fully compatible with people understanding law to be a purely predictive system. The harsh condemnation is unlikely to be *about lawbreaking* unless the instance is one that really does put the effectiveness of the legal system in jeopardy, such as a lawgiver's attempt to add to the law through words that the existing system predicts will not be issued, words that the existing system calls illegal or unconstitutional. If you murder your aged aunt to speed up your inheritance, the condemnation and disgust of your neighbors will be for the substance of what you did, not for the fact that your behavior happened to break a law or two. On the other hand, if you drive at 70 miles per hour in the left lane of a California freeway under conditions reasonably judged safe to do so, and you encounter another driver pulling parallel to gesticulate angrily, it will *not* be to condemn you for exceeding the 65 miles per hour official speed limit; it will probably be because he thinks you ought to go *faster still* if you are going to drive ahead of him in the fast lane. A moral duty to obey lawgivers does no work in any of these stories. In thinking about what makes law matter, we so often end up using speed sign hypotheticals precisely because our encounters with them are one of the few contexts in our lives where we may frequently have no reason to conform to law *other than* the fact that it is *law*.

Suppose that on hearing this parade of good reasons that we often have for doing things, someone says: "That's what I *mean* by authority! When I get a message that coordinates me well with others or tells me something else I didn't know that helps reveal what I should do or reminds me of stuff I already knew that helps reveal what I should do, and when the message is *law*, I say it came from authority!"[34] What is our response? He is welcome to the word, but news of these good reasons for behavior could equally have come from sources *other than* law. If he wants to use the word "authority" only for occasions when news of these reasons came from law, then he is just using the word as a synonym for law, and he is no closer to figuring out *what law is*, what makes some messages law, and others not, and what difference it should make to his decision making when messages are law. If he were to say that he follows the law because following law is *in itself* good, we are finally onto a reason for action that really is about the message being law. But what is it about following law that could cause us to call following *in itself good*? We need to know that, in order to know what impact the reason we call "following the law" deserves to have on our thinking about what to do. If what makes following the law good is that it helps us do the will of someone who really has a right to be *obeyed by us*, if law's messages tell us what a master wants, then the impact of that reason on our thinking is *preemptive*. It means we *must* follow. It shuts down the rest of our thinking and sends us off in service of the master. That is the old idea of authority. But if what makes following the law good is that it helps us have a way to understand each other and live together, if law's messages tell us what others in our community will likely do and expect, then the impact of that reason on our thinking is just a prod that shepherds us in the direction of living in sync unless we see weightier reasons for moving against the flock's momentum. *That* is systematized prediction.

What we understand law to be, and so what we understand our *purpose* in consulting law to be, affects how we use it. Law obviously does affect our lives together so much that we have a strong reason to want to be as clear, as accurate, as we can be about law's character and purpose so that we can live with it and each other in the best way possible. We do not need a clear definition of *science* in order to figure out who among those who call themselves scientists are bright and believable when they make claims to us about the natural world. We do not need a clear definition of *art* in order to figure out who among those who call themselves artists are creating works that captivate us or move us in more modest measure. The reason we do not need clear definitions of science and art is that our *purposes* in paying attention to science and art *are* clear, and enough to guide us to who counts *for us* as a scientist or an artist.[35] Any old nutcase can call himself a scientist or an artist and use whatever method he pleases to come up with whatever he touts. And we can choose to ignore him without any need to consult a definition of science or art. But we *do* need a clear definition of law in order to know when and how to pay attention, because until law's definition is established, *our purpose* is up for grabs. If I am not sure whether words are law because they were issued by someone who has a right to be obeyed by me or whether words are law simply because they systemically predict what people in my community will likely do and expect, then I am not sure what I should do with a claim that words are law. I do not know whether my purpose in looking for law and consulting it should be to find out *conclusively* what to do or to find out merely relevant information that has a weight related to its relevance, to be put on my decision-making scales along with lots of other information and thinking about what to do. That is why it is so important that we have this conversation and reach the right answer about what law *is*. If someone has a theory of law that is riddled with complexity and qualification, if he thinks that the moral status of law is a difficult question with no forthright answer, then what use is his thinking to ordinary people who need to know what to do in response to claims that some of the things said to them are *law*? Our lives together need an accurate working understanding of what law is.

In his *Practical Reason and Norms,* Joseph Raz sets forth a concept of preemptive or, as he calls them, exclusionary reasons for action. These are, he says, "reasons not to act for certain reasons."[36] He gives three examples. First, refusing to make an important decision when too tired to trust one's own judgment—in Raz's example, refusing to consider a time-sensitive investment opportunity. Second, obeying a commanding officer's order without deciding for oneself whether the ordered action is on balance the right thing to do—in Raz's example, appropriating private property for military use. Third, keeping a promise to consider only specified reasons and no others when deciding on something—in Raz's example, promising to consider only a child's interests when deciding where to send the child to school.[37] As these examples reveal, Raz is not merely making the obvious point that one fact may change another fact's relevance to what we should do, perhaps stopping that other fact from being a reason for action. If you were acting in self-defense, that fact stops the fact you killed someone from being a reason to punish you. Raz is talking about situations where the preempted or excluded reason remains a real reason for action. The opportunity offered for enhanced financial well-being in the first example, the rights of private property in the second example, the interests of persons other than the child in the third example, remain relevant to the decisions being made. Raz observes, through his examples, that people sometimes treat impaired judgment, authority, and promise keeping as reasons not to consider other good reasons when deciding what to do. And maybe some of us sometimes do. But is thinking this way ever morally justified?

It is good not to act when our judgment is impaired, but it is not always the best thing to do, and when it is not the best thing to do, treating impaired judgment as an exclusionary reason really amounts to giving it the wrong relative *weight*. I may think to myself that I won't make important decisions when I am tired, and when the decision that life actually presents to me in a particular moment is merely about whether to invest in a particular stock fund, my tiredness probably makes passing up the opportunity the best thing to do, all things considered. There will be other investment opportunities. Indeed, the fact I am not in top form may be reason enough to reject the opportunity regardless of whether I had precommitted to doing so—promises to ourselves are just working hypotheses and don't really even change the weight of our reasons for action, let alone exclude other reasons. Now let us change the important choice that life is presenting to one that presents a weightier competing reason for action. If a mugger jumps out at me and demands "your money or your life!," there is no chance that my response will be "sorry old chap, I don't make important decisions when I'm tired." No dozing off-duty airline pilot has ever refused to take over mid-air from a *dead* on-duty pilot because she hasn't slept enough. Likewise, having promised to consider only my child's interests when choosing his school may outweigh some competing considerations, but not necessarily all that the promise purports to exclude. When the decision that life actually presents to me in a particular moment is merely about whether to quit my job and to try writing the great American novel, my promise may help make passing up that opportunity the best thing to do, all things considered. Indeed, the fact that my child's education independently matters may be reason enough to prioritize it over my midlife crisis regardless of whether I earlier made a promise to do so. The good of promise keeping just adds extra weight to that side of the scales. Now let us change the competing interest to a worthier one. Suppose that keeping my promise to consider only my child's interests when choosing his school will leave no family funds to educate another child, born subsequent to the promise. Now keeping the promise and focusing solely on the first child's interests is, all things considered, the wrong thing to do. There are weightier reasons to approach the choice of school differently. I am not morally justified in treating my promise as excluding regard for those other reasons. Whether to keep the promise turns out really to be the usual matter of weighing reasons for action. It turns out that we are morally justified in treating a reason for action as excluding regard for other reasons for action only when having regard to them reveals that those other reasons for action are in fact less weighty than our so-called exclusionary reason. Calling it exclusionary therefore does no moral work.[38]

The truth of our moral circumstances is that deliberation never ends on what to do until we do it. Every day, at every moment in time, every decision we make is made on the balance of reasons that we see in that moment. Supposed precommitments are always revisable as our reasons evolve. At one moment in time, we may judge that one reason will always be outweighed by another and may say, to ourselves or to others, that where the second applies, the first will not be considered. But if tomorrow the first reason in fact outweighs the second, then refusing to act on the first will be the *wrong thing to do.* I may promise my mother that I will never drink and drive. I may say that if I have been drinking, I will not even *consider* driving. But if tomorrow, after one drink, I encounter a friend whose car has broken down and who is running late for a flight that will take him to an interview for a dream job, or to propose to the love of his life, or to see a terminally ill relative for the last time, then saying "sorry, I don't consider driving when I've been drinking" may be the *wrong thing to do.* If those examples don't strike you as yielding that conclusion, it will be because you think they do not *outweigh* the good of keeping your promise to your mother. We can make that clear by changing them up to some that do—make driving after a drink your only way to see *your mother* for the last time; make driving after a drink the only way to get to the hospital when someone's life depends on getting there fast; make the amount of drink consumed smaller.

Perhaps Raz began the reasoning process that led to the idea of exclusionary reasons by noticing how we humans have used the idea of authority, how often one person has claimed a right to be blindly obeyed by others and has not been booed off the stage for saying so. Perhaps Raz treated the potential truth of the authority claim as a *reality* for which an account needed to be given. The idea of authority as right to be obeyed has origins in a claim about reality that if true would justify thinking of authority as real and an exclusionary reason. The claim about reality was that leaders were delegates of the divine. Obeying the divine could justifiably be treated as an exclusionary reason, because the will of the divine was a reason of infinitely great weight. There was no chance that any other considerations could morally outweigh what the divine wanted, even when everything else was considered cumulatively. There was therefore no point in even considering anything else. The divine was the master, the divine necessarily knew best, and the divine had boundless ability to affect human life adversely. Once we drop the idea of a divinely delegated right to be obeyed, we are in a world of reasons that each have finite and relative weight, and we are never morally justified in refusing to treat them as belonging on the same set of scales. We are never morally justified in not doing the weighing.

If, as this book argues, law is just systematized prediction, can we handle that? Don't we *need* the idea of authority to give us relief from deciding what to do? Can we get where we need to go without taking an "authority" shortcut? Are we up to the task of deciding for ourselves? Is it realistic to conceive of ourselves as taking account of everything we have reason to think morally matters when we decide what to do each day? The answer is that we morally must, and actually can. If Corporal Meyer could manage it, so can we. And that is so whether we are Ronald Dworkin's Judge Hercules deciding how to decide a case and what words to add to the law in explaining our decision,[39] or an ordinary member of the public deciding whether to act in the way that Judge Hercules' words predict we will. It takes more thinking, but that thinking is something we owe ourselves and each other. Law is not a morality meter. Some of us may find the old authority vision of law comforting, but we cannot justify holding our moral decision making hostage to the hang-ups of unsupple minds. To treat law as a morality meter is like using a pocket calculator to save ourselves from doing sums in our heads when we know full well that the calculator is defective and sporadically spits out wrong answers. We *have* to do the sums in our heads. And we have abundant evidence that we can.

Consider how much daily decision making we obviously manage. A day of writing this book involved constant decision making about which words would best convey what I am trying to talk with you about. Every conversation you have is full of judgment and reasoning about what it is best to say to others, given what they are saying to you, including what they are communicating through tone and manner and other nonverbal cues. Every trip to a supermarket is suffused with choosing among options. If you are on a tight budget, you are forced to think a lot about trade-offs among possible purchases—which to get and which not to get. If you are on a bounteous budget, you still have to think a lot about how much of the store you are going to cart home with you. How do we manage all of these choices? As Malcolm Gladwell recounts in his bestselling book *Blink*,[40] much of our decision making, including much of our most important decision making, happens extremely quickly and subconsciously, yet accurately—more accurately than if we second-guess ourselves. We often do in fact take Obi-Wan Kenobi's advice and "use the force" of our own subconscious.[41] Fighter pilots are trained to operate quicker than conscious reasoning processes ever could, because their operational environments are changing too fast for reflection. When after a training that inculcates him with authority rhetoric a soldier enters a village in wartime and is ordered by his superior to massacre unarmed inhabitants, we expect him to think swiftly for himself and say no.[42] As the proceedings of the Nuremberg and other genocide tribunals have reflected, we *do* think we can morally hold people accountable if they make moral choices wrongly, and deference to lawful government is no defense. Given what we know about how human minds work, it is self-contradiction to say that we can adequately think through a moral decision to obey authority but cannot think through the full range of reasons that we morally have when choosing our actions each day. If we can think through authority, we can think through everything else. The very ability to reason morally that would let us absorb and act on a claim of right to be obeyed if the claimant could give us good reason to believe he had that right, also explains why we never need pretend that someone has that right when he has failed to prove it. We are never right to accept "because I said so" from anyone. We can always think through for ourselves what is best to do, giving the information others supply only the weight that it actually deserves on its merits. And the information that law supplies simply *by being law* deserves at least, but not always more than, the weight that comes from our valuing a social system that tells us about the likely actions and expectations of others.

David Hume came close to saying this in all respects but one, despite preceding Charles Darwin and the Darwinian evolution of evolutionary ideas about our collective origins. Hume saw that thinking about what to do involves comparing, involves *weighing*, the reasons life gives us for doing one thing or another. He saw that deciding whether to follow the law involves weighing competing reasons, that law supplies reasons for action no different in the way they get considered from all the rest of our reasons, that everything we find relevant to whether we do something has to be weighed together when deciding what to do. Using "authority" as a synonym for law and government, he wrote: "We ought always to weigh the advantages, which we reap from authority, against the disadvantages."[43] And Hume saw that our reason to value doing as law signals just because it is law is the "public interest" or "the sense of common interest"—the fact that having law and government helps us live together better. He dug down into how having law and government makes our lives better deep enough to see that law and government prevent anarchy, that law and government supply us with "security and protection."[44] But then he stopped digging. In any community, there are only people doing actions and harboring expectations. *How* does the law and government that evolves over time through *some* of those actions and expectations affect the actions we do and the expectations we have *today* in a way that lets us see ourselves as *secure* and *protected*? Law and government do that by, as Luhmann put it, "stabilizing expectations."[45] Law and government let us *expect* of each other, even of people we do not know, by giving us a way to know what people in our community are likely to do and to expect.

Hume did not dig deep enough to expose law's essence as a prediction system. He did not see a way to think about how law *works* to do us good other than as a hierarchy of "because I said so" delegated rights to be obeyed. He thought that law and government could not really exist, could not really achieve the good that they do us, unless we *treat* our law and government *as if* it expresses and has a "because I said so" right to be obeyed. He knew that the right was illusory, that "time and custom"[46] do not really create moral rights. If time and custom could create moral truth, that would be an "is" creating an "ought," contrary to his celebrated insight that such is never so.[47] But time and custom *could* create a widespread *illusion* that someone had a right to be obeyed—that would be an "is" creating an "is." And if everyone around us is treating someone as having a right to be obeyed, then what that someone says people will do supplies very valuable information to us about what everyone around us is likely to do and to expect of us. That information is often very relevant to what we *should* do, for reasons we have explored earlier in this chapter. There might as well be a duty to obey, thought Hume, "because every one thinks so."[48] Because Hume did not see a *constructive* way to contest the idea of a duty to obey, he thought that the good of *having* law and government called for all of us to buy into the illusion of a duty to obey, because if we dispelled the illusion, all the good that law and government do us would disappear. The good of "security and protection" called for treating those in government as having a "because I said so" right to be obeyed unless and until they were behaving so badly that on balance it was better to *get rid of the government*, take on the costs, the harms, of transitional anarchy, and have ourselves a revolution. The good of having law and government could be outweighed in our decision making about what to do "only in cases of grievous tyranny and oppression." Up till things got that bad, the good of having law and government called for treating law's words as if they tripped an authority switch and shut down our independent judgment about what to do. In Hume's words, "blind submission is commonly due to magistracy."[49]

No it isn't. We can fine-tune our conformity to law far more than Hume acknowledged, and in fact we mostly do. We can tell when our actions risk jeopardizing law's predictive effectiveness and when they really don't. We can calibrate our conformity according to its likely consequences, for the legal system, for ourselves, and for each other, throwing those consequences onto the scales with whatever other reasons we have for doing one thing or another. We can and should and mostly do make real use of our moral scales to weigh what we should do *each* day, not only on days when revolution is in the air.

CHAPTER 7

How Law Works

LAW AS UNDERSTANDING EACH OTHER

Through Magna Carta, bad King John was forced to promise not to kill, lock up, exile, or take property from the free men of England except "by the lawful judgment of [their] Peers, or by the Law of the Land."[1] That promise painted an enduring picture of our relations with government, a picture very different from what the idea of authority had given us. John's promise to comply with the law of the land would have been pointless if the law of the land was whatever the king wanted it to be. The law of the land was higher and older and bigger than the king. The law of the land preceded and ushered in his kingship. The law of the land made him, he did not make it. The customs of the English people had evolved to include a custom of paying attention to particular people as leaders. The king's ability through his words to signal what the English people were likely to do and to expect depended on law not of his making that signaled his kingship, his ability to lead, his power among the English people. The expressions of custom on which the kingship depended could shape the contours of kingship, could signal limits on what being king let someone succeed in doing. Magna Carta reminded of this truth. It enduringly expressed the idea that we live together under our community customs, not under anyone's "because I said so" right to be obeyed.[2]

Pope Innocent III swiftly saw the threat that this thinking posed to authority claims and purported to annul Magna Carta at the request of the furious John.[3] The words that the Pope tried to annul were likely the handiwork of his own Archbishop of Canterbury. What Stephen Langton wrote was at odds with the authority claims of popes and kings, and so in writing it he went against the hand of his patron, much as his predecessor Thomas á Becket had gone against John's father. The life of the medieval church afforded a unique chance for the actually talented and insightful to influence life in the wider community without having high aristocratic pedigree, and among those who rose through that route we see hints of recognition that the authority claims of the elites were dangerous, vacuous, and self-serving. As the story of John's monarchical maneuverings reflected, authority claims were mostly extravagant pretexts for power games, rhetorical flourishes amid amoral struggles for dominance.

In *Dr. Bonham's Case,* Edward Coke made the point about parliaments that Langton had earlier made in Magna Carta about kings: institutions of government owe their life to the law.[4] The idea that a king's words or a parliament's words are part of the law is itself a proposition of an existing common law. Law comes first. The lives, freedom, and property of the English people were foretold by English law, which gave account of how lives were likely to go in England. Shared understandings—conventions or customs—are the bedrock of the law and express what community is, what life in law's community distinctively involves.

Australia's Holmes, the great Owen Dixon, called the common law an "ultimate constitutional foundation."[5] The *reason* that courts when deciding disputes respect the words coming out of constitutional conventions and legislatures and give those words priority over what our law would otherwise be is that we have a customary law that says to do so. The common law tradition makes that clearer, but it is just as true in other legal traditions that more pervasively obscure its truth through top-down authority rhetoric. We have community *customs* of taking the words that come from certain people in certain settings seriously. An institution of government is just a collection of people who have been brought together and coaxed into interacting by many cross-referenced sequences of sayings that are part of the law. The law tells people both inside and outside institutions what each is likely to do and to expect, and so gives them reasons for actions that fulfill law's predictions.

Law's words can do that for us. Law's words can let us live in sync, even very intricately in sync, with people we personally know little or not at all. Language is the way a community communicates with itself. *Law* is the way a community communicates with itself *about* itself. That law is *only words*[6] coheres with law's task of telling us truths about others in a *big* group, of letting us live with people we do not know, including lawgivers we never meet. The distinctive value to us of custom and ultimately of law comes with social scale—its value lies in learning information about what others are likely to do and to expect that we cannot obtain directly from those others because we do not know them well enough.

To live together, we need ways to know where we stand in the eyes of each other. In a small group, we can and do sometimes communicate in ways beyond words—physical presence lets us use gestures and other nonverbal expressions of expectation and emotion. Inside small communities our understanding of each other depends far less on *law*. In a small group, there is little need to distinguish between what we say to each other *as individuals* about what we will likely do and expect and what we say to each other about what *members of the group* will likely do and expect. A family sharing a household may have sayings that they call customs, rules, and traditions, but the line between those and everything else that family members say to each other is often not well defined, because there is no strong reason to define it.[7] In an intimate group, the distinction between the law of the group and other things that we say to each other is less clear and matters less than when we grow as a group to a scale where we need to know what strangers are likely to do and to expect. With those who are actually near and dear, the line between law and everything else we say to each other can stay unclear. The line can be less clear, because we have less need of it. *The smaller the community, the less clear the line, because the less value is to be obtained from the line.*

The boundary between expressions of small group custom or law and everything else that we say within that small group can stay unclear, because being custom or law among people who know each other well and communicate directly does not *distinctively* add much to our reasons for action. "We have a custom of convening for Christmas every year," does not add much to Mother simply saying: "It would make me happy if you came home for Christmas this year." In many families, these would be alternative ways of saying the same thing, and the second way would be the more accurate expression of the real reason to come home. The personalized statement supplies all that we really need to know, and as we get to hear it from Mother directly, our knowledge of her expectations does not depend on detecting family customs. Indeed, *how* Mother says it may tell us more about her expectations than what *words* she uses. Contrast that with the laws of a big group, where all we have to go on in getting guidance about each other are the words themselves. Using the language of rules, traditions, or customs in family discourse has both sentimental and emphatic overtones—"it's our family custom" is a way both of alluding to a history of intimacy and of emphasizing the depth of already-appreciated expectation. Having expressions of custom that convey what is likely to be true of people just because they are in the group only becomes a distinct and necessary category of information when a group grows beyond the people we personally know well. Law is words and only words because our need for law is a need for remote and anonymous communication, away from the people we really know, and all of their nonverbal ways of letting us know them.

Law tells us about more than just the people it credentials as lawgivers. Law even tells us about more than just the people it calls government. Law helps us understand and trust each other, not just those in the group whom we may call officials.[8] The law of a community helps us know people throughout that community, because law's signals to us are *multifaceted*. Law's signals embrace the likely actions and expectations of those in government, the likely actions and expectations of everyone else around us, and, ultimately, the actions and expectations that are likely to be our own. Oliver Wendell Holmes, and those legal realist scholars who followed his lead, focused on the governmental aspect of law's predictive project. They focused on what law tells us about the likely behavior of "officials," and particularly of judges.[9] But law's *systematized* prediction tells us much more than that, because by opening up a way for us to live together, law makes and self-fulfills predictions for all of us.

We may think of the way law helps us understand how to live in community as like helping us solve a jigsaw puzzle. To see law's predictions as only about government action is to treat law as putting in place only a few isolated pieces, indispensable but disconnected from all the *other* pieces—other pieces that help reveal why the placed pieces belong where they do, other pieces whose places are in turn partially revealed by the pieces already in place. In any community, there are just people doing actions and harboring expectations, all with eyes on each other. Law's success at predicting the actions and expectations of those few among us who from time to time successfully participate in governing depends on law's success at predicting the actions and expectations of everyone else, because in any community, law will not succeed in telling a true story about the few who are governors if it fails to tell a true story about the many who are governed. Law and government exist only in and through what we are all mostly doing and expecting. Lawgivers are only lawgivers because the rest of us are treating their words as good guides to what everyone in our community will do and expect. Lawgivers are only lawgivers because existing law predicts that *we* will treat their words as effective to tell true stories about our lives together. And those stories stretch well beyond our isolated experiences of "official" action. So far as its words go, law can tell an all-encompassing story about our lives in law's community, a story that we have reason to value for what it tells us about ourselves and each other, not just for what it tells us about officials. Law predicts what we will do by being addressed to what we will do. And law's guidance about what others will likely do and expect contributes reasons for doing as law predicts we will do. A red traffic light in one direction and a green light in another valuably tell us about *everyone* approaching the intersection. They predict how each person will likely behave and what each person will likely expect, ourselves included, not just the police.

In arguing against predictive understandings of law, H. L. A. Hart observed that we sometimes speak of a draft dodger as having an *obligation* to report for military service even when that person has run away or bribed someone and is at no risk of actually being punished for draft dodging in the way that the law predicts.[10] Having read this far, you may be bewildered that this example would be given against a predictive understanding of law. Law's predictions are not just about *punishments*. Law gives us multifaceted, *interactive* accounts of how people in community are likely to behave and what people in community are likely to expect. Law predicts the very attitude of the draftee's neighbors that Hart described. Once we see this, the draft-dodging story becomes authentically a moral one into which a predictive understanding of law fits far better than the idea of authority. En route to considering this, let us reflect on what law may tell you about any particular action that you are contemplating.

When you are thinking of doing something, law may, and often does, tell you about a whole range of relational consequences that are likely to follow. Law may predict particular responsive action by identifiable other persons. Those responses may be supportive or punitive. The persons predicted to act may include persons whom law calls government officials. The persons predicted to act may include persons whom law does *not call* governmental but who law nonetheless predicts will respond in particular ways to what you do. For example, if you contemplate building a new house, law's prediction that you will receive an electricity supply upon request may be just as effective when law calls the electricity supplier a private corporation as when law calls the supplier a public utility and a government institution. If you then fail to pay your electricity bill, the responsive supply cutoff may be just as predicted by law when law calls the supplier private as when law calls the supplier public. Law may also predict whether other community members in comparable circumstances will likely act in your contemplated way and how they will likely react to your contemplated action. For example, if you are deciding whether to recycle, what a local recycling law tells you about the likely actions and expectations of your neighbors may be more significant in your decision making than what that law predicts as punishment for nonconformity, both because you want them to think well of you and because recycling might actually "make a difference" if lots of people are doing it. And so, partly through what it tells you about everyone else, law predicts what you will do. You will pay the electricity bill; you will recycle. A red traffic light predicts not only what police will likely do if you drive through it on their watch but also what other drivers will likely do, and what they will expect you to do, and therefore *what you will do*. To see law as *just* about what your neighbors will likely do and expect is to see law as if it has no *spine*. To see law as *just* about what government officials will likely do and expect is to see law as if it has no *soul*. Law's multifaceted predictions of our lives together have both spine and soul. That is why law can be so effective at predicting what we each will likely do and expect.

Law is effective at predicting what you will do because law gives you reasons for doing it. Usually reasons arise from law's contribution to your understanding of what others will likely do and expect. And always, when there is law on point, a reason for action arises from the fact that law's value as a signaling service, law's predictive effectiveness, has in some small (or not so small) degree been staked on your actions. Law's predictions contribute information that is integral to our independent moral thinking every day. When we say that the draft dodger has an obligation to report for service, we mean a *moral* obligation. There isn't really any other kind.[11] We mean that reporting for service is the *right thing to do*. Law may add concrete detail to the draftee's moral duty to help defend his community, much as road rules may add concrete detail to our moral duty to drive safely by, for example, telling us which side of the road other drivers will expect us to be on. If invading Viking ships have just been spotted on the horizon and the order goes out to assemble for your village's defense, that order tells you what everyone likely will do and will expect of you. If you don't show up to help defend the village, your nonconformity with law may be a moral failure as surely as if you drove on the wrong side of the road into oncoming traffic. Joining in the fight for the village's survival may be the right thing to do as surely as driving safely. Law will have supplied information that helped you know the detail of what you *ought* to have done, whether or not it predicts punishment for nonconformity, let alone whether any punishment is in fact likely to happen in your case. On the other hand, if you are a Viking and the order from your community's legal system is to join the marauders, the expectations that law conveys might not track what you ought to do, however accurate the order's predictions of the likely actions and expectations of others may be. If we think that the war for which the dodger has been drafted is an immoral war and nothing really to do with defending the community, then we might end up saying that the draftee has an obligation *not* to do as law signals, a moral duty not to report for service. During the Vietnam War, we heard some people say just that, and others robustly dispute the claim. That debate was a *moral* one. What law signaled did not *preempt* the debate. What law signaled did not resolve conclusively what should be done. What law signaled deserved some *weight* in any debate about what a draftee should do but did not necessarily outweigh moral reasons for doing differently.

Law often looks as if it is *prescribing* what we must do. Counterintuitively, criminal law looks that way less often than some other parts of the law. As John Finnis observes, criminal laws are often framed as mere forewarnings that particular behaviors will be punished.[12] We find talk about *duties* to behave in one way and not another more often in torts and contract law, even though what criminal law predicts will be punished more often tracks what we really *should not* do. As a whole school of scholarly thought devotes much energy to explaining, keeping our promises and performing *contractual* "duties" is *not* always the right thing to do.[13] Law's reality is not prescription, it is *description*. Law describes what we are likely to do and to expect, because we belong to law's community.

Recognizing law's *descriptive* character lets us reconcile our use of the word about human relations with our use of the word about the rest of the natural world. John Stuart Mill claimed that the two uses were wholly distinct. In H. L. A. Hart's approving account, Mill saw a "perennial confusion between laws which formulate the course or regularities of nature, and laws which require men to behave in certain ways. The former, which can be discovered by observation and reasoning, may be called 'descriptive' and it is for the scientist to discover them; the latter cannot be so established, for they are not statements or descriptions of facts, but are 'prescriptions' or demands that men shall behave in certain ways."[14] In truth, the law of a human community expresses the course or regularities of that community and may be discovered by observation and reasoning. We communicate among ourselves about the laws of science to understand the world better—to understand how the physical world around us is likely to act and to react in our encounters with it. We communicate among ourselves about the laws of our community to understand *each other* better—to understand how those around us are likely to act and to react in our encounters with them. Mill contended that a community's laws could be broken and remain laws, whereas scientific laws could not. If a "law" of science fails to describe accurately, it ceases to be seen as law. But that is just as true for the "law" of a human community that fails to describe what people in that community are likely to do and to expect. Law describes a regularity and successfully predicts the continuation of that reality. Words that fail to describe and to predict accurately do not fulfill for us law's function. Mill's error was not seeing the true element of nature that "human" law describes. Our law describes the character of our community, not the isolated behaviors of individuals. The laws of the Medes and Persians succeed in telling us what life was like among the Medes and Persians, even though doubtless the occasional Mede did differently.

All law works in the way that *international* law most obviously does. International law sometimes has its status as law questioned precisely because it is so obviously just a prediction system for the world community of nation states. International law's signaling system among nation states tells what they are likely to do and to expect of each other just because they are members of the international community. The system of international law quite obviously emerges from the *practices* of states, practices that have evolved over time into customs.[15] Those customs include the reciprocal promising and promise keeping that we call treaty making and treaty performing. Everyone acts with eyes on each other, and we hear the word *sovereignty* used to express everyone's independence of each other and the absence of any master puppeteer atop the system.[16]

Worries about whether international law really is law come from two sources that may sometimes sound the same but really are different. First, concern comes from the obvious absence of a higher *authority* in the system, of anyone with a right to be obeyed by everyone else. That evaporates as a distinguishing worry when we discard the old idea that some humans have a "because I said so" right to be obeyed by others. Authority is an illusion that deserves to be dispelled wherever we encounter it. Many of us have long seen that the idea of authority does not help us understand the true character of the international community's law and government. But that fact just reflects the greater truth that the idea of authority does not help us understand the true character of *any* community's law and government.

A second source of worry about international law is genuine. The legal system of the international community has yet to evolve lawgiving institutions that enjoy the degree of predictive effectiveness, the degree of *power,* that lawgiving institutions take for granted inside most national communities. That lesser *degree* of predictive effectiveness makes the predictive nature of the international legal system just that much more transparent to us. We can see that international law depends for its effectiveness on the accuracy with which it signals the likely actions and expectations of its community members, because international law so often conspicuously fails to do that. Over the past century, international law has failed to fulfill its function on occasions when we had strong reasons to want it to work. Events leading to World War II and the Holocaust marked only the most shocking occasion, and we see other serious instances arising still. If, for example, the members of the international community choose to endorse words in an international convention that condemn genocide wherever it may occur in the world, but in practice do not lift a finger to stop that evil from occurring outside their own borders, then the international words condemning genocide less deserve the label of law. But we can well envision that the degree to which international law fulfills law's function will continue to evolve. If one day the United Nations or some other global institution has its own standing military and frequently intervenes with force when the genocide convention looks at risk of being flouted, we will be that much more confident in calling that convention law. That will be so *not* because the convention has suddenly acquired a new author with a right to be obeyed, but because the effectiveness with which that convention predicts what will be done and expected in the world has improved.

WHOSE WORDS ARE LAW?

In 1729, Charles-Louis de Secondat, Baron de Montesquieu, visited England. It was an enjoyable time to be there, so much so that he stayed until 1731. As his name suggested, Montesquieu left a very nice life in France to take this extended trip,[17] but that did not blind him to how well people were living in England. One particular quality of their lives jumped out at him as much more present in England than in France. Montesquieu called it "political liberty." What was that? Montesquieu defined it as "a tranquility of mind arising from the opinion each person has of his safety." People in England seemed to feel quite free to speak their minds. You could walk into a Fleet Street pub and hear people loudly saying rude things about *the government*. Yet despite this widespread insouciance, law and government were just as present in people's lives in England as elsewhere and seemed to be functioning fine. It would have been impolitic for Montesquieu to have said that law and government were functioning *better* in England than elsewhere, but at our distance we certainly can say that. How was this possible? It was possible, said Montesquieu, because in England, the government was "so constituted as one man needs not be afraid of another."[18] People in England felt as though they knew where they stood in the eyes of each other. They did not live like squirrels, furtive and afraid of their own shadows. They did not especially worry that someone in government might whimsically take a dislike to them and treat them in unpredictably bad ways, ways that we hear lawyers call *arbitrary*. They did not seem to see any real risk of randomly losing their lives or their freedom or their property at the hands of those in government. Why not? Montesquieu set out to answer that question. The answer, he said, lay in how the government was set up. English government was set up so that no one person held the fate of other people in his hands.

On any given day, the people who governed England came into their roles through channels not completely controlled by anyone. Thanks to the revolution that John Locke had so dextrously defended four decades before, England's government was now genuinely *shared* by many minds.[19] In the spirit of Magna Carta, three generations in Parliament had spent the seventeenth century fighting the divine-right-driven authority claims of the Stuart monarchs. That protracted power struggle culminated in the revolution that, David Hume observed, "has had such a happy influence on our constitution, and has been attended with such mighty consequences."[20] Now it was clear that no one person in England had an open-ended ability to get his own way. The *constituting* of government that accomplished this was, said Montesquieu, a *separating* of three ways that we experience government in our lives so that each way came to England through different people who arrived in their roles independently of each other. There was still a king, but the king's word was no longer law. The *law-giving* role was fulfilled by people who became members of Parliament, whether by election or by birth. The *law-applying* role was still with the king, but if there was a dispute about whether the law was being rightly applied by the king's officials, other people were brought in from the community to decide that question, to exercise the power of *judging*.[21] Before government could affect your life, Parliament would have to pass a law, the monarch's officials would have to enforce the law, and a jury of your peers would have to agree that the law was being rightly applied to you. This let you know from day to day where you stood. It let life in your community feel comfortingly predictable. It let you say that you lived under the *rule of law*. John Locke's idea of consent[22] was neither sufficient nor necessary for achieving this happy outcome. As Thomas Hobbes had elaborately explained, people could in principle consent to being governed by a dictator.[23] And as the history of the actual revolution revealed, law and government could evolve into something much better than dictatorship without any credible way to say that all or even most people had actually agreed to the change.[24]

Sixty years after Montesquieu's visit to England, the Americans would experiment with a written constitution that called for more than one lawgiving assembly to issue laws at the same time for the same people, and that experiment would prove successful enough to endure. But in Montesquieu's time, the prevailing opinion was that power to govern could not be split up in a lasting way. Widely read commentary criticized the relationship between the Habsburg Holy Roman Emperor and the princes of Germany as unsustainable precisely because it was unclear who was in charge.[25] Montesquieu's innovation was to say that power could be split up in a lasting way if the power of each governing institution was different in *kind* from the powers of the other institutions. So long as there was only one ultimate lawgiving institution, the law could be clear. So long as there was only one chief executive, no one would be stepping on anyone else's toes. This, he said, was what had happened in England. This idea of a separation of powers let Montesquieu explain why the government of England was working well, even though there was no one person ultimately in charge. But there was one problem with his claim that three kinds of power had been separated in England: it wasn't really true.

What was really doing the trick in England was power *sharing*, not power *separation*. In each of the institutions of government that Montesquieu noticed, lawgiving and law executing were *both* going on. Montesquieu half-acknowledged this in identifying the importance of *checks and balances* among the institutions. For example, he called the king's power to say no to new laws a *check* on Parliament, and Parliament's power to remove the king's officials a *check* on the king.[26] But really the king's power to say no made him a third chamber of Parliament, with more ability to get what laws he wanted in exchange for saying yes to other laws than any individual member of Parliament enjoyed. What made that less true was a custom that was still evolving in Montesquieu's time, the convention of responsible or cabinet government, by which the king acted only on advice of officials whom he chose because they led dominant factions in Parliament and could get their way there. In 1729, the monarch still looked very much like someone who might decide for himself whether words became law, indeed the monarch had said no to Parliament as recently as 1708. Conversely, Parliament's power to remove the monarch's officials looked awfully managerial. And the biggest gap in Montesquieu's vision of English government concerned the courts.

Montesquieu missed the whole common law. He missed seeing that people whom he classified as officials of the king had for centuries done far more than *apply* law to the facts found by juries. For centuries, those officials, the king's judges, had said *words* to *explain* their decisions when applying the law. Those words had been reported to the wider community and had been added to the words that *counted* in the eyes of the English people as English law. Those words of the judges had told readers what life was likely to be like in England and had shaped the actions and expectations of the English people accordingly. What evolved a rule of law in England, what nurtured the experience of political liberty by the English people, was that separate people in separate institutions of government were *sharing* the power to shape the law of England, so that no one person in government could conclusively settle the reach of his own power. A circle of second-guessing was formed by the members of Parliament, the officials outside courts, and the officials inside courts, with each adding to the words that counted as English law through documents respectively called statutes, regulations, and judicial decisions.

The *lawgiving* aspect of what each institution was doing was marked out by the extent to which it was *adding words* to the legal system that contributed to how everyone thereafter was understanding the law, was understanding what people in England would likely do and expect. The predictive effectiveness of those words was in turn promoted by the fact that the people in the institutions from which the words came had to live with each other, that no person in any of the institutions was situated to run roughshod over everyone else. The words of the law were not the mere say-so of someone pretending to have a right to be obeyed by everyone else, who might switch those words out on a whim. The words that were law belonged to a system that was bigger than and beyond the will of any one person. The law of England had evolved into a system that safeguarded itself enough to let the English people feel real confidence that the words of the law let them know how their lives together were likely to go.

When we celebrate the rule of law, we are celebrating the fact that law can become for us a way to experience a stable sense of standing in the eyes of each other. Our legal systems can evolve to involve many minds, growing our confidence that law lets us see to distant horizons of our lives. If law depended on *authority,* on a right to be obeyed coming from some source outside the law, then there would be no rule of *law,* there would be only rule of the authority source. If the supposed rule of the authority source is in fact experienced as the will of a human person, then that rule is held hostage to the vagaries of human personality, and in particular to the corrosive effects of power on human personality. So far as this is true, we experience in our relations with each other a fear of arbitrariness. And on the receiving end, arbitrariness feels no different from anarchy. It does not matter to me as one who thought we understood each other, that we were together *community,* whether that has ceased to be so because all those around me are behaving unpredictably and in ways that may hurt me, or whether community has been lost because all those around me are behaving in absolute obedience to one person who is behaving unpredictably and in ways that may hurt me. An erratic tyrant and social anarchy each feel much the same to us, and each evidence our loss of any community identity that would let us celebrate the character of our lives together.

What was shielding the English from tyranny and anarchy, those twin terrors that all too often ruined human hopes for community? What was letting a rule of law feel real? The answer is that lawgiving in England had become a *shared* activity. For Parliament to turn words into law, large numbers of people through a voting process had to agree upon those words becoming law. That was the point of its multimember, multichamber assembly. For the king's bureaucracy to turn words into law, there had to be preexisting words from Parliament or the courts predicting bureaucratic power to do that. For the king's courts to turn words into law, again multiple people through an appellate process had to agree upon those words becoming law. And in addition to those *participatory* ways to include many minds in lawgiving, there were *expository* ways too. When someone disputed the way the government was treating her, that dispute was not necessarily about whether the government had its facts wrong, a question for juries. Sometimes, the dispute was about whether the government had its *law* wrong, a question for judges. And where the law was in dispute, the judges could resolve doubts by *adding* words to the law, words that explained, expounded, elaborated law's existing words. The king's bureaucracy could not treat Parliament's words as meaning just whatever the bureaucrats wanted to do, both because Parliament could act to remove bureaucrats who behaved that way and because the courts were open to hear complaints that law's words were not being applied rightly. The king's courts could not treat everyone else's words as meaning just whatever the judges wanted the world to look like, both because Parliament could act to remove judges who misbehaved and because dissatisfied litigants could appeal to Parliament itself, where the House of Lords exercised an ultimate appellate jurisdiction.[27]

During the period when American state conventions were deciding whether to adopt the draft document that became the U.S. Constitution, Alexander Hamilton tried to defend the drafters' choice to leave out any way to appeal the rulings of the proposed Supreme Court. As some of the Constitution's brighter opponents realized, unappealable decisions about what law's existing words meant could enduringly *add* words to the law that would change the law into whatever the decisionmakers wanted the law to be.[28] Hamilton downplayed that risk both by emphasizing that Congress could remove misbehaving judges[29] and by mischievously quoting Montesquieu on the political insignificance of judicial decision making. "The celebrated Montesquieu, speaking of them, says: 'Of the three powers above mentioned, the judiciary is next to nothing.'"[30] That quotation was mischievous, because when Montesquieu spoke of the judiciary and its power of judging, he meant juries, and the fact-finding that they do.[31] Montesquieu did not see that the judges in England were lawgivers, that their decisions added to the words that counted as law in England. Trained in the common law tradition, *Hamilton* knew perfectly well that the judges on America's Supreme Court would be lawgivers, that their decisions would add to the words that counted as law in America. Hamilton knew perfectly well that the Court he was helping to create would decide far more than the fates of the individual litigants who reached it. Hamilton knew that through its words, the Court could add to the law that it was expounding, the law of the Constitution, and so shape what people were likely to do and to expect in America. But for misleading arguments of the kind that Hamilton advanced, the American founders might well have made the Court's lawgiving appealable in a way comparable to the legislative review of judicial decisions that then existed in England and in some American states. If more of the American founders had seen that the Court's decision making could add to and effectively *amend* the law of the Constitution, they might have fashioned a review process for that decision making to stand in for the *amendment* process. They had said in the Constitution that three-quarters of the state legislatures could change it, and they had provided for state legislatures to choose state representatives to the new national Senate. Letting three-quarters of the Senate substitute their words for those of the Court would have been an obvious way to involve more minds in settling the law of the American Constitution.

What lets us feel that we live under a rule of law is not that lawgiving is separated from other "governing" but that lawgiving is shared among many. We feel that we live under a rule of law when our law emerges from an interplay of evolving institutions, of evolving combinations of people who are *ourselves,* people whose interactive behavior grows out of existing law and in turn grows that law in ways that conform to predictable patterns and that are predictably considerate of our well-being. We feel that we live under a rule of law when the lawgiving institutions that emerge in our community help grow each other in ways that achieve predictable changeovers in personnel through principles distanced from the self-interest of incumbents, something that crucially depends on no person having the last word on what he can do, on no person conclusively settling the reach of her own role. That is what gives us that sweet sense that no one is really in charge, but somehow we are yet governed, yet enabled to know what we can expect of each other.

How our communities' signaling systems travel the distance from crudely individualized lawgiving by a dominant person to beautifully interactive lawgiving by many persons depends on wheels that each community must reinvent for itself. When we have together achieved that evolution in who we are as a group, we can only look back and marvel at the feat of spontaneous self-organization that occurred. The influences of individual humans may in retrospect have been pivotal, but were always contingent on the evolving dispositions of everyone else. Sometimes, perhaps often, the spread of leadership from one mind to many may have come opportunistically through weaknesses in the character or situation of the one. Courts as contributors to law may accumulate their influence through the laziness of a leader who cannot be bothered himself holding court and playing Solomon. Assemblies as contributors to law may accumulate their influence through the vulnerability of a leader to rebellion by dominant persons in distant regions, the reality that the leader "cannot be everywhere at once" and so needs to lure potential rivals and rebellion leaders into loyalty through "consultation." What we share when we look back, though, is a sigh of relief to have moved on from a form of leadership that felt in need of a "because I said so" right to be obeyed. It is no accident that in the English language, the word *authoritarian* is pejorative. We know that law and government resting on such a notion is necessarily suboptimal, as surely as any exasperated parent who blurts out the phrase realizes that giving his child *real* reasons would be better.

GIVING LAW AND BEING GOVERNMENT

Having come this far, we can see that to speak of someone as leading, giving law, or governing, are three ways to say the same thing. There is only one human activity that we are noticing when we distinguish leadership, lawgiving, governing from everything else we do. That activity is adding to the words that count as law, sending out words that succeed in joining the system that signals what life is likely to be like in our community. How that community's legal system classifies the *rest* of what we say and do, which institutions the system *calls* governmental or *calls* nongovernmental, is inconsequential. We have no reason to care whether law calls institutions public or private. Law may shape our relations with persons who belong to those institutions just as much either way. Attempts to define essential functions of government for purposes of intergovernmental relations have been conceptual failures, both internationally and within those national legal systems we call federal.[32] Even fighting wars can be "outsourced" to eighteenth-century Hessians or to twenty-first-century "independent contractors." The only essential function of government is lawgiving. It is no accident that the institutions most likely to be called government by a community's legal system are those that host the most lawgiving for that community. We all do law *applying*, at least to ourselves. In your relations with your "private" bank, you will probably encounter as much law applying by people who belong to that institution as you will encounter in your relations with the Department of Motor Vehicles. When you take a dispute to "private" arbitration, you will encounter an abundance of both fact finding and law applying. And notice that in these examples we are speaking of the law of the wider geographic community being applied by the private institutions, not to mention all their applying of the distinct and derivative bodies of words that are the internal law of those institutional communities.

We are each members of multiple interrelated human communities, each with its own dedicated, community-defining legal system, each opening up opportunities for some of us to do lawgiving, each shaping all sorts of things we do in ways that render our actions law applying. Think of all the rules that shape relationships among people in your workplace. The larger that community, the more clearly you will be able to distinguish the law of that community from everything else that you and its other members say to each other, and the more reason you will have to draw that distinction. If you wait tables in a small restaurant, the discernible law of that community will be mostly what your boss tells you he expects of you. If you work for a huge corporation, the law of that community will look much more like the law of a geographic community—there will be documents, such as an employee handbook, through which lawgivers for that community set out to be systematic in describing what community members will do and expect. The law of your workplace community expresses the terms on which you have come together to be community, ways in which your togetherness in that community shapes what you are each likely to do and to expect. The internal legal systems of your institutional communities have a derivative relationship to the law of one or more geographic communities—cities, states, nations—covering parts of the planet where the leaders of your institutions have reason to care what outsiders will likely do and expect. When we notice that an institutional community lacks a derivative relation to the law of a geographic community in which the institutional community operates, we call the institution a community of outlaws, and sporadically we see such phenomena, from Spartacus's army of rebelling slaves, to Robin Hood's band of merry men, to modern criminal syndicates and gangs. Communities of outlaws sometimes succeed in bringing revolutionary change to the legal systems that called them so, as Spartacus might have done in Rome, as William of Orange did in England, as Libyan insurgents did in 2011. On this, we will reflect more in the next chapter.

Returning to the more prosaic story of derivative institutional communities, we can see that if your boss wants to fire you, the laws of one or more geographic communities may intrude upon his decision making even more than internal workplace rules do, indeed internal rules may exist to conform to the law of a geographic community within which your workplace operates. Your organization's internal laws may have been issued with an eye on what the law of a geographic community predicts about workplace relations. Your boss has reason to care whether a court in a place where he does business may order him to keep you on or to pay you damages. And that is just as true in organizations that law calls private and "nonprofit" as it is in "business."

How and how much the law of a geographic community affects the activities of people in an institution, including the internal word-issuing activities that shape the internal law of that institution, does not depend on whether the law of the geographic community calls the institution governmental or private. The law of the United States calls American banks private but heavily regulates many of the activities in which people in banks engage. The law of the United States shapes many of bankers' actions, including their internal lawgiving actions for their institutions, as surely as it shapes the actions of people whom the law of the United States *calls* officials in a government department. Persons classified by the law of their nation as acting privately within private institutions may through their actions be applying the law of their nation just as much as do persons whom law actually classifies as government officials. And the law-applying actions of "private" persons may affect *other* people just as much as, and in similar ways to, the law-applying actions of "officials." To be sure of that, we need look no further than recent American experience with privately run prisons.

Sometimes words we say that predict the actions of others are said within scope predicted by existing law, but come at the end of a signaling sequence and add no new words to the system. They add no new words to the system because they are expressed in settings that render them for that day and person only. If a police officer told you to "step out of the car, please," when Corporal Dakota Meyer's superior told him "stay put" in a dangerous situation, we could say that the words were law in those moments, for you and for Corporal Meyer respectively, but added nothing to the consultable law of the community because they did not help others predict what would be done and expected in the community thereafter. But if those words, and the facts that prompted them, were faithfully recorded and reported to the wider community, and if people deciding whether to issue comparable orders in the future developed a practice of consulting those reports, then the words would have joined the legal system. That is, after all, how we got the English common law. How much those words contributed to the law would have varied with how much the persons issuing orders explained their reasons for issuing those orders. The more they elaborated their reasons, the more we could draw predictive value for the future from their words. In any event, where words come within a scope signaled by existing law, they are law for the people to whom they are addressed, whose behaviors they predict, regardless of whether those words contribute to our community's consultable guide for the future. We say that refusing to comply with a lawful instruction is unlawful. The person who does not comply with a lawful order is a lawbreaker, because existing law predicted that within specified scope, his actions would conform with the signals of someone else. Issuing those instructive signals to others, as the police officer did to you, as Corporal Meyer's superior did to him, is predictive of what will be done, and is lawgiving in the same sense as an unreported judicial order is lawgiving. Lawgiving at the tail end—an umpire's call of "out," an unreported court order to pay damages, a police instruction to step out of a car—is law for us when given, even if it does not add words that will affect others over time, even if it provides no predictions for others of the world to come. Such an end-of-sequence order is lawgiving for the person to whom it is directed, it is law for the person whose behavior it *does* predict, and like most of our lawgiving, it is law-applying too. Such an order applies the laws earlier in the signaling sequence that signaled scope for issuing it.

THE MYTH OF "THE STATE"

Law does not exist to justify the behavior of some big brooding beast called "the State." Too often our thoughts about how law helps us and what justifies humans in using force have been distracted and diverted down a dead end by depictions of government like that in the cover art of Thomas Hobbes's *Leviathan*.[33] In a human community, there is *just us*. Just people, doing things, including forceful things. Dressing up in uniforms never changes the truth about who we are and what we owe each other. When deciding whether to behave forcefully toward someone else, we each individually face the range of reasons we happen to have on that occasion for and against behaving that way. Whether the law of our community predicts that we will or will not act forcefully on that occasion is morally relevant, and may be weighty, but is never preemptive. Law does not shut down our thinking about everything else that is relevant to the rightness of what we do. That law happens to call us "officials" of "the State" is, as we have already seen, inconsequential. Law may predict for or against forceful actions by people whom law calls officials or by people whom law calls unofficial. Law may predict privileges or punishments for people who do particular forceful actions, regardless of whether law calls those people governmental or private. The only essentially governmental actions that law may predict we do are those communicative actions that we call lawgiving. And all that law's predictions distinctively and consistently add to our reasons for or against doing as predicted is the good of having the legal system, the good of understanding each other better in the way that a predictively effective legal system distinctively lets us do.

Knowing law's purpose helps us distinguish law from other words we hear and say and lets us see what good law distinctively does us. As Wittgenstein observed, we can draw a boundary when we identify a purpose.[34] Law's purpose is to help us understand each other better, so that we can live together in community. It is not to supply "a general justification for the exercise of coercive power by the state."[35] No human who is deciding whether to use force on another human, or to tell others to do so, can ever hide even partially under cover of any label other than his own name. We individually own our actions. That through law we have been led into an institutional community and have been helped to coordinate our actions with others rescues us not at all from moral responsibility for every action we do. Describing some institutional communities as components or instruments of a "State" has *in itself* no consequences for the moral responsibilities of the individual humans who in those institutions daily decide what to do. The concept of a nation state is an artifact of international law. The choice to call some geographic communities with some institutional arrangements "nation states" is a self-referential choice made by people in institutions in those communities when talking with each other over recent centuries of human history. It adds nothing to our understanding of law's moral contribution to our individual choices of what to do. Law's predictions of likely action and expectation may contribute reasons of similar strength for or against using force in particular ways, whether we are marines defending an embassy from a protesting mob or private prison guards subduing a drug-addled inmate or nightclub bouncers breaking up a bar fight. In our lives together, there are just human communities, shaped and reflected by their unique signaling systems, including those aspects of the systems that regulate the internal life of derivative institutions. Wherever we have talked to each other enough to experience group identity, there is community, and wherever there is community, there is law and government, regardless of whether anyone talks about "the State." What value for our life choices we obtain from information supplied by the law and government of any community to which we belong depends not at all on whether it calls itself, or anyone else calls it, a "State."

RETROACTIVE LAWS

"Taken by itself, and in abstraction from a system of laws that are largely prospective, a retroactive law is truly a monstrosity," said Lon

Fuller in his classic *The Morality of Law.*[36] Well might we think that to live under the rule of law is to be able to know what law says about actions we might do *before* we do them. It would be rather unsporting of a lawgiver to predict new bad consequences for actions done at times past, times when we had no way to know that the law would later change to make our lives worse for having done those things. When we see that law's purpose is to help us make good life choices by understanding the community in which we make those choices, we have to agree with Fuller that retroactive laws potentially stink. We might be tempted for a moment to think that the rule of law and retroactivity really cannot be seen in the same room together . . . until we notice how we got the common law.

The "political liberty" that Montesquieu noticed in England, the sense of a rule of law among the English people, emerged within a community whose law had mainly come through treating new judicial decisions as expressing what the law had always been.[37] When a new judicial opinion held that a soft drink manufacturer could be liable to pay damages for the tort of negligence when a dead snail showed up in one of his bottles,[38] not only did that manufacturer become at greater risk of having to pay up for any snail that had slithered in at an earlier time, but manufacturers throughout the community suddenly faced more exposure to paying off dissatisfied consumers for manufacturing they had *already done*. That exposure might have been nice to know about back when they were deciding whether (and how) to do that manufacturing. And the retroactive character of judicial lawgiving did not stop with the common law. When courts had to decide disputes about what a statute meant, their words of explanation effectively became part of the law, as if the statute had always contained those words.

Thanks to the judges, retroactivity is pervasively present in English law, and always has been. Once we concede that courts in adding to the words that we watch are adding to the law at all, we expose the fiction that the common law courts were merely expressing what always *had* been law. They were issuing *new* law, and doing so in an intrinsically retroactive way. Why, then, was Montesquieu nonetheless able to present England's law and government as showcasing "political liberty?" Because the English people's sense of a rule of law came from the way many minds were interacting to evolve the law of England. The sharing of lawgiving among many gave English people confidence, reinforced by their experience of English life over time, that legal change would follow a path of *reason* that was sufficiently foreseeable to feel fair. The soft drink manufacturer really should have realized that likely he would not forever get away with letting half the back garden crawl into his drink bottles. Retroactivity did not necessarily destroy law's potential to make life in law's community substantially predictable, and certainly had not stopped the English people from celebrating English justice. Law sometimes extended new predictions of bad consequences to past instances of behavior, but English life, including English business life, remained foreseeable enough to encourage English people to invest, and to innovate, and to lead the industrial revolution.

Law as a prediction system can live with a nontrivial level of retroactive addition. Law as a way to express moral duties to *obey lawgivers* cannot live with retroactivity at all. That was Fuller's point about monstrosity. "To speak of governing or directing conduct today by rules that will be enacted tomorrow is to talk in blank prose."[39] The old idea of authority, that law implements the lawgiver's right to be obeyed and imposes duties to obey, cannot sit with applying to the past. To announce that people's duty to obey requires behaving in a way never mentioned before and that they have already disobeyed if they did not behave that way in the past is absurd. But in fact, retroactive laws are not absurd. They just resemble laws that predict consequences for other unalterable attributes, such as age or disability. What you have done in the past is now part of your unalterable story, as surely as how old you are. We might think it rarely right for a lawgiver to pick on you by predicting bad consequences for things you cannot change. That is why the U.S. Constitution prohibits American legislatures from adopting "ex post facto laws,"[40] which the Supreme Court has held to preclude retroactive *criminal* laws.[41] On the other hand, we might be happy about a lawgiver predicting new nice things for you, such as someone paying you a pension, based on past events you cannot change, such as war service. Fuller's example of a morally justified retroactive law was one validating (that is, recognizing) marriages that had failed to meet a minor procedural requirement of which the parties had been unaware, and with which through no fault of their own they could not actually have complied.[42] We would have to hold a very dim view of marriage not to like *that* law.

THE INTERNAL POINT OF VIEW

One of H. L. A. Hart's celebrated contributions to our understanding of law was the idea of the internal point of view—that those who live inside a legal system view the law differently from people on the outside. People on the inside view the details of the law not just as interesting facts about the world but as relevant to what they and other insiders *should* do. Hart considered that people might have all sorts of reasons for holding this internal point of view, but the important fact about legal systems was that people on the inside did in fact share the view.[43] But how likely is it that a shared attitude toward law would *often* exist without a shared reason for the attitude? If I am dancing because I like dancing to the particular tune that is playing and would do it on an empty dance floor anytime that tune started up, and you are dancing because the dance floor is full of people dancing and you enjoy matching your movements to theirs, and a third person is dancing because he thinks his creator wants him to dance all night to whatever tunes this particular band should happen to play, then the three of us are engaged in activities that *to us* are essentially different. It is pure happenstance if those activities all look the same to an observer. If our reasons for dancing differed, they would cause us to start and stop at different times, based on whether our differing reasons applied, and we would *not* present any convergent behavioral pattern to a *persistent* observer. We would not always share a favorable attitude to dancing because our differing reasons for favoring dancing would not always apply simultaneously. Yet what we find in every human community is a crowded dance floor, with almost everyone dancing in sync. For that to be mere coincidence of attitude is improbable; it would not arise so consistently if there were not a common denominator reason to dance, which all share, even though some may have additional reasons. And the common denominator reason, the reason that draws the crowd, is the second person's—the benefits of moving in sync, of being in community.

Hart emphasized that the internal point of view involves using law as a standard for appraising our own behavior and that of others.[44] Though Hart was reluctant to say so, for that notion of appraisal to have the sort of significance in our lives that law obviously does, the appraisal has to gain its focus from a moral reason for behaving one way rather than another, as John Finnis explained in his monumental *Natural Law and Natural Rights*. Finnis observed that we can connect law distinctively to a particular reason for using it as a standard for appraisal where we can justify calling our having that reason the central case of the internal point of view, even if that reason is not shared by everyone who takes the internal point of view toward law.[45] But the case for connecting law distinctively to a particular reason for using it is obviously stronger if in fact that reason *is* shared by everyone in law's community. One moral reason for doing what law signals would be a belief that lawgivers have a moral right to be obeyed. But as we have seen, such a belief is difficult to defend. Another moral reason for doing what law signals is the value of preserving and promoting law's effectiveness at helping us understand each other. That reason is easy to defend, especially when we acknowledge that it will vary in weight from one occasion to another. And however much people may say that they accept the first, "authority" reason, they certainly accept the second, predictive reason for paying attention to law. They may not all explicitly acknowledge a moral obligation to help make law predictively effective, but by their actions they reveal understanding that law's predictive effectiveness is valuable to their lives. It is valuing law's predictive effectiveness, not belief in lawgivers' moral rights, that pushes people into lawyers' offices despite the big bills that inexorably follow. If we want to know what people really think has value in their lives, we could do worse than take Mark Felt's attributed advice to Woodward and Bernstein, and "follow the money."[46] We humans may often disagree about what deserves our attention and concern, but our species is sufficiently social and our lives are sufficiently interwoven for us to find common ground in caring about what those around us will likely do and expect. Anyone who thinks otherwise really should try to get out more.

CHAPTER 8

Evolution and Revolution

GOING FOR IT

"What you suggest is treason," objected the noble Eddard Stark in a scene from *Game of Thrones*. "Only if we lose," replied his would-be coconspirator, eyes atwinkle.[1] Although said on that occasion by a self-serving scoundrel, we can be sure that variations on that conversation were had all over the Middle East during the Arab Spring uprisings of 2011, as they had been in Iran in 2010. And saying such things did not necessarily make speakers scoundrels. Sometimes revolution is the right thing to do. On August 20, 2011, many people in Tripoli "came to the point where they wanted to go for it."[2] They took the risk of rising up, were predictably attacked by the tyrant Qaddafi's fighters, but nonetheless succeeded in joining up with liberators from the outside and freeing themselves.

How does a whole community "come to a point" where they together succeed in doing something without the aid of the community's existing law and government? How do people act with others whom they do not know without *law* to bring them together and to guide their way? If you are thinking of refusing to follow an evil leader, how do you know you won't be a lone voice in the public square, that yours will not be the sound of one hand clapping, that you will not be isolated and what good there is in your world destroyed, that the evil one will not stay the leader? You try to figure that out by glancing from side to side, by talking with others as much as you can, by searching for reasons to believe that enough people think and feel as you individually do to let your not following mean that the evil one no longer leads. You need to know that your action will be collective action, that your action will be vindicated by the actions of others which, together with yours, will shift the deep community customs that tell whose words count as law. That is very difficult to discover, even with the new tools for understanding each other that have arrived in our midst through the Internet. For revolution to happen, enough people have to be willing to risk being wrong—not only to risk being wrong about whether revolution will on balance have good consequences but also to risk being wrong about whether revolutionary action will achieve even the initial, displacing change for which it strives. We know that rising up against what existing law and government predict for our lives involves potentially ruinous risk, risk that helps support the existing system's predictive effectiveness. We know that evil leaders are often adept at picking off their opponents one by one. We know that this is why whole communities of largely like-minded people have so often and for so long been oppressed by evil systems of law and government. But when it happens, when we *together* stop paying attention to existing law and government, we expose in the blinking of an eye law's purely predictive character. All that law's being law ever told you was what those around you were likely to do and to expect, and when that ceases to be so, the words that were *law* cease to be so. On that day in Tripoli, Qaddafi's say-so went from being lawgiving for a group to being news only of the goings-on inside one half-mad mind.

For those with substantial stakes in an existing system of law and government, the calculation about when to treat rival candidates as lawgivers may resemble the calculation about when to sell that someone holding a hefty stock portfolio makes in turbulent markets. Both calculations are made with an eye to likely consequences that are all about the actions and expectations of others. During those early 2011 days of national protest, many a well-padded Egyptian general might have reflected on his prospects of emulating the legendary Talleyrand and remaining privileged and pivotal, revolutionary change notwithstanding. Reactions among the well-situated to prospects of revolutionary change can resemble reactions inside an intellectual or religious community to a new idea that threatens the standing of existing ideas. There is often a moment of silence, in which everyone is trying to figure out how others will react and what reaction is the right one, all things considered. People whose social standing or sense of self is tied to threatened ideas will themselves sometimes feel threatened and may fight to suppress the new idea by whatever tactic looks to them most likely to work. When they see that the new idea is nonetheless catching on, they may then maneuver to switch positions as seamlessly as possible to avoid being left behind.

THE WILL OF THE PEOPLE

Whenever we witness wholesale revolutionary change, and oftentimes even without that provocation, we hear lots of talk among the community's big talkers about the *will of the people*. Sometimes we hear even loftier language about the *sovereignty* of the people.[3] Such sayings are meant to make us feel good, but a sovereignty of the people is either a truism or an oxymoron. Sovereignty of the people is a truism if it merely expresses the obvious reality that no one is a leader unless most of us are treating her as one. It is having our collective attention that affords someone power; to have power in a group is to have one's words treated by those in the group as good evidence of what everyone is likely to do and to expect. That was as true for a time of Saddam and Qaddafi and Hitler and Stalin as ever it was of people who were nicer and whose leadership was more regularly put to various forms of voting within their groups. That tyrants can be tyrants only because we collectively let them be was said with irresistible eloquence by Étienne de la Boétie almost half a millennium ago.[4] On the other hand, sovereignty of the people is an oxymoron if it translates as *leadership of the followers*. In any human community, there will always be some who lead and most who follow. Most people in most communities through most of human history have been heavily preoccupied by the business of survival, and following whoever happens to be leading has for most of us most of the time been just another element of what it takes to get through the day. In those rare instances in our history when groups got rich, we sometimes saw a shift in the predominant preoccupation from survival to self-gratification and creative expression, but still only in a small subset of the group did we witness desire to *lead*, let alone abilities and other circumstantial advantages that held out promise of leadership.

In defending the proposal to put the draft U.S. Constitution to a vote at specially elected state conventions, James Madison memorably argued that "the people" were the source of all power, and when presented to them, new words could become law, no matter what the words of the existing legal system said.[5] That would have been true enough had he meant it as a truism. If you want the outcome of a process to succeed in being lawgiving for a group, then you want that outcome to get everyone's attention. For the outcome of a process to get everyone's attention, it helps if *the process* had everyone's attention and started everyone believing that *this* was going to be *the thing.* A method of bringing words to widespread attention within a group that prompts most people to treat those words as telling what everyone in the group will likely do and expect *is* a method of issuing words that will be lawgiving for the group. But what Madison said was not true if taken to mean that the Constitution would become law because somehow, for at least a moment, everyone was leading, everyone was lawgiving. Think about what it would have taken for you, had you been a member of the American community in 1787, to affect what the law of the group was set to become. To begin with, you would have needed to be able to spare the time to get involved and to be inclined to use your spare time for that purpose. If you were poor and needed to work long hours to feed your family, that would have taken you out of the game before the opening whistle. If you *were* free from other more personally pressing priorities, you still would have needed to be a dextrous self-positioner. You would have needed to be or become situated within the group suitably for your words to have an audience among other well-situated people, and this probably would have required a history of adept and adroit maneuvering by you and your family. That may have seemed less true in the new America than in old Europe, but in fact it was still true, as the professions, property holdings, and educational qualifications of delegates to the adopting conventions reflected. We see how much people vary in their abilities, opportunities, and inclinations to maneuver for leadership in *any* human community, starting in the school yard. Most humans who were breathing American air in 1787 had no real prospect of affecting what American law was set to become.

What everyone in America had reason to want was a way of choosing law and government that was likely to be considerate of their well-being. What our history tells us is that *power sharing,* lawgiving through the interaction of many minds, is the path to confidence that our community's moral understandings, our understandings of what matters in our lives and what we owe each other, will make their way into our law and government. Power-sharing processes for choosing leaders and for leading, for adding to the words that count as our law, best promote our prospects of being led well. Obviously those processes need to be configured to keep lawgiving possible—adopting a unanimity principle would rarely be right, and recent American parliamentary experience with a procedural super-majority requirement colloquially called the Senate "filibuster" shows that with power sharing, as with so much else in life, more is not always better. But *some* is vital. We can hope to evolve power sharing within our communities in ways that help to optimize our experience of law and government. We can hope for legal systems that rotate leaders in predictable ways and that compel those who lead from time to time to work together in ways that maximize their prospects of leading well. And both in choosing ways we choose leaders and in choosing ways we let them lead, we can see that power-sharing inputs are likely to produce power-sharing outputs. Simply giving free rein to a particular leader through a moment of mass majority voting by everyone turns out to be a terribly ineffective way to achieve good law and government. Too often, the rhetoric of "will of the people" has been deployed at the dawn of dictatorship, exploiting our oft-experienced human predisposition to fall under the spell of charismatic authority, of *auctoritas*. Too often, we see someone who through happenstance of history is flavor of the month obtain a mass vote of community support, only to champion change that pushes power sharing out of the legal system through the psychological weight of his transient popularity. Too often, mass voting is exploited to turn a passing community mood into power-concentrating change that sets the stage for tyranny. And so a Boris Yeltsin can pave the way for a Vladimir Putin.[6]

Why did Madison's invocation of the "will of the people" in America not do the kind of damage that Yeltsin's did in Russia? Two factors loom large. First, the method Madison proposed for gauging the "will of the people" was not in fact the obvious one of a mass vote but rather a representative process that was genuinely deliberative and involved genuine power sharing among many minds. The fix was not in. The votes were close in the state conventions most crucial to success of the enterprise. There was genuine compromise, both during the Philadelphia drafting process and through the adoption of the first ten amendments. An inclusive and deliberative process—one that involves many minds and engages those minds actively and extensively—has comparatively good odds of achieving inclusive and deliberative outcomes that are considerate of the interests of many *and* has comparatively good odds of being treated by everyone as truthfully telling what everyone will do and expect. Second, the charismatic figure in American life who might have concentrated power in his own hands had he been so inclined and campaigned accordingly, was not so inclined. General Washington was there, presiding at the drafting convention, but he did not push for an overbearing presidency. Had he been otherwise disposed, the outcome might have been very different. Even in a big group, the *auctoritas* of one who captures the public imagination is a mighty force. It can attract us like moths to a flame. On the three occasions when the American people experienced the kind of total war that really gets everyone's attention, they turned the victorious general into the president—Washington, Grant, Eisenhower. America got lucky that at its unsettled beginnings, the one person who could have obtained mass support for concentrating power in his hands had no desire to be dictator, much as South Africa got lucky with Nelson Mandela. And the fact that a noble person was filling the leadership space kept less noble types at bay.

"Will of the people" discourse draws some of its appeal from moral ideas about our shared humanity that may be in the backs of our minds and may help inform our understanding of how we want leaders to behave, including ideas of human equality and of human autonomy. We can certainly count on campaigning politicians, whatever their real agendas, to speak fervently of their representativeness and of their consequent solicitude for the interests of "the people." But too often our competing would-be leaders resemble bad parents in a custody dispute who invoke the "interests of the children." Too often the squabbling adults are altogether full of themselves, and the poor kids are pawns in the contest. That is why *shared* custody is so important. Mass voting, whether for particular laws or for particular lawgivers, has a precious part to play as an additional hurdle that those who would be pivotal leaders must surmount, but it is no substitute for power sharing among many minds in *all* of the lawgiving that shapes our lives together. And as we have seen, much of the major lawgiving that happens in "democratic" legal systems, America's included, is shared by people whose names never appear for a mass vote—judges and other regulation-writing officials.

Mass votes often evidence what even more often is true anyway—that everyone is treating someone as the leader. But mass votes have a deep virtue within our communal lives that gives us reason to care that they be regular and real, even though the options among which they let us choose are often uninspiring. Mass votes help rescue a people from the terrible risk-taking that the Libyan people faced in trying to change leaders and that other oppressed peoples have faced throughout human history. Mass votes are part of the answer that Karl Popper astutely sought when he said that we should "replace the question: *Who should rule?* by the new question: *How can we so organize political institutions that bad or incompetent rulers can be prevented from doing too much damage?*"[7] For mass votes to help fulfill that precious service, two things must be and stay true about them. First, the voting has to be real, not rigged, with rival candidates able to speak and able to be heard *safely*. Second, no vote can ever be enough to let a leader call it the last one—no vote should ever hand anyone a mandate to determine conclusively the reach of his own powers. For these two stories to stay true, we always need power sharing in the meantime. We need our voting to be for people who will always have to share power with other people. We need those who are our leaders for the time being to interact in ways that John Hart Ely elegantly called *representation-reinforcing*.[8]

Ely was particularly noticing the crucial role that courts may fulfill in policing the rules of the game that a modern legal system sets up for rising to leadership, exercising leadership, and leaving leadership. But judges, however chosen, cannot do all the police work by themselves. Their hands are much strengthened if the system apportions the rest of government among many minds too. That way, we can hope that no one person will ever think he can get away with disregarding what our community's dispute resolvers say about the rules of the game. The power sharing that Montesquieu noticed, and that we see redoubled in *federal* systems, helps safeguard the predictive effectiveness of a legal system's core elements.[9] For example, the U.S. Supreme Court's ability to settle disputes about what the U.S. Constitution signals has been little affected by the Court's having saddled itself with a misconceived doctrine that the U.S. Congress can make "Exceptions" to the Court's jurisdiction. That doctrine is misconceived, because there is compelling historical evidence that the constitutional words on which the doctrine relies are really about *how* the Court hears cases (as a trial court or on appeal), not about *whether* the Court hears cases.[10] But Congress has in any event rarely been tempted to take away the Court's ability to decide the reach of Congress's powers, because Congress *needs* decisions about the reach of Congress's powers from a source that the President and state governments will respect.[11] Congress has been tempted to strip the Court of jurisdiction only in cases affecting those whom Justice Harlan Fiske Stone memorably called "discrete and insular minorities"[12]—people who lack enough champions among those who share in lawgiving under the Constitution. The most recent instance concerned access to courts for the noncitizen detainees at Guantánamo Bay.[13] The power sharing for which the Constitution provides is extensive enough to make such instances rare.[14] A system that brings many people into lawgiving roles for the same community independently of each other can force everyone to respect the roles of everyone else, and make takeover by a would-be tyrant very unlikely.[15]

Well-structured power sharing can help homogenize the degree of predictive effectiveness that lawgivers enjoy. The power sharing we see in many modern legal systems helps to reduce the risk that any leader will have opportunity to subvert the system by exploiting a disparity between the degree of predictive effectiveness that his words enjoy and the predictive effectiveness of other lawgivers. Military coups are nothing more than those leaders we call generals exploiting the extent to which people in soldiers' uniforms are more likely to do what generals say than they (and everyone else) are to do what civilian leaders say. The power sharing on display in long-lived modern legal systems helps counteract the risks that arise when military discipline exceeds civil discipline. Power sharing can become so part of community culture that all of us, even soldiers, internalize the idea that the moral duty we see when we see *law* is a duty to help maintain a good system, often described as a duty to "uphold the Constitution." If an American military commander were toying with ordering his forces to occupy the White House and the Capitol and to arrest the incumbents, he would have reason for grave doubt that those under his command would comply, and even more reason for confidence that many others would rise to act against him.

CONSENT AND THE DYNAMICS OF REVOLUTIONARY CHANGE

"Sovereignty of the people" rhetorically reflected our reaching a way station on the slow death march of the empty idea of authority. Those words expressed our enlightenment with the truth that our leaders' status as leaders comes *from us*. During the Enlightenment we started to say more often and more openly that power rises from the ruled, rather than descending from the divine. But at that stage of our journey, we still thought that leadership somehow had to involve a *right to be obeyed*. When Enlightenment scholars demolished the divine right of kings, they should have disabused us of the right, not just of the notions that it came from the divine and belonged to kings. But their thinking was not yet ready to let their rhetoric reach that far. The artificial bridging idea that let them keep talking about rights to be obeyed was *social contract*.

When thinking about how we *ought* treat each other in our lives together, we may see value in thinking about treatment to which we could reasonably *consent*. Ideas about what a hypothetical contract among us all might look like feature prominently in moral philosophy.[16] But the value to be found in that thinking translates not at all into truths about what makes words law. We can blame the false idea of moral right to be obeyed for putting us at risk of conflating ideas about what makes actions moral with ideas about what makes communicative actions *lawgiving*.

John Locke thought he needed to salvage a life raft for law and government from the wreckage of a wooden world view we called the divine right of kings. In doing so, he substituted one wooden vision for another, and his substitute had more holes than its predecessor. We have already seen in chapter 3 that the idea of contract *should not* shape our thinking about law and government. And what we see in the world around us suggests that it *does not* either. Under Locke's binary vision of a social contract that gives leaders a right to be obeyed, obedience is due for so long as the leader keeps his side of the deal. When the leader behaves badly enough to break the contract, the duty to obey disappears all at once. Yet in none of the real-world revolutions that we see around us does the idea of social contract help us understand actual events. When revolutions happen, they do tend to happen fast. But the timing of attempts at revolutionary change bears no particular pattern of correlation to the timing of bad behavior by leaders. The calculations of potential revolutionaries about whether and when to act are not focused on whether leaders have forfeited a right to be obeyed, they are focused on whether risking an attempt at change would be *worth it* to the attempters, all things considered. Often, horrible law and government persist for years before wholesale revolutionary change happens, and the idea of promises, kept or broken, contributes little or nothing to the thinking and acting of anyone involved.

And in the meantime, life goes on. If you were a Libyan judge or bureaucrat in 2010, the right thing to do on many days when you went to work might have been to apply Libyan law as it then was. Your thinking about the role of law in guiding your action may have been little different at your office desk than it was when you were driving home and attending to street signs. You could do *good* with your life, possibly more good than was visible down any alternative path, by acting within a legal system that was having some good consequences for the lives of Libyan people. On occasions when you judged that applying the law was on balance the *wrong* thing to do, you might have found discrete and discreet ways to be a small-scale revolutionary. If, for example, a law imposed an exceedingly vicious punishment for treason and defined treason to cover any criticism of the government, you might, depending on your moral vision, have avoided applying that law honestly to someone charged with treason either by inaccurately finding that facts had not been proven, or by inaccurately elaborating on the law, such as by holding that the words of the law did not *mean* whatever would have covered the case. You might have hoped that your misstatement of existing treason law would be taken up by other judges and achieve a mini revolution that took the law of treason off in an unpredicted but better direction. You might have concluded that messing with the legal system in this way is in some circumstances the right thing to do. Whether being dishonest in dealing with evil is the right thing to do was, of course, something every good person who hid their Jewish neighbors from the Nazis had to think about. The worse the system is, the more likely acting contrary to its predictions will be the right thing to do, not only because the more likely are the applicable predictions to be of bad behavior but, more fundamentally, because promoting the predictive effectiveness of the legal system matters only in proportion to how much good is coming to the community from having that system. Being morally conscientious would not have called for deciding whether the Libyan leadership still had a right to be obeyed and quitting if they did not. They *never* had any such thing. Being morally conscientious *would* have called for deciding each day whether acting contrary to the system's predictions would in particular instances be better than behaving as predicted.

In 2011, amid all the uncertainties of transition, we can imagine a morally conscientious judge who happened to discover that his rulings were still somewhat predictively effective using that ability to continue deciding disputes in a predictable way under existing law, even though the leaders who issued the law were gone. If the words of a Libyan civil code were still in fact being treated by most people as signaling what everyone would likely do and expect, then those words could continue to fulfill the function of law, regardless of how they came to be law. In any revolutionary transition, some elements of existing law will stay part of the system and others will go. The residents of Tripoli doubtless drove on its streets in much the same way in the days after their liberation as in the days before, even though the regime that issued the road rules was gone. Ultimately, all law comes from and expresses custom, including customs of treating particular people's words in particular settings as effective to tell us what those around us will likely do and expect. And customs can persist and continue to evolve even after the lawgivers who helped get them started have ceased to be lawgivers.

The idea of authority cannot adequately account for lawgivers remaining lawgivers and laws remaining laws after revolutionary change has ousted those whose actions credentialed the ongoing lawgivers and issued the ongoing laws. If being a lawgiver involves exercising a delegated right to be obeyed, then that status ceases when the delegating lawgiver disappears. But in fact it is perfectly possible that when a revolution wipes out senior leadership, much of the law issued by that leadership, and many of the lesser lawgivers put in place by that leadership, may *stay* and affect life in that community much as before. And that does not depend on new leaders reinventing the wheel. It would be wholly artificial to say that the Libyan civil code now implements a new leadership's right to be obeyed when in fact the new leaders have said not a thing about it, just as it is artificial to attribute long-standing customs to later-arrived lawgivers merely because the new arrivals do not try to wipe those customs out.[17]

The reality of our communal circumstances is that lawgivers become credentialed and law is issued inside an existing system whose evolution is as continuous as the life of its community.

Revolutionary events affect the system's evolution like storms affecting a ship's course on an unending journey to an unspecified destination. If the ship does not sink, if the community survives, some parts of the structure may be replaced, while others stay as before. What gets replaced, what stays unchanged, and what disappears without replacement, depends on the vagaries of the storm and on both the inventiveness of, and relations among, those on board. Signals well along one of the system's predictive sequences may survive as effective predictions of what will be done and expected and may stay recognized by other surviving elements of the system as such, even though their origins lay in extending a branch that has been lopped off. Customs that came from other customs, expressed through laws that came from someone who was treated as a leader, may grow their own roots and attach down to the foundational customary plane of the legal system. For example, if a now-deposed leader set up a special court for hearing commercial causes, or declared a particular date to be a public holiday, or lowered the highway speed limit to 60 miles per hour, the court and the holiday and the speed limit may all stay effective aspects of the community's life even if a revolution restructures much else and the new leaders never say anything at all about the court or the holiday or the speed limit. Sequential relationships among predictive signals inside a system are a typical feature of law's emergence in human community, because leadership chains are the fast-track way to form new customs, new shared understandings of what everyone is likely to do and to expect. But once the customs are up and running, they may retain a recognized life of their own within the system even when the signalers whose actions started them off have lost effectiveness. Or they might not. In times of transition, such as Libya's experience in 2011, people who want to know how others are likely to behave are pushed back to whatever they have reason to think stays customary. That may be very little, resulting in real risk of what we shudderingly call anarchy. Anarchy is not a condition of inaction, it is something far worse—a condition of unpredictable action, of absent understanding, of failed community. How dependent on effective current leadership people are for their understanding of each other is a community-specific story. Some communities may have intricate webs of customary relations that reliably shape their understanding of each other regardless of who sits in some palace in a distant city. Once we see that the foundation of the legal system is custom, then the whole system is really an expression of custom, and whatever stays customary stays part of the system.

The uncertainties of transition starkly expose the purely predictive character of law and government. Amid our doubts about who if anyone leads and even about what community there still is, keeping our eyes on what we can predict about the actions and expectations of others is the way to see whatever valuably survives to be seen through the social confusion. Arguing about the "locus of sovereignty" is pointless. No one has a *right* to lead—the only question for those who encounter opportunities to lead is whether, all things considered, they should do so. Whether postrevolutionary life stays largely predictable or descends into anarchy depends on psychological dynamics among people in the group and particularly on the quality of leadership that in fact emerges. If you are a participant with potential for leadership, such as our hypothetical judge, the way you conduct yourself during the transition time may significantly shape what the legal system becomes. Of course you cannot do much alone. But if enough of those whom the old system called police and judges continue to go to work and to act in various ways as the old system predicted they would, and if most other people go along with their doing so, then in those various ways, the predictive words of the past may remain the law of the land. And if they do not, then substitute lawgivers issuing substitute laws will likely emerge eventually, not because a right to be obeyed has returned and alighted on the shoulders of those substitutes, but because the group has survived and somehow within the group those new people have become situated to be good guides to what everyone will likely do and expect.

Legal systems have lives of their own that are all about group dynamics, to which particular revolutionary changes contribute in idiosyncratic ways. Sometimes the revolution may be *sub silentio*, as it has been in Canada. The British North America Act's place within the Canadian legal system[18] never really depended on the British Parliament having a right to be obeyed by Canadians. What made that British statute central to Canada's legal system was simply that it succeeded in signaling what Canadians were likely to do and to expect, and was recognized within the Canadian community's legal system as a central element of that system. The British Parliament had no more *authority* over Canadians than the Roman Emperor Justinian had over medieval European communities that latched onto the Corpus Juris Civilis.[19] The analogy is imperfect only because many in Canada once *thought* that the "Imperial" Parliament at Westminster had a right to be obeyed, whereas the medieval Europeans thought a right to be obeyed belonged to local leaders who adopted Roman law by reference. But in fact, following the Westminster Parliament in Canada and following local leaders in Europe was always just down to changeable custom, and custom for the Canadians has certainly changed. If the British Parliament were to legislate anew for Canada in ways unsolicited by the Canadians, few legal facts are more certain than that Canadian courts would refuse to treat the new measures as part of Canadian law, while continuing to acknowledge the centrality to Canadian law of words that earlier came from that source.[20] That is so even though the British Parliament's enacted promise not to legislate any more for Canada[21] would probably be treated by British courts as not fettering later Parliaments.[22] Staying part of the system depends on staying customary, not on coming from, or being picked up by, some master puppeteer. Anyone in the system who looks like such a puppeteer in fact owes his status to custom, old or new, which is the essence of the system.

Locke's vision of social contract did not allow for the possible rightness of revolution against a *good* system of law and government. As we have noticed, even a lawgiver, such as a judge, who acts within a very good legal system may sometimes make the judgment that it is better to act contrary to existing law than to conform to the system's predictions. The better the system, the less likely that judgment is to be *right*, because the weightier will be the reason for action supplied by the goodness of keeping the existing system predictively effective. But ultimately we humans have to decide for ourselves what it is best to do each day, all things considered. And quite aside from mini revolutions in the law that we may hope will not compromise the overall predictive effectiveness of our existing legal system, sometimes we may judge that it is best to seek outright overhaul of a whole existing system even though it is quite good, simply because we have thought of a better one. James Madison incited that kind of wholesale revolution when he proposed adopting the U.S. Constitution by a method not contemplated in the existing Articles of Confederation.[23] And the words of the new Constitution implicitly condoned such revolutionary behavior by signaling that treason against the new system would consist only in taking the wrong side in armed conflict.[24]

The goodness of revolutionary change turns on *outputs*, not *inputs*. What made the 1688–89 English revolution in which Locke participated *good* was not that the former leader had lost a right to be obeyed and the revolutionary leader had picked one up, but that the revolution led to changes in law and government that made life in England better. When contemplating revolutionary change, our reason to care about the inputs is their likely effect on the outputs. What would have given us reason to get behind Prince William's revolution against King James was its prospects of producing better law and government through the quality of power sharing promised by the circumstances of the change. That promise we would have seen magnificently on display through the 1689 Bill of Rights.[25]

Whether the revolution's promise would be fulfilled remained to be seen, and the absence of encouraging precedents circa 1689 afforded ample grounds for doubt. England's seventeenth century had been one long, bloodstained power struggle between monarchs and those who sought to secure *power sharing* in English life. Locke not only needed William to succeed, he needed to keep William's monarchical favor. To secure William's success, Locke published before victory was certain. James was gone from England, but he had not gone far. After a sojourn in France as guest of the Sun King, James had moved to Ireland, where he was assembling a new army with Louis XIV's support. And in England, Locke could hear murmurings—by what *right* was William king? Locke argued that William had received a right to be obeyed by tacit consent of the English people. Had that been true, we might wonder why there was the very debate in England that prompted Locke's contribution. The facts on the ground were not wholly helpful. William had arrived in England with an army, at the invitation of a small circle of Protestant grandees. Though bolstered by desertions from James's army, the core of William's force, like the troops of the previous conquering William, were not even English. It was true that many among the English *elite* had welcomed William, and the English Parliament had subsequently offered William the English crown, to be taken up jointly with his wife Mary, who was James's daughter. But that did not demonstrate the attitude of the English people, even on a representative basis, because back then hardly anyone could vote—only men who owned substantial property had a say in who was elected to Parliament.[26] Crowds always come out to cheer victory parades—so what? Celebrating someone's success in a prizefight hardly counts as choosing him to run your life. The prize was leadership, but it was question-begging to assume that leadership involved a right to be obeyed. Even assuming that the desire for change in leadership displayed by Parliament was shared across the population, nothing Locke said showed that ordinary English people *promised to obey* William, let alone addressed the Law and Economics 101 insight that promise keeping is not always the right thing to do anyway. If today you contracted with another ordinary person to do *whatever* the other party might in future tell you to do, courts would likely hold your promise unenforceable on grounds of public policy, at least in many of its potential applications. And as government is what government does, there is a sense in which those who tell you tomorrow to do what you have not previously been told to do are a *different government,* not the one to which you may have previously made promises. If tomorrow the Supreme Court reads the Bill of Rights to protect you less than previously, would a previous promise to obey apply to what government has become?

Aside from helping William succeed, Locke's consent argument also served to help keep William's favor. What would have been Locke's fate had he advanced the central claims of this book—that law is just a prediction system and that the idea of "because I said so" rights to be obeyed is and has always been a fabrication of self-interested claimants? That was just not something that people in Locke's day could safely say. In many communities even now, it cannot safely be said. As it was, Locke had spent much of his adult life feeling frightened.[27] From his writings we taste the flavor of his feelings, as when he asked of the divine right claims of James, "what Security, *what Fence,* is there in such a State *against the Violence and Oppression of this Absolute Ruler*? The very Question can scarce be born. They are ready to tell you, that it deserves Death only to ask after Safety."[28] Reflecting the same worries that must have weighed on many a Middle Eastern mind during the 2011 uprisings, the so-called Immortal Seven who invited William to invade showed how very mortal life in a dictatorship made them feel, using words much like those that leaders of the Libyan insurgency addressed to NATO:

> We have great reason to believe, we shall be every day in a worse condition than we are, and less able to defend ourselves, and therefore we do earnestly wish we might be so happy as to find a remedy before it be too late for us to contribute to our own deliverance. . . . [T]he people are so generally dissatisfied with the present conduct of the government, in relation to their religion, liberties and properties (all which have been greatly invaded) and they are in such expectation of their prospects being daily worse, that your highness may be assured there are nineteen parts of twenty of the people throughout the kingdom, who are desirous of a change; and who, we believe, would willingly contribute to it, if they had such a protection to countenance their rising, as would secure them from being destroyed, before they could get to be in a posture able to defend themselves. . . .[29]

And destroy them was what existing law set out to do. The self-serving character of authority claims was reflected in lawgivers' calling revolutionary endeavors the highest crime conceivable and predicting punitive responses of the most vicious kind that humans could dream up. At the 1660 restoration of the Stuart monarchy, revenge against old opponents took the traditional grotesque form of hanging, drawing, and quartering.[30] Nothing could morally justify the severity of such treason laws. Nor was there a moral defense for their overbreadth. Even Locke, in arguing the case for revolutionary change, timidly emphasized that the case depended on "the miscarriages of the former reigns" that broke contractual faith, without which "our complaints were mutiny . . . and we ought to return as fast as we can to our old obedience."[31] Well, why? Treating treason laws as justifiably stretching that far would have condemned Madison for proposing change to American government in a way not contemplated by existing law.[32] That kind of incumbent coddling had far less to do with moral truths about our relations in community than it did with serving the self-interest of authority claimants. A tragedy of our history is that so rarely have our leaders seen law's true purpose as *conveying* something to promote the *receivers'* well-being. All too often they have seen law as all about them, all about control. They did not mind using lead, because they did not think they were making pipes, they thought they were making bullets.

The same morally defenseless self-service that prompted overcondemning revolutionary actions has been on display throughout our human history in our leaders' overclaiming prestige and privilege. However did humans start speaking the hyperbole of honorifics such as "Majesty" and "Highness" that our leaders have so frequently draped over themselves?[33] The answer seems to lie deep in nature. When a bird lands on a satisfactory perch, from which there are no discernible threats to its survival, it promptly begins . . . preening itself. Established leaders, like show business celebrities and tenured intellectuals, are just so many birds on perches. For many of the well situated, whose real needs are more than abundantly met, life becomes increasingly about having one's feathers plumped. Misled by the old idea of authority, we too often treated our leaders like plantation overseers, exercising an owner's delegated rights. Our old folk stories of "good" kings reflect the low expectations we have historically had of our leaders. We too often took for granted their pomposity and privilege, and were grateful if they showed the slightest scintilla of actual concern for the well-being of anyone but themselves.

Locke was right to characterize the conflict between William and James as about *contracts*, but not of the kind about which Locke wrote. If, as Locke argued, government first emerged in early human communities through contract,[34] what reason was there to think that the deals differed in character from those that Locke could actually see around him—James's negotiations and agreement with Louis; William's negotiations and agreement with the disaffected English aristocrats?[35] Life around Locke was a story of agreements alright, but none to which most of the affected populations were party. Rather than through a contract among us all, was it not more plausible to suspect that leadership emerged among us through a mix of violence and negotiation among those few community members whom the happenstance of genetics and genealogy had optimally situated to lead?[36] Would not what those persons signaled soon become self-fulfillingly most likely to happen, interweaving their identities with emerging conceptions of law and government? Far from occurring behind a veil of ignorance,[37] the human actions that began our experience of government were likely all about realizing and responding to the variations in who we are.

Our early experiences of leadership, like those we have now, may well have owed more to someone's ability to inspire than to any ability to threaten. But that should not blind us to the dangers underlying the drive to lead, dangers that make power *sharing* so important. If you only listened to the rhetoric of campaigning politicians, then and now, you would marvel that there should be on this earth such a unique breed of exceptionally selfless servants of everyone else. But if you closed your ears to their rhetoric and focused solely on their actual behavior, you would swiftly see patterns indistinguishable from the maneuvering among dominant males that may be witnessed in the chimpanzee enclosure at the San Diego Zoo.[38]

Choosing who among our campaigning politicians will lead us does not necessarily involve promising to obey those we choose. The word "consent" has always been a deeply ambiguous way of expressing the idea that promising produces rights to be obeyed, because whether we *agree* to someone being a lawgiver for our group does not necessarily say anything about whether we are promising obedience. Ever since Locke and Rousseau, many of us when considering the value of widespread participation in deciding who will be lawgivers (a feature often labeled *democracy*) have conflated two totally separate questions. The first question is whether it is a good thing for lawgivers to be selected through processes that achieve widespread *agreement* on who the lawgivers will be. We may answer that question *yes*. We may think that democratic selection helps morally justify someone in acting as a lawgiver—we sometimes say that it helps make the person a "legitimate" leader. The second question is whether being morally justified in acting as a lawgiver involves having a "because I said so" right to be obeyed. This book answers that question *no*. *Being a lawgiver* has nothing to do with having a right to be obeyed. The word "consent" contributes to conflating these questions, because it is used in a contractual context to mean "agree to promise." Agreeing to someone being a lawgiver in our community need not imply promising to do what she says. Consent theories of authority presuppose the old conception of what law and government *are* (namely, that "true" law and government grow out of and implement "because I said so" rights to be obeyed) and then try to identify circumstances in which law and government *so conceived* can morally exist. Consent theories just assume that law and government are *about* someone saying "conform to what I say because I say so," and then argue that this demand may be morally justified when the audience has promised to obey the speaker. Once we see that law and government are not *about* obeying lawgivers, consent theories of authority lose their point. But that does not at all diminish the enthusiasm we deserve to have for ways of choosing our lawgivers that involve our widespread agreement.

CUSTOMS AND SYSTEMS

When we reflect on words' predictive effectiveness for life in a community and the ways that words may interconnect and recognize each other within a community-defining *system* of predictions, we must always keep in mind that direct expressions of custom come first, and count. It is no objection to words being treated as truly law that those words "just describe a custom." Quite the opposite. In working out what words are law, our felt need to trace the *legal pedigree* of words comes from the fact that those words do not *obviously* express customs—our need, fulfilled by the systemic nature of law, is to trace those sayings *back to custom*. When you trace a sequence of signals back from a bailiff's words at your front door to a court decision to a regulation to a statute to a written constitution, you are letting the legal system lead you back to words that you know express group custom—ultimate constitutive documents clearly rest on that and nothing else. We are unsurprisingly more careful to call words *law* when there is more need to make the case for their being so—either when the behaviors they predict have not yet in themselves obviously become group customs, or when the stakes are high—when the behaviors at issue are a big deal in community life. We might see no reason to pay an alleged tax but for the fact that words predicting that we will pay it came from someone who is credentialed by someone else whom we have a community custom of treating as a leader. Tracing the sequence of signals back to the deep custom of conforming to ultimate expressions of leadership may be essential to seeing words later in the sequence as law at all. In many systems, proving that words are law for us depends on showing a sequence that runs from the words of a written constitution to the words of a legislative assembly. What makes the words of the written constitution part of the law is the deep constitutive custom of our all treating them as such.

What of words that obviously express customs but do not now derive legal status from showing up in the sequences of signals that emanate from our leaders? What if the custom we are noticing is not one we obtained on the fast track supplied by our customs of treating signals from some sources as expressions of new customs, or . . . laws? Whether to call *law* the words that express the British behavior of queuing at bus stops depends on the same enquiry as whether to call *law* the words that express the British behavior of the monarch choosing as prime minister the person most likely to be able to get his way in the House of Commons. The question is whether the *community* understands words expressing those behavioral patterns to be part of what defines community life. If so, those expressions of behavior are *law*—they truly express custom and stand on the foundational plane of the legal system. The British monarch's choosing as prime minister the person who can command in the Commons is a deep constitutive custom of British life on a plane with the deep constitutive custom of American life we call following the Constitution. Of those two customs, the British one has so far lasted longer. The British bus queue may be considered on that plane too, and less importantly so only because the aspect of British life covered by that custom is minor. Expressing any of these customs is relevant to life in their communities because those expressions inform us of likely actions and expectations in those communities.

Conforming to customs always has at least one thing to be said for it—the good of keeping the customs alive. If we see value in having a custom of queuing, that is a reason not to try queue jumping. If we do not see value in having a custom of queuing—if we think a general scramble when the bus arrives is a better way to handle things—then our only reasons to avoid queue jumping will come from what the current custom *tells* us about the likely actions and expectations of others and what other information we may have about those in a contemplated queue, such as what we can glean from their appearances. If we suspect the current custom to be fervently favored by others, that may supply abundant reason to follow the custom anytime we have reasons to care what others think. Such reasons may include that we do not want to cause unnecessary unhappiness in the world or that we do not want others to dislike us or that we see risk that our flouting the custom may cause a breach of the peace and possibly even an injury-causing physical altercation. Congruently, conforming to law that owes its status to appearing in a sequence of signals traceable back to those we have a custom of following *always* has at least one thing to be said for it—the good of keeping alive the custom of "following the leader," on which depends the predictive effectiveness of the whole system of signaling sequences from that leadership. *That* is a custom we will almost always have strong reason to want to keep alive, and even when we do not, we may still have abundant reasons for conformity coming from what law and other information tell us about the likely actions and expectations of others.

Whether lawgivers, who themselves owe their status to custom, can succeed in overriding, in displacing, *other* customs is something we and they cannot know for sure until they try. In the nineteenth century, A. V. Dicey famously claimed that in Britain the custom of conforming to words from Parliament would override anything else. Parliament could "make or unmake any law whatever."[39] But as soon as we ask what *counts* as Parliament (what rules for composition and voting?), we see the self-refutation in saying that those who owe their life to custom can always kill or change custom. Parliament has often enough successfully changed itself in ways that made it more representative of the wider British community.[40] Could Parliament change itself in ways that made it less representative, or shut down the institutions who resolve disputes about the reach of lawgiving powers? Not so fast, we hear contemporary English judges say. Parliamentary supremacy would make sense if the combination of humans we at some moment call "Parliament" had a "because I said so" right to be obeyed delegated from some higher source. But that "hypothesis of constitutionalism" is false. Parliament is what it is only because the British people have a custom of seeing it so. Here is Lord Steyn in the recent *Fox Hunting* case:

> The classic account given by Dicey of the doctrine of the supremacy of Parliament, pure and absolute as it was, can now be seen to be out of place in the modern United Kingdom. Nevertheless, the supremacy of Parliament is still the *general* principle of our constitution. It is a construct of the common law. The judges created this principle. If that is so, it is not unthinkable that circumstances could arise where the courts may have to qualify a principle established on a different hypothesis of constitutionalism. In exceptional circumstances involving an attempt to abolish judicial review or the ordinary role of the courts, the Appellate Committee of the House of Lords or a new Supreme Court may have to consider whether this is a constitutional fundamental which even a sovereign Parliament acting at the behest of a complaisant House of Commons cannot abolish.[41]

Custom is always ultimate, and how custom evolves is a story that no lawgiver can conclusively tell, any more than he can dictate other aspects of life that depend on group dynamics, such as the condition of the economy. As Steyn observed, preserving power sharing in the system might be a compelling reason for courts not to treat every word that ever comes out of "Parliament" as law.

When do we *have* a custom? When do words succeed in describing what people in our community are likely to do and to expect? That, like so much else in life, is a question of degree.

> [T]he downgrade reflects our view that the effectiveness, stability, and predictability of American policymaking and political institutions have weakened at a time of ongoing fiscal and economic challenges to a degree more than we envisioned when we assigned a negative outlook to the rating on April 18, 2011.
>
> *From* Overview Statement, Standard and Poor's Report on Downgrade of United States Government Long-Term Debt Rating from AAA to AA+, August 5, 2011.

Suppose that in early 2011 you sold a house and decided to invest the proceeds in some more accessible form for a while. Suppose that your investment adviser brought various possible investments in government bonds to your attention. In exchange for your money, the borrowing governments would promise to pay you interest periodically for an agreed term, and if you wanted your cash back before the term was up, you could sell the bonds to someone else in the world market for their prevailing market price. When looking over your bond purchasing choices, you noticed that the interest payments you could get by investing in Greek government bonds were a lot higher than what you could get investing in U.S. government bonds. Why not invest in Greek bonds?, you asked your adviser. Didn't Greek law signal that the Greek government would pay you as promised? Indeed it did, your adviser advised. But then he earned his title by explaining to you that the difference between the interest rate on Greek bonds and the interest rate on U.S. Treasury bonds reflected the difference in probability that law's predictions would come true. The higher returns demanded by investors in Greek government bonds reflected their judgment that the Greek law predicting repayment in full was less likely to be accurate. Can we still rightly say, then, that the Greek law is about prediction? Of course we can. You and other prospective investors glanced at it for no other reason. We get grumpy when law is a poor predictor precisely because prediction is all we want and hope to get from it. Some law in some communities predicts poorly, but to the extent we bother consulting those words at all, we do so for the purpose of prediction. That we do not derive as much value from our scrutiny of that law as we would in some other communities does not alter the fact that whatever value we do derive from consulting words because they are law we derive from the *degree* of their predictive accuracy. That law varies greatly in how well it fulfills its predictive purpose is no argument against prediction being law's purpose—it merely reflects the character of predictive effectiveness as a "how much" question, a question of degree.

Law's success at fulfilling its predictive function varies both from one community to another and inside a legal system from one law to another. That some laws in many communities are poor predictors of what people will likely do and expect, that many laws in some communities are poor predictors of what people will likely do and expect, counts not at all against the truth that law's purpose is prediction. A lousy fortune-teller is still a fortune-teller. The purpose of a stopped clock is still to tell the time. The fact that the stopped clock fails to fulfill its function at all times of the day but two does not give us reason to think that its purpose is something *other* than telling the time. And while we may say that it loses its title to be called a clock if it fails to fulfill its function, that does not help it acquire some other title. The signaling systems of some communities more fully deserve the label "law" than do the signaling systems of others. But the less predictive, less deserving ones do not deserve to be labeled on some *other* basis. Helping us understand what others are likely to do and to expect is what we seek from law. To the extent that law's information is inaccurate, it less fulfills its function, it is a little bit less *law,* but that supplies no support for saying that law is *about* anything else. However much law predicts accurately or inaccurately, however much people in a community may or may not self-fulfillingly treat their law as predicting accurately, prediction remains the point of law's existence.

Everywhere law predicts the character of life imperfectly.[42] But if you have ever been a tourist, you may have noticed that local law predicted the character of life more fully and accurately in some of the communities you visited than in others. In some places, the weight of expectation emanating from law might have been enough to put you off jaywalking for fear of bystanders' rebukes, while in other places, not so much. Yet we can see that if the legal systems that seemed less successful at predicting how things were likely to go in their communities bore *no* predictive relation to the character of life in those places, then they would not be legal systems at all, and in the absence of sufficiently predictive substitute systems, there would be anarchy in the literal sense of chaos. Every uptight northern European who buys a vacation villa on the Mediterranean depends on the relative accuracy of what the local property law predicts about how people will treat the purchased premises. Simultaneously, he may recognize that when driving to his new getaway spot, the government-issued road rules may not tell him as much about the behavior of other drivers as he is accustomed to learning from the road rules back home.

Sometimes, we find that law's multifaceted predictions prove more accurate across some of their aspects than others. The laws that predict that you and your neighbors will stop at red lights and will pay income taxes and that predict punishment if you do not may be highly accurate accounts of what you and they are likely to do, even if the laws' predictions of punishment for noncompliance are not all that accurate. That may be partly because people overestimate the risk of being caught by highway patrols and auditors, partly because people are risk averse, and, believe it or not, partly because people conscientiously conclude that there are good reasons apart from the risk of punishment for them to stop at red lights and to pay prescribed income taxes.

When we see that the law of some communities deserves its description more than does the law of others, we can see that life in places that are more predictable is in a sense life more in community—we are more community to the extent we understand each other better. Like other feats of spontaneous self-organization, the accomplishment of law always has potential to wax or wane. Central and marginal instances of legal systems correspond to central and marginal instances of community; law and community are two sides of the same coin. What makes persons living in parallel a *community* is communication, and the understanding of each other that communication gives us. That understanding is itself a question of degree, and in a large group, the degree of our shared understanding derives from the degree to which we have *law*. Where we are unsure whether we can see a legal system, we are unsure whether we can see a community.[43] Our understanding that we belong together is expressed through the sayings that are our law, and where law is in doubt, community is too. Where the predictive value of law in a wider community falls into doubt, we see a turning inward to those we personally know, a retreat from dealing with those of whom we can only know what law tells us. When law does not tell enough for trust, the most immediate, most visible consequence for life in community is a curtailing of economic potential. The less convincingly we are community, the less willing we are to work together.

We see the durability of communities in the endurance of their deep customs, shared understandings that are rarely in doubt and that supply an underlying basis of togetherness even during times of transition in leadership. Where there are insufficient of these shared understandings, we may see the scope of community itself change, as we did when the Soviet Union and Yugoslavia successively fell apart. In 2011, deep customs were doubtless most of what Libyans had left to let them feel any predictability about their lives—much else was set to stay radically uncertain until competing candidates for leadership had resolved what would newly emerge to help guide the evolution of Libyan life. What sources of guidance would prove effective and complementary and what former guides would be lost to the legal system must have been very unclear. What counted as law across significant sections of social life may for a time have been actively contested, with rivals vying to define life in the community. It was not a good time to enter a contract with a stranger in Libya. The economic consequences of such uncertainty are incalculable, but predictably terrible.

Even highly predictive lawgivers may completely fail in some of their attempts at lawgiving. Our community may, for example, have a well-settled custom of following leadership in most respects, but not all, and not in ways that would alter some other customs. When our leaders try to change some of our customs, they may fail—the custom of treating them as leaders may just not extend to any attempts to mess with those other customs. The idea of authority does not know what to do with community-wide disregard of, and divergence from, some but not all of an ultimate leadership's signals, except emptily to condemn it. Suppose that pursuant to treaty commitments, the leadership of a European nation issues new laws about cheese- and sausage-making. Suppose that the nation's cheese and sausage makers disregard the new rules in favor of their traditional methods, and those persons predicted by the rules to punish for noncompliance do not do so. After time for things to shake out, our assessment of that community may frankly be that those who issued the purported cheese- and sausage-making laws are not lawgivers with respect to cheese- and sausage-making, however much they may be lawgivers with respect to other matters. The community's custom of treating them as leaders just does not extend to cheese- and sausage-making, as reflected by the behavior of everyone in the community who is predicted by the cheese- and sausage-making "laws" to *apply* those "laws," including the cheese and sausage makers themselves and the persons predicted to punish for noncompliance. If the European Union gets on the community's case and applies various forms of pressure, such as by threatening to ban exports to other parts of the Union, maybe that will change—maybe the community's custom of making cheese and sausage in its traditional way will cave and people will start applying the law on the books.

In a 1910 article, Roscoe Pound distinguished "law in books and law in action."[44] That distinction points to differences between what some of the words we call law predict about what people will do and expect, and what the patterns of behavior in a community turn out to be, some of which we may perpetuate through talking about them, as in "the law on the books technically says this should be done, but no one ever does it, instead we all do that other thing." The phrase "law in action" is, however, apt to mislead about what law is. Only *people* are ever "in action." Some of the actions people do are communicative. Some of the words that are communicated among people in a human community come to be understood as expressing community law. The truth that Pound's distinction highlighted is that sometimes the articulated customs of a community include both a custom of treating words coming from a particular institution as law and other customs that qualify and cut down the reach of the primary custom. Sometimes even those within the very institutions that issued the law on the books consistently act in ways that differ from what the law on the books signals, and these patterns of differing behavior become talked about in ways that spread the word about what is really likely to be done and expected. Whether a community's custom of paying attention to particular people as lawgivers will prevail over other customs is always something we do not know until it happens.

Law supplies a starting point for figuring out what is likely to happen in a community. Belonging to a community's signaling system, being pedigreed as a signal in sequence, is prima facie evidence of words' predictive value in that community. News we get from other sources may, however, add to our understanding in ways that rebut the presumption of law's predictive value. For example, law in predicting some bureaucrat's actions may call those actions performances of duty, or exercises of power, or both those things—obligatory exercises of power. From the bureaucrat's perspective in making daily choices of what to do, law's characterizing his likely behavior in one way or another is relevant to what he should do, but not conclusive. Life inside his department may reveal that those around him really *do* expect him to exercise a formally discretionary power, and will react adversely if he does not, or that those around him really do *not* expect him to perform a legal duty, and will react adversely or indifferently if he does. If he is a fairly low-level functionary, he may never read the applicable law at all—law's guidance about what to do at the office each day may come comprehensively mediated and filtered through conversations with other persons in that office. Those on the outside with whom he deals will discover soon enough through their dealings how closely law's predictions of the bureaucracy's behavior track what actually happens. Bureaucracy is, however, a setting in which law shapes life a lot, often in minute detail. Some of that law comes from inside the institutional community, some from the wider geographic community in which the institution operates. What we find when people have to spend their whole workdays together in closely coordinated activity in a *large* group is that the group needs a lot of law, because those issuing instructions are not personally interacting regularly with most of those whom they are instructing. This notoriously produces inflexibility. Innovation and resort to the reasons behind the rules when deciding what to do is inhibited, because the benefits of innovation are unlikely to be personally felt by the innovators, and the risks bureaucrats incur by even minor nonconformity may be substantial. Often their immediate superiors will take credit for any successes and be swift to attribute blame for any missteps. This is all just as true inside General Motors as it is inside the Department of Commerce; just as true inside Citibank as it is inside the World Bank. Higher-ups often get caught up in valuing conformity with their rules as in itself a measure of success, wholly aside from actual effects of the institution on the wider world. During my stint in bureaucracy, a memorandum circulated from the division head to all of us, reminding us that in all of our documents we should be using courier font. The marvel of this to me was, as you might guess, that such a senior person would spend even a second thinking about such a thing, let alone the time he took to issue the memo.

The confidence to deal with people we do not know is a legal system's signature accomplishment. Corruption may put that accomplishment at grave risk. A former student of mine, whom we shall call Carlos, practices law in Mexico. Recently, he represented a foreign corporate client in litigation over a business transaction that had gone awry. He advised his client that existing law was overwhelmingly in their favor, and the case proceeded to court. On intermediate appeal, they lost, despite a dissenting judge confirming that the existing law was compellingly in their favor. The majority's published words did nothing to rebut that conclusion—they just verbosely recited the facts in the record without any real attempt to justify their decision. The backstory turned out to be that the majority acted under instruction of a higher-up who is influential in affecting the promotion decisions of the Mexican Judicial Council. If this sort of thing goes on much in any community, it must corrode the confidence that people need for doing business with those whom they do not know. Notice, however, that the deep source of potential economic harm is not the moral dubiety of behavior, it is the unpredictability of behavior. We might think that if corruption follows predictable patterns, if it is knowable custom, then to an outsider contemplating the costs of doing business it may look little different from formal regulation. It might be just another instance in which a community's custom of paying attention to lawgivers is limited by the vitality of another custom. In practice, however, a culture of corruption eats away at the predictability of life, because the motivations that invigorate a custom of corruption are limitless and always on the lookout for new angles to exploit. Corruption is like effluent from a broken sewer pipe in a high-rise, ever searching out extra points of penetration. When we encounter entrenched customs of corruption, we are reminded how pervasively our thinking about law as the expression of our customs is thinking about questions of degree. Not only is being predictive for life in a community a question of degree but so is the moral weight that law's predictions deserve in our thinking about what to do. That "everybody is doing it" is good to know, it is relevant information, but never conclusively resolves for us what *we* should do.

CHAPTER 9

Reading to Understand Each Other

Imagine that to great fanfare a colorful sporting personality announces on late night television that he has devised a new sport. He then begins a book tour for his heavily hyped rule book. Suppose that you buy the book, and on a nice sunny day, you and some friends decide to wander out to a park and try playing. After one game, you all agree that you have enjoyed playing enough to want to play some more, but one of you points out an aspect of the rules that seemed overly complicated with little real payoff, so he proposes that for the next game you change that rule.

As the second game gets underway, it so happens that the sport's celebrity inventor is being driven past the park. He notices the variation in rules by which you are playing, tells his driver to pull over, jumps out, and comes rushing across to you. "Stop!" he bellows. "I did not intend the game to be played that way. If you're going to play, you have to stick to the rules." You all stare at him, stupefied and bewildered.

Our celebrity was already known to have a filthy temper, so why does this little performance still strike you as strange? And why, once he has departed, do you not feel the slightest inclination to do what he said? If you have persisted with this book to chapter 9, you are probably ahead of the story and already muttering: "What a control freak, what makes him think he has a right to be obeyed?" And that would, of course, be the right response. The author of the rule book has no right to be obeyed. We as a group of would-be players are free to play by whatever rules we please. He has no *authority* over us.

Is it any different when rules are written for the wider life of a group and not just for one group activity? Not really. No one gets a right to be obeyed just because he came up with some ideas for contributions to the rule book. What makes the words in the rule book *the rules* is our choice as a community to play by them, regardless of whether that choice is made through a negotiated agreement among us all or under the bullying or persuasion of dominant people, or just by happenstance of converging on behavior that seemed to work out well for ourselves and others. The story of law is the story of that long sporting season that is the life of a human community. The rules by which the sport is played evolve over time as we play it, and good changes come when we notice ways to make it a better game for us. No one who succeeds in shaping the game does so through any right to be obeyed. Where she succeeds, it is because we all happened to be paying attention, and once it seems likely that other players will abide by a possible rule change, we do too, because a generally shared understanding of what the rules are is what makes the game possible and worthwhile.

If you were asked at any moment during a game to say what the rules are, how would you know what to say? The right answer would be for you to express as well as you could how everyone was understanding the rules, not what any particular contributor to those rules intended. If there is a dispute about the rules, we have to exit the game to settle the dispute unless our existing rules signal a way to add clarifying words to the rules as we go along. Maybe, for the law as much as for the facts, we already share an understanding of who can umpire, who can referee, who can issue words that we expect each other to treat as an effective rule change or explanation. The clarifying words will mean to us what we think they mean to everyone else. Language lets such connective thoughts achieve shared understanding. Maybe the person who contributed the clarifying words is multilingual and actually intended a meaning that the clarifying words would have in some language that the rest of us don't share. For the purpose of the game, the meaning that matters to us is the meaning that we *do* share. And if there is no such thing, then the clarification is a failure and further clarifying words may be needed to let the game go on.

Obviously the game will descend into chaos if extensive rule changes happen too frequently, because the whole point of the rules is to let us be able to understand how others are likely to behave and what they are likely to expect of us *over time*. Our goal in reading law is to understand what life in our community is *going* to be like in respects that matter to us, and words issued at one moment in time cannot help us learn about that unless those words are understood in the same way across the community and over time. That will never be achieved perfectly, but if it is not achieved at all, then law fails to fulfill our hopes for it.

The words that we call the rules of the game do not in themselves have *purposes*. The words that we call the rules of the game do not in themselves have *perspectives* on what we *should* do.[1] Only *people* can have purposes and perspectives. What usually causes us to care about words is concern to understand the people who say those words to us. We pay attention when we want to know *those people's* purposes and perspectives. But law, like the rules of a game, is different. We care about and pay attention to the words that are law *not* because we want to understand *lawgivers,* but because we want to understand *each other.* It would be different if lawgivers had a right to be obeyed. That would set us off on a quest to understand them—their purposes, their perspectives, their will for our lives. But once we see that law is just systematized prediction, then the only reason to focus on trying to understand lawgivers is if we think that *others* will do so. The role of a community's language in conveying community custom is deeply different from the role of the community's language in conveying particular communicators' personal truths. What makes someone a lawgiver and her words law is our seeing her as a lawgiver and her words as law. That is so whether or not she intends even to be a lawgiver, let alone whether or not she intends her words to be understood in the way that the receiving community understands them. She could be as reluctant to lead as the hapless protagonist in *Monty Python's Life of Brian,*[2] perhaps not even aware that her words are being used by a human community to help constitute its customs. When the significance of communication *for us* comes from the fact that the communication self-constitutes community custom, discovering likely "reader response" is our reason for reading.[3]

What we need to know from law is what we all will likely do and expect, and that depends on what everyone else is treating as the way to work out what law's words mean. If everyone else is scouring beyond law's words for evidence of lawgiver purpose to second-guess what they would otherwise understand law's words to mean, then we have reason to do so too, as surely as we would have reason to consult the Cheshire Cat[4] or the little boy who said the Emperor had no clothes[5] if that was what everyone else was doing. What we need from law is news of what everyone else will likely do and expect. We need to find that out, by whatever means necessary, or law is useless to us. And others *may* be looking for lawgiver purposes and perspectives, because we are in collective recovery from indoctrination with the idea of authority, and because in so much of the rest of life our reason to read and hear words is to know their authors.[6] When we have conversations in community about *why* we pay attention to law, we may point out to others that all we want from law is to understand each other. Law can help us do that most effectively if we cut to the chase and read law's actual words with our eyes only on what the context of their appearance in our community lets us together understand. We can admit that our courts *add* to the law through clarifying words in our shared language when law's existing words don't help us share understanding enough.[7] We can encourage each other not to think about law in ways that compromise law's capacity to make our lives together more certain. We can tell each other to stop chatting with the Cheshire Cat.

Let us go back to a time long before 1997, a time when Hong Kong was a British colony and the automobile had just been invented. Imagine that at that earlier time, the Parliament of the United Kingdom enacted a law that it called the Hong Kong Traffic Act. In parliamentary debate on the measure, the responsible minister explained to the House of Commons that the Government's purpose in proposing the bill to the House was to ensure that Hong Kong traffic laws would conform to British ones in various salient ways, including that motorists drive on the left side of the road. To be user-friendly to the people of Hong Kong, the Government proposed that Parliament enact a text written in the local language, Cantonese, rather than in English. The minister's speech was duly recorded in *Hansard*. Unfortunately, the Cantonese words actually enacted said that motorists were to drive on the *right* side of the road. Suppose that the text of the law arrives in Hong Kong, and everyone dutifully drives on the right side of the road. Suppose that you step off a ship from England some time later, jump straight into a waiting car, and speed off on the left side of the road. You wonder why oncoming drivers seem to be rather over on your side, why they wait so long to correct their errors that they have to swerve, why they are honking and looking at you strangely. You guess it must be to do with your being so obviously foreign and exotic. Eventually you cause a huge multi-vehicle pileup, and the next day find yourself in court, charged with the criminal offense of dangerous driving and buried under a blizzard of civil lawsuits too. When asked how you plead, you say: "Not guilty, your Honor. I read in *The Times* not long before I left London that Parliament had passed a law to ensure that Hong Kong traffic behaved the same way as the British. The law is on my side, and the prosecutors have charged the wrong person. They should have charged everyone else." Are you right about that?

Now switch to being someone who is driving over the border from mainland China and who happens to have checked the text of the new Hong Kong Traffic Act beforehand. As you are fluent in Cantonese, your perusal of the law's text leaves you in no doubt about what to do to stay safe in Hong Kong—you drive on the right. Unfortunately, in the meantime, litigation over the earlier accident has prompted communication with London, a copy of *Hansard* has arrived, and a court has ruled that the law should be understood to mean "drive on the left." Everyone has switched over to driving on the left because of the ruling. The next day, you are in court over yet another accident, and when asked how you plead, you angrily brandish a copy of the Hong Kong Traffic Act.

How should these court cases go? We can see that what drivers in Hong Kong really have reason to care about is what other drivers and government officials in Hong Kong will likely do and expect. Whatever that is, that's what we want to know when we consult law. If law fails to tell us that, then law fails in its function. If law succeeds in telling us that, then law succeeds in its function, however that success is achieved. What the lawgiver intended is *in itself* irrelevant to what law *means*. The lines of symbols we call law succeed in predicting what law's receiving community *understand* them to succeed in predicting. The law of a community is what its receiving community understands it to be. Where that understanding changes, the law changes, regardless of what triggered the change. Drivers caught up in the moment of confusion might be forgiven by the judicial system through some sort of excuse doctrine, but we would be surprised if those who went with the flow of traffic were so much as charged over either accident. And whatever the people of Hong Kong treated the words of the Traffic Act as meaning in the long term, there would be little sympathy a year later for someone who drove against the traffic because he had a different theory of meaning. If Hong Kong continued to drive on the right, everyone would understand that the law's literal meaning in Cantonese was the law's legal meaning. If Hong Kong switched to driving on the left, everyone would understand that the court ruling conveyed the law's legal meaning, not because Parliament actually had a right to be obeyed, but because law's predictive words had been expounded, had been elaborated upon, by more words (in this instance, from a court) that everyone is treating as adding to the law and telling them what everyone else in Hong Kong is likely to do and to expect. How would people *know* that the words of the court ruling succeeded in saying that "right" in the Traffic Act meant "left"? Because the *public meaning* of the words used *in the court ruling* is "right in the Traffic Act means left." If the court ruling had literally said "right in the Traffic Act means right," everyone would have continued driving on the right, even if the court typist had messed up and the judge had *intended* for people to switch over to the left. Ultimately, we as a community cannot have a shared understanding of law's words other than what we can access through our shared language. That is our source of common reference. Law is only words. All that words can achieve as law is to tell us about each other.

If they don't do that, they don't do anything *as law*. Living together in a large group depends on a shared language. Only the words of that language can convey throughout the group news of what is likely to be true of people just because they are in the group.[8] Law can fulfill its predictive function only through a shared language that lets law's words have a *public meaning*.

In the second half of the twentieth century, the Supreme Court of the United States issued many opinions whose words changed the law of the United States and limited what American governments could do in ways that courts had not previously held those governments to be limited. The Justices claimed that the new limitations were signaled by the words of the U.S. Constitution, and cited words from that document that had been there for a very long time. Among reactions to these changes there arose a claim that the Court was behaving *illegitimately*—that the Court was acting in ways contrary to what the Constitution's words signaled.[9]

The first formulations of the complaint were that the Court was holding the Constitution's words to mean things that the Constitution had not been *intended* to mean by people whose intentions morally mattered—people whose intentions should have guided the Court. Early suspects were the "framers" who had drafted the document, but soon critics of the Court began to focus on the fact that the Constitution had become *law* atop the American legal system through ratifying conventions in each of the states. The intentions of the ratifiers, the actual lawgivers, were said to matter when deciding what the law signaled.[10] Contributing to the moral force of this argument was the idea of authority. If the reason that the words of the Constitution matter to life in America were that those words have been approved by people who had authority in the sense of a "because I said so" right to be obeyed, then what those people thought they were achieving would seem to matter. If you are listening to someone because you think she has a right to be obeyed by you, then you necessarily care about what she *intends* to say. The intentions of someone with a right to be obeyed are surely what those with a duty to obey should care about when reading her words.[11]

But as the criticism matured, many so-called "originalists" evolved their claims to be that the Supreme Court should adhere to the original *public meaning*[12] of the Constitution's words—the *understanding* of the American community, of law's recipients, not its issuers, at the time that the law was issued. The idea that law's words should be understood to mean what they meant to their receiving community in the community's language at the time of receipt was in fact the historic common law approach to reading legislation. Not until very recently did the English courts let themselves so much as peek at parliamentary debate when deciding what statutes meant.[13] The refusal by some prominent jurists, notably Antonin Scalia[14] and Frank Easterbrook,[15] to focus on trying to discover "legislative intent" reflects the old common law principle that laws with a discernible "plain meaning" should be treated as having that meaning. Still, when law's words are as old as much of the U.S. Constitution, finding out about public meaning may involve consulting history books. If you were set to inherit under an old trust deed that contained the words "no Attainder of Treason shall work Corruption of Blood, or Forfeiture except during the Life of the Person attainted,"[16] you as a member of today's audience would realize you needed to do some research to work out what they were talking about back then. If an old law gives you a right to "bear Arms,"[17] you might need to check your history to be sure it is about carrying weapons and not about wearing insignias or keeping your upper limbs or something else that had never occurred to you at all. What the history books reveal about public understanding of the law may mostly come from what the lawgivers said about what they were doing, but if we are searching for public understanding, our attention to what lawgivers said will be not because they were the lawgivers, but because their commentary helps reveal how the receiving community understood the law.[18]

In other communities with more recent constitutions, from Canada[19] (whose Charter of Rights and Freedoms was added only a generation ago) to South Africa,[20] courts take for granted the shared understanding made possible by their community languages, and in doing so are effectively seeking out original public meaning. They do not use that phrase, because where constitutions have more recent origins, there is no distinction between original public meaning and . . . public meaning. The reason "original" belongs in the phrase is merely to emphasize that our concern is to give law's meaning continuity over time, so that it can achieve for us law's predictive purpose. The whole point of writing judicial opinions in a community's shared language is to help those in that community *share* an understanding of law through that language. The whole exercise of lawgiving, whether through enactment or opinion writing, presupposes that law can have a public meaning. When the Supreme Court of Canada issues its opinions in both English and French, it strives to say the same thing, to convey the same understanding, in each language. Any extent to which it fails to do so would upon detection be seen as a serious misstep, totally at odds with the whole point of the exercise. When foreign constitutional theorists are heard to deride American "originalism," they typically turn out to be deriding the claim that drafters' or legislators' *intentions* dictate law's meaning.[21] Deriding originalism understood as a search for lawgiver intention misses the mark when original public meaning is the question. When reading law, most of us most of the time, inside court and out, follow the logic of original public meaning.

Once we see that law's value to us is systematized *prediction,* we can see that asking about public meaning is definitely the way for dispute-resolving courts to go. Law's value to us depends on its words having some potential for meaning fixedness across our community and over time. That is the only way that law can achieve its purpose of helping us understand each other better. The good of *having* the legal system calls for courts to read law according to its public meaning. As we have noticed, the good of having the legal system varies in weight as a reason for action and sometimes may be outweighed by reasons for acting contrary to what law predicts we will do. As we have noticed, even lawgivers may sometimes be justified in trying to do lawgiving beyond or even contrary to what existing law's public meaning predicts they will do. In thinking about this, let us consider the notorious scenario addressed by a New York state court in the case of *Riggs v. Palmer.*[22] If existing law predicts that someone will inherit under a will, newly signaling an exception where that person murdered the testator may be the right thing for a lawgiver to do. If the existing system predicts that the lawgiver will be effective at adding to the law in that way, then we are noticing nothing *legally* controversial. We all regularly see such examples of legally uncontroversial change when legislative assemblies amend statutes or when courts newly express elements of the common law. And if not legally controversial, this particular addition would not be morally controversial either, even if it were applied retroactively to existing murderers. Retroactive change bothers us when it newly predicts bad consequences for past behavior that we judge might on balance not otherwise have been the wrong thing to do. But retroactive change does not bother us much when it newly predicts an additional bad consequence for having murdered someone, because law's moral value in helping us decide not to do something is superfluous anytime we know anyway that we definitely should not do that thing. We know that we should not murder people, regardless of what the law signals about the likely actions and expectations of others. As the preexisting inheritance law in *Riggs v. Palmer* was a statute, and as the New York state constitution signaled scope for the state legislature to enact retroactive noncriminal statutes, a new statute retroactively adding the exception for murderers would have been both legally and morally uncontroversial.

But the addition to New York law that we saw in *Riggs v. Palmer* was not issued by the New York state legislature, it was issued by a New York state court. How do we think about situations where the existing system does *not* predict that a lawgiver will be effective at adding to the law in the way that the lawgiver purported to do? If the lawgiver is acting outside the scope for lawgiving that the existing system signals for him, then that purported lawgiver is engaging in an attempted mini revolution. He is then at heightened risk of being told by others in his community that he is behaving *illegitimately*. He is essentially elbowing in on someone else's job. That the *predicted* lawgivers (in *Riggs*, the state legislature) are too busy or too lazy to do their job properly is a reason for revolutionary action that will vary in strength depending on its truth and the consequences of that truth. Everyone is busy. When a court announces that a statute or constitution means something different from what that court's community understood their existing law to mean, the court is being revolutionary. That may be the right thing to be, but only if the good consequences achieved outweigh the adverse consequences for the legal system's predictive effectiveness. The court has strong reason to care about the system's predictive effectiveness, not least because the significance of the court's own words depends on that systemic effectiveness. It could be self-defeating for courts to behave as though the words of constitutions and statutes *never* have a public meaning, as though applying *that* existing law always involves making it up. If courts behaved that way, and the rest of us took our cue from their behavior, we would treat the *courts'* words as without a public meaning too, and no lawgiver, courts included, would ever succeed through law's words in helping us understand each other better. And even if this consequence did not occur, what reason do we have to want judges to be the only *real* lawgivers in the system? It would be very shortsighted to favor that outcome just because we like the people who currently sit on courts more than we like the people who currently sit in legislative assemblies, as wherever power shifts, every faction in the community will soon enough shift their attention to getting seated there.

But what if some of law's words really do lack a public meaning? What if law's words genuinely generate different understandings among us, compromising their capacity to help us understand each other better? What if we really disagree about what a sign is signaling when it says: "No vehicles in the park?"[23] Notice that what worries us is *not* whether some creative person can come up with another *interpretation* of words' meaning. As Wittgenstein pointed out, that is always possible.[24] What worries us is whether or not the words of the law are helping us understand each other's likely actions and expectations by in fact being understood by us in the same way.[25] If words never achieved that, then we would likely give up trying to use them in many of the ways we currently do, and would certainly give up trying to have the use for them that we call *lawgiving*. Inevitably, we will sometimes find uses of words in law to be vague or ambiguous, but over time those uncertainties can be resolved and law's predictive value increased so long as law sufficiently signals who within our community will likely succeed in adding to the law through clarifying signals. And the U.S. Constitution does just that, both through its elaborate provision for its own amendment, and through its nod to a dispute-resolving institution for which it provides and which it calls the Supreme Court. The existing system signals that the amendment route can be used to add to the law of the Constitution either to *change* the existing law or to *elaborate* upon the existing law. The existing system signals that the dispute-resolving route can be used to add to the law of the Constitution only to *elaborate* upon the existing law. The dispute-resolving route for adding to the Constitution is predicted to be available only to resolve *actual* differences in understanding, *actual* disputes about what existing law means. The Constitution predicts that the Court can effectively add words within the Constitution's zones of actual vagueness or ambiguity to resolve those uncertainties. That dispute-resolving function lets the Court add to the law of the Constitution to the extent necessary to let the Constitution's words *mean* for us. Once we see that law's purpose is to help us understand each other in community, we can see that law's true potential to *mean* for us depends on its potential to let us *share* an understanding. Where we lack a shared understanding of the Constitution's words, the Constitution signals that the Court can add words to the law of the Constitution within the zone of doubt. Within that zone, the Justices are predicted to be lawgivers who make all-things-considered judgments about what law would be best, as surely as courts do when evolving the common law or assemblies do when enacting statutes. If the Court's additional words let us share an understanding of the law, then they help us understand how our lives in community are likely to go. They help us understand each other better, and so let the Constitution fulfill for us law's function.

Increasingly we see much of this conceded by defenders of the Court's decision making, but the point made by some that adhering to the original public meaning of the Constitution does not stop the Court from announcing lots of new restrictions on what governments can do, because the Constitution's words include expressions of big moral ideas, and the public meaning of big moral ideas is vague enough to allow abundant scope for new limitations on government. For example, expressions of equality such as the Equal Protection

Clause of the Fourteenth Amendment[26] convey in the English language the idea that we should not distinguish among people unless we have a good reason to do so. Applied to the content of laws, the abstract idea expressed by "equality" language is that laws should not draw *immoral* distinctions among people. Laws that signal reactions to and expectations about human behaviors and characteristics inevitably distinguish among people. A law that signals punishment for murder discriminates against murderers—the distinction it draws just happens to be one we are readily willing to call *moral*. This example should not lure us into thinking that an equality principle never protects *behaviors*. There is no easy line to draw between what we do and who we are. A nineteenth-century California law that signaled the length of male prison inmates' hair discriminated against Chinese men who at that time had a cultural tradition of wearing their hair in a long braided "queue." The law's words were about behavior we would now call hairstyling, not about the unalterable characteristic we call race, but Justice Field of the Supreme Court held the law's discrimination against a long-haired Chinese inmate to be so immoral that it was a *cruel and unusual* punishment.[27] We know from the history of the Fourteenth Amendment that the people who put the words "equal protection of the laws" in the Constitution were worried about distinctions drawn on the basis of race. But does the abstract guarantee of "equal protection of the laws" protect only against race discrimination? The people who put "Arms" in the Second Amendment[28] were particularly thinking about muskets and the other comparably clumsy old weapons with which they were familiar. Does the more abstract word "Arms" not cover any of the other handheld weapons we have now?

We all know that words may have multiple meanings. A narrower meaning may be not simply the expected application of an understood broader meaning[29] but rather may be the whole of what the words mean to their reader—that is simply to say, a word or phrase that is vague is also ambiguous and may be understood in one way and not at all in any other.[30] But where ambiguity comes through *abstraction* and there are alternative ways to express narrower notions, we have to credit the community with appreciating the whole abstract idea that was actually announced. To see why this is so, contrast two sources of doubt we might have about what the Second Amendment means when it guarantees "the right of the people to keep and bear Arms." First, we might be unsure whether "Arms" refers to heraldic symbols, to actual weapons, or to upper limbs. English-language dictionaries do not dispel that doubt, and the amendment's opening words about a "well-regulated Militia" do not resolve it either, as wearing identifying insignias is a species of regulation akin to wearing uniform clothing and might sometimes be quite useful on a battlefield.[31] Having upper limbs is handy for fighting too. So we turn to history, and from history we find a conclusive answer as to how people in America understood the Second Amendment when they received it. They understood "Arms" to be weapons. Because the ambiguity has nothing to do with abstraction, we can hope to discover that pretty much everyone in the law's receiving community understood that law in a particular way. And in this instance, history lets us discover just that. A comparable ambiguity in the Fourteenth Amendment is whether "the equal protection of the laws" limits law giving or only law applying.[32] Now turn to a second source of doubt about what the Second Amendment means. Does "Arms" refer only to particular kinds of weapons with which everyone was familiar at the time when they received the Second Amendment in the late eighteenth century, such as muskets, or does the word also embrace weapons then unimagined, such as rifles and revolvers? This ambiguity arises because in the Second Amendment, the word "Arms" is relevantly *abstract*. When you say "Arms" to an audience, some of them might think of possible future weapons, and others really won't. In any human community, abstract words will be understood by different people in different ways, depending on their differing abilities and predispositions to think abstractly. In any human community, some people will see the big picture to which abstract words point, and others will miss it. Now come to the Fourteenth Amendment, in which the word "equal" is relevantly abstract.[33] As Lawrence Kohlberg analyzed through his stages of human moral development,[34] some people can think in principles, while others think only in current concrete applications. For those who could handle abstraction, the Second Amendment's reference to "Arms" instead of muskets embraced arms not yet imagined, and the equal protection guarantee reached immoral distinctions not yet appreciated. We know that many in the American generation who received the Fourteenth Amendment well knew that our understanding of equality can grow deeper over time, because they could see that it already had. When through Thomas Jefferson's pen their predecessors had declared that "all Men are created equal,"[35] the focus had not been on race. Now it was, but the abstract word was the same. Whatever those who voted for the Fourteenth Amendment intended (and their intentions were likely disparate), the public's understanding of the new constitutional language, like the public's understanding of many other new laws, likely varied with the intelligence and erudition of the readers.

At one of the Australian constitutional conventions in the 1890s, someone proposed including the American equal protection language in the Australian document, but the proposal foundered after another delegate pointed out that in the United States the provision was understood to guarantee equal treatment to *all* races.[35] Law is full of language that the man in the street might need advice to understand. In the case of abstract language, as in many other instances in the life of the law, where relatively intelligent and educated people understand words in one way and less sophisticated users of the language understand in another way or not at all, we inevitably privilege the understanding of the erudite and tell the others to consult lawyers when they want to know what the law signals. That is a big part of why lawyers are in such demand. That is our universal approach to making law predictively effective for life in a complex society. That is the only way we can hope to let law's words be a source of *shared* understanding across a community and over time.

It is possible to write a constitution without broad expressions of "rights" that nonetheless signals the shape and interplay of power-sharing institutions in ways likely to let us experience most everything that we understand by "liberty" and "equality." We can evolve a system of law and government that lets us feel free and fairly treated without open-ended mention of those ideas in our constitution's text. Twentieth-century life in Canada before its Charter of Rights and Freedoms arrived was not appreciably less free and equal than life in America. The substantial achievement for which we can hope when mentioning abstract moral ideas in law's text is to hand much more power, much more scope to signal effectively the likely character of life in the group, to those whose words settle disputes about what law's existing words *mean*. That is why even the most beautiful bills of rights have achieved little in legal systems that failed to share power among many, in legal systems that let a monolithic lawgiver decide the reach of his own powers. Stalin's 1936 Constitution of the U.S.S.R. promised freedom of speech, press, and assembly, inviolability of the person and of the homes of citizens, privacy of correspondence, and many other gems.[37] Never mind that it appeared during the purges and was law of the land at their height. But that is also why bills of rights have successfully shifted lots of power to the courts in legal systems that *do* share power among many, that assign to courts the job of settling disputes among everyone else, and that leave the highest court as the one institution in the system with significant scope to settle the reach of its own powers.[38] That is what gives the U.S. Supreme Court so much say in shaping American life.[39]

Does the shift in originalist reasoning from intentions to understanding leave any force to complaints against the Supreme Court's decision making? Force remains in those instances where the Court has gone outside the public meaning of the Constitution's words. The Due Process Clause of the Fifth Amendment,[40] for example, came from Magna Carta's guarantee that freemen would not be killed, locked up, or lose property except by the lawful judgment of their peers or by the law of the land.[41] Some state constitutions, such as Virginia's 1776 prototype,[42] kept Magna Carta's explicitly disjunctive formulation, but the national Bill of Rights' drafters split the alternative protections and made separate, more specific, more detailed provision about jury trials.[43] The Supreme Court has since held that the general alternative to jury trial protects freedom to do whatever things a majority of the Court think people really should be free to do—an open-ended "liberty" guarantee.[44] On occasion, the Court has held that the words impose an open-ended *equality* limitation on the federal government, too.[45] That is a strange journey's end for the text, as John Hart Ely eloquently observed in his classic *Democracy and Distrust*.[46]

The Supreme Court's reading of the Due Process Clause looks linguistically strained because the Court has really read the words to *illustrate* bigger moral ideas than the one that those words express, rather than reading the words as just expressing the idea that they express. We saw a hint of that when Justice Douglas claimed in *Griswold v. Connecticut* that government in America is limited by "penumbras, formed by emanations" from the Constitution's actual words.[47] Illustrative reasoning is the method of the common law, a method that treats text's relevance to law as that of an example of a bigger idea rather than as a definition of the relevant idea. Reading the Constitution's text that way frees the Court to make constitutional law *even outside* the Constitution's zones of actual vagueness or ambiguity. "Due process" is vague, it has a fuzzy fringe, but freedom to do whatever the Supreme Court thinks people should be free to do is not one of the possible meanings we can find inside the zone of doubt. For its receiving public at the American founding, due process was the general alternative to jury trial; it was about the *same kind of thing* as jury trial. Had it been kept explicitly in the alternative to jury trial, as it was in Virginia, then whatever it required would *not* have been required anytime there was a jury trial.[48]

To reason illustratively when reading the Constitution lets the Court write a constitution that covers far more than the actual words of the Constitution plausibly do. To reason that way hugely increases the power of the nine people on the Court to shape American life. If the Constitution's Fourteenth Amendment explicitly prohibited only "race discrimination," we would question a choice by the Court to hold that the Constitution succeeded in prohibiting other kinds of immoral discrimination because the text *illustrated* a bigger, abstract idea called equality. Reasoning of that kind happens at common law, where the words of judicial opinions do not definitively predict the scope for lawgiving by *the same courts* in later cases, but merely exemplify or illustrate that scope. The whole point of issuing a constitutional document is to *set* the scope for adding words to the system. A written constitution is a predictive source of power, a device for credentialing lawgivers, and therefore a definitive document, not an illustrative one. If Americans had wanted the common law approach to constitutionalism, they would have taken Britain's route, and let the customs of paying attention to people that turn those combinations of people into institutions of government evolve *without* overarching textual definition. Instead, the Americans contrived to turn everyone's attention to a document that defined how lawgiving would happen, and they succeeded in starting up a custom of treating the words of that document as effective to predict the reach of lawgiving in America.[49] James Iredell memorably made that point right back at the beginning of the Court's life, when rejecting the illustrative approach overtly adopted by his colleague Samuel Chase:

> It has been the policy of all the *American* states, which have, individually, framed their state constitutions since the revolution, and of the people of the *United States*, when they framed the Federal Constitution, to define with precision the objects of the legislative power, and to restrain its exercise within marked and settled boundaries. . . . If . . . the Legislature of the Union, or the Legislature of any member of the Union, shall pass a law, within the general scope of their constitutional power, the Court cannot pronounce it to be void, merely because it is, in their judgment, contrary to the principles of natural justice. The ideas of natural justice are regulated by no fixed standard: the ablest and the purest of men have differed upon the subject; and all that the Court could properly say, in such an event, would be, that the Legislature (possessed of an equal right of opinion) had passed an act which, in the opinion of the judges, was inconsistent with the abstract principles of natural justice.[50]

The Supreme Court does not read the words of the Constitution's first three Articles that provide for a Congress, a President, and one Supreme Court as merely illustrating the scope for setting up a system of government. The Court reads those words as defining that scope. For the Court to read the Constitution's words illustratively to extend the limits on what others in government can do is to reach beyond the scope for lawgiving that the Constitution predicts for the Court.

To see what is wrong with being cavalier about whether we read the Constitution definitively according to its original public meaning, just ask yourself how American law would work if other officials in state and national governments read the words of the *Supreme Court* in ways that step outside the original public meaning of the text. If Supreme Court opinions were read by other courts, by other officials, and by all the rest of us to mean what we each individually think it would have been best for the Court to have written, we would not learn much from those opinions about life in America. Words so read would not contribute much to American law, because our understandings of those words would often not be *shared*. Only public meaning is somewhat reliably *shared* meaning. We need to know the original public meaning of law's words if law is to fulfill for us its predictive function. Ronald Dworkin's iconic Judge Hercules' expository syntheses of our community's moral commitments would be lost to us if we lacked a *shared* understanding of the words through which he expressed himself.[51] His words would not help us know what to expect of each other if we were not reading them the same way. His words would not be law for us. As they unanimously made clear in a follow-up case to *Brown v. Board of Education*,[52] the U.S. Supreme Court Justices are all originalists when it comes to how *their* opinions should be read.

The debate about whether the original public meaning of the Constitution's words matters is really about whether the Constitution's words are our ultimate source of American law, or whether only the Supreme Court's words are. The issue is whether the ultimate issuers of signals in the American legal system are the people who participate from time to time in adopting the words of the U.S. Constitution, or only the people who sit from time to time on the Supreme Court.

Do the Constitution's words limit the Court in the way that the Court takes for granted *the Court's* words limit everyone else? With occasional exceptions, such as some states' initial disregard of the Supreme Court's desegregation decisions, the words of the Court have been very good guides to the character of life in America. And that is precisely because those words are almost universally understood according to their original public meaning.

CHAPTER 10

The Life of the Law

> The life of the law has not been logic: it has been experience. The felt necessities of the time, the prevalent moral and political theories, intuitions of public policy, avowed or unconscious, even the prejudices which judges share with their fellow-men, have had a good deal more to do than the syllogism in determining the rules by which men should be governed. The law embodies the story of a nation's development through many centuries, and it cannot be dealt with as if it contained only the axioms and corollaries of a book of mathematics. In order to know what it is, we must know what it has been, and what it tends to become.
>
> Oliver Wendell Holmes, Jr., *The Common Law* (1881).[1]

"That is not the Hopi way," we hear a Native American parent tell her child. To what is she appealing? A reason to do differently that is at once plausible and profound. Alongside it, any claim that one human has a "because I said so" right to be obeyed by another human looks strained and improbable. Law frees us to live together by revealing a way of living and rendering it ours. Law lets us fulfill more fully our life's potential by being in community with many people we do not know well. Life in large numbers needs a way for us to know what those around us are likely to do and to expect. Law is our way.

For too long we have thought of prediction, of understanding each other, as a gratifying side effect, not law's main attraction. Law's main event, on the old account, is, hold your applause . . . that law tells us how to *obey another human*. The idea that law comes from authority is now a brittle artifact of a world view we have in other respects discarded. How we fell for that notion we now well know. And many of us probably never did fall for it, but had reason to act as though we did, because we could see that for us law was fulfilling its true function of telling us what everyone else was likely to do and to expect. Well might we always have doubted the idea of authority, when the brightest minds who argued for its possibility in principle had such trouble pointing to its real-world presence. We can readily see that the human leaders whom our history records visibly and loudly proclaiming their own right to be obeyed were obviously wrong. Once we disbelieve the notion that they were delegates of the divine, we find no satisfying substitute for that status that would let the authority claims live on. Attempts to refine a moral case for authority as about consent or expertise or anything else miss the mark, they miss the actual psychological dynamics of human relations and end up artificial and unavailing exercises in contrived complexity. Too often over our history we sat silently through such performances, reluctant to be the ones to say that the Emperor wore no clothes.[2]

Darwin made telling the truth easier, by spreading among us a vision of how *who we are* might have come to *be* in a way previously unimagined. One of Darwin's admirers and correspondents, the Boston-based intellectual Chauncey Wright, co-convened a scholarly discussion group dubbed the Metaphysical Club,[3] in which the young Oliver Wendell Holmes actively participated. Also in attendance was Charles Sanders Peirce, author of the seminal pragmatic maxim: "Consider what effects, that might conceivably have practical bearings, we conceive the object of our conception to have. Then, our conception of these effects is the whole of our conception of the object."[4] And from Holmes thereafter we received a phrase that helps impart a fresh vision of *what law is* and of how law comes to *be* among us: *systematized prediction*.[5]

Much of what humans have managed to discover about our world enhances the daily lives of those who do not understand the discoveries as much as the lives of those who do. Many of us benefit in our day-to-day living from scientific advances as much as the scientists do. But benefiting as much as we can from the truth about law requires understanding. Experiencing law's value to the full depends on seeing what law is telling us. Law is about living together, we cannot avoid it, and we need to know how to respond to its presence in our lives. When people say "it's the law," what is supposed to follow from that? We need an answer to that question, an answer that can be used in our daily choices of what to do, of who to *be*. This book's ambition has been to offer an answer.

Law's words let us live in community with people we do not know. In chapter 2, we traced the path by which law's words spread the story of custom in a large group and how, through customs of leadership, law's words exponentially increased what the story of custom told us about the shape of our lives together. In chapters 3, 4, and 5, we explored the causes and the consequences of our leaders' all-too-frequent pretense that law comes from something altogether different from custom, that law comes from people who have a "because I said so" moral right to be obeyed. We also considered what of value we could salvage from the rhetoric of authority. In chapter 6, we investigated law's rightful place in our thinking about what to do each day.

In chapter 7, we considered a range of ways that understanding law as the expression of our customs clarifies our thinking about law and government, and particularly about what helps to make law and government *good*. In chapter 8, we integrated our understanding of law as the expression of our customs with our thinking about *change* in what is law and in who governs. In chapter 9, we saw that understanding law as the expression of our customs makes clear what we are trying to learn when we ask what law *means*, and points us in the right direction to find the answers we really need.

When we understand law as systematized prediction, when we see the sequences of signals that come from our leaders as just part of a bigger picture of who we communally are, of what is *custom* for us, then we can finally answer the questions posed in the opening paragraph of this book. The words that are law are the words that express our customs, either obviously so or because they come to us through sequences of signals from those whom we have customs of following. The words that are law *mean* to us what they mean to most everyone else—law *means* for us only so far as language lets us *share* an understanding of law's signs, sounds, and symbols. And the words that are law do not preempt our own deciding what to do each day. Law's value, its service, to us is to inform of what those around us are likely to do and to expect. That knowledge has deep value to us and may help contribute many reasons for acting one way rather than another. But however much else law helps contribute to our thinking about what to do on any occasion, law always contributes at least one reason for going the way that law's multifaceted predictions point us—the good of having a prediction system that lets us understand each other better. The stories this book tells are threads in the fabric of one big story—the story of how we humans found a way of understanding each other and living together in a big group. "Law" never sits out on its own, it is never in a vacuum. Law is always law *of*, law always belongs, and through law's words we can trace the shape of human community.

Our communal signaling systems, our networks of knowing about each other, vary in their effectiveness at telling truths about our communal lives. Some predict the character of life in their communities better than do others. They also vary in the virtue of the behavior that they predict—some may come close to predicting paradise, others close to predicting hell. Striving to situate good people as signalers and striving to suffuse our signaling systems with *power sharing* will always be worthy goals, not because anyone's goodness or their being situated to signal gives them a right to be obeyed, but because signals have consequences, they self-fulfill their predictions, to some degree or another.

We lived lawful lives long before we found that label for our expressions of shared understanding. But when we came to talk about law's place in our lives, too often we were blind to or blindfolded from the beauty of law's evolution into self fulfillment. Instead we were told a creationist story. Someone had a right to oblige the rest of us to do what he said, and that indirectly let us all know about each other. "Pay no attention to that man behind the curtain,"[6] we were told by self-serving claimants while we stood captive audience to the smoke and mirrors of the authority show. In fact, we have good reason to think that no one ever had a right to be obeyed, and that nonetheless we evolved a way to find out about each other's likely actions and expectations. Claims that we need authority are at their core about our need to know what those around us are likely to do and to expect. Once we see this, the authority claims themselves fall away from law's vibrant presence in our lives.

So much of the joy in life comes through understanding and belonging. We cannot experience the joy of belonging together without *understanding*, for the joy of belonging together comes to us through understanding each other. Law lets us belong far beyond the boundaries of personal experience. Law extends our understanding to embrace far more of our human family than we can personally ever know. Law helps us open up our lives to the fullness of our possibilities, well surpassing what life in smaller circles would ever have let us imagine. Law does this, because law widens the world in which we can live together.

NOTES

CHAPTER 1

1. Oliver Wendell Holmes, Jr., *The Path of the Law*, 10 HARV. L. REV. 457, 458 (1897) (laying "down some first principles for the study of this body of dogma or systematized prediction which we call the law").
2. David Lewis used the phrase *signaling system* more generally to describe successful communication among sentient beings. *See* DAVID K. LEWIS, CONVENTION 122–59 (1969). We will focus on the systems of signals that convey community customs and that help distinguish expressions of custom from everything else that community members say to each other.
3. 1 FRIEDRICH CARL VON SAVIGNY, SYSTEM OF THE MODERN ROMAN LAW 15 (William Holloway trans., 1867) (1839):

   > In fact we find so far as history informs us upon the matter, that wherever men live together, they stand in an intellectual communion which reveals as well as establishes and developes itself by the use of speech. In this natural whole is the seat of the generation of law and in the common intelligence of the nation penetrating individuals, is found the power of satisfying the necessity above recognized.

4. *See* LUDWIG VON BERTALANFFY, GENERAL SYSTEM THEORY: FOUNDATIONS, DEVELOPMENT, APPLICATIONS 36–37 (1969):

   > While in the past, science tried to explain observable phenomena by reducing them to an interplay of elementary units investigable

independently of each other, conceptions appear in contemporary science that are concerned with what is somewhat vaguely termed "wholeness", i.e., problems of organization, phenomena not resolvable into local events, dynamic interactions manifest in the difference of behavior of parts when isolated or in a higher configuration, etc.; in short, "systems" of various orders not understandable by investigation of their respective parts in isolation. Conceptions and problems of this nature have appeared in all branches of science, irrespective of whether inanimate things, living organisms, or social phenomena are the object of study. This correspondence is the more striking because the developments in the individual sciences were mutually independent, largely unaware of each other, and based upon different facts and contradicting philosophies. They indicate a general change in scientific attitude and conceptions.

5. The term coined by systems theorists is *autopoiesis*, from the Greek for self (αυτό) production (ποίησις). *See* Humberto R. Maturana & Francisco J. Varela, Autopoiesis and Cognition: The Realization of the Living xvii (Robert S. Cohen & Marx W. Wartofsky eds., 1980) (1972). *See also* Niklas Luhmann, Law as a Social System (Fatima Kastner, Richard Nobles, David Schiff, & Rosamund Ziegert eds., Klaus A. Ziegert trans., 2004) (1993); Autopoietic Law: A New Approach to Law and Society (Gunther Teubner ed., 1988); Gunther Teubner, Law as an Autopoietic System (Zenon Bankowski ed., Anne Bankowska & Ruth Adler trans., 1993).
6. "Our understanding (of the meaning of Being) is an understanding *that* we share understanding between us and, at the same time, *because* we share understanding between us. . . ." Jean-Luc Nancy, Being Singular Plural 99 (Robert D. Richardson & Anne E. O'Byrne trans., 2000) (1996).

CHAPTER 2

1. Niklas Luhmann, Love: A Sketch 14–15 (André Kierserling ed., Kathleen Cross trans., 2010).
2. *See* Fernanda Pirie, *Law Before Government: Ideology and Aspiration*, 30 Oxford J. Legal Studies 207, 217 (2010) (discussing anthropological evidence from the Kabylia villages of northeastern Algeria): "Law-giving, both as a foundational act and an ongoing activity, was intrinsically bound up with local notions of community. . . ."

3. WILLIAM GOLDING, LORD OF THE FLIES (1954).
4. ELMAN R. SERVICE, ORIGINS OF THE STATE AND CIVILIZATION: THE PROCESS OF CULTURAL EVOLUTION 83 (1975).
5. *See* JANE GOODALL, THE CHIMPANZEES OF GOMBE: PATTERNS OF BEHAVIOR (1986). *See* ch. 12 ("Aggression"), 313–56 (especially 318–19, "Coalitions and Snowballing"), and ch. 15 ("Dominance"), 409–42 (especially 418–24, "Coalitions," 424–29, "Motivation and Alpha Status," and 429–36, "Loss of Rank").
6. *Compare* CHARLES DARWIN, THE ORIGIN OF SPECIES 153 (1859) (describing natural selection as preserving "variations in some way advantageous, which consequently endure" and observing that "any form represented by few individuals will, during fluctuations in the seasons or in the number of its enemies, run a good chance of utter extinction"). *Id.*, at 154:

   > The forms which stand in closest competition with those undergoing modification and improvement, will naturally suffer most. And we have seen in the chapter on the Struggle for Existence that it is the most closely-allied forms,—varieties of the same species, and species of the same genus or of related genera,—which, from having nearly the same structure, constitution, and habits, generally come into the severest competition with each other. Consequently, each new variety or species, during the progress of its formation, will generally press hardest on its nearest kindred, and tend to exterminate them.

   On the evolution of evolutionary theory since Darwin, *see* EDWARD J. LARSON, EVOLUTION: THE REMARKABLE HISTORY OF A SCIENTIFIC THEORY (2d ed., 2006) and EDWARD J. LARSON, EVOLUTION'S WORKSHOP: GOD AND SCIENCE ON THE GALAPAGOS ISLANDS (2001).
7. Readers who wish to explore the relevant anthropological literature might like to start with the following: THE EARLY STATE (Henry J. M. Claessen & Peter Skalník eds., 1978) (includes studies of twenty ancient communities); ORIGINS OF THE STATE: THE ANTHROPOLOGY OF POLITICAL EVOLUTION (Ronald Cohen & Elman R. Service eds., 1978); JARED DIAMOND, GUNS, GERMS, AND STEEL: THE FATES OF HUMAN SOCIETIES 265–92 (1997) (ch. 14: "From Egalitarianism to Kleptocracy"); TIMOTHY EARLE, HOW CHIEFS COME TO POWER: THE POLITICAL ECONOMY IN PREHISTORY (1997); MORTON H. FRIED, THE EVOLUTION

of Political Society: An Essay in Political Anthropology 185–226 (1967) (ch. 5: "Stratified Societies"); Max Gluckman, Custom and Conflict in Africa 41 (1955) ("The Barotse . . . state explicitly that it is the lot of leaders to be hated, because they are the Law itself."); Max Gluckman, Politics, Law and Ritual in Tribal Society (1965); Jonathan Haas, The Evolution of the Prehistoric State (1982); Bronislaw Malinowski, Crime and Custom in Savage Society (1926); Elman R. Service, Origins of the State and Civilization: The Process of Cultural Evolution (1975).

8. Max Weber, *Theory of Social and Economic Organization*, *in* On Charisma and Institution Building: Selected Papers 46–62 (S. N. Eisentstadt ed., A. K. Henderson & Talcott Parsons trans., 1947) (1968). John Locke shared, though with an improbable utopianism, Weber's opinion that leadership likely emerged among early humans through recognition and appreciation of some persons' "exceptional powers or qualities. These are such as are not accessible to the ordinary person, but are regarded as of divine origin or as exemplary, and on the basis of them the individual concerned is treated as a leader." *Id.*, at 48. In Locke's optimistic speculation on leadership in ancient communities, "some one good and excellent Man, having got a Preheminency amongst the rest, had this Deference paid to his Goodness and Vertue, as a kind of Natural Authority, that the chief Rule, with Arbitration of their differences, by a tacit Consent devolved into his hands, without any other caution, but the assurance they had of his Uprightness and Wisdom. . . ." 2 John Locke, Two Treatises of Government § 94 (Peter Laslett ed., 1988) (1690).
9. *Compare* John Finnis's account of the "clumsiness of custom formation" as a method of solving coordination problems in a group. John Finnis, Natural Law and Natural Rights 244–45 (1980).
10. *See* John Austin, The Province of Jurisprudence Determined (1832). Austin's vision was shaped by the earlier work of Jeremy Bentham. *See* Jeremy Bentham, Of Laws in General (H. L. A. Hart ed., 1970) (written approximately 1782).
11. Kareem Fahim, *Slap to a Man's Pride Set Off Tumult in Tunisia,* N.Y. Times, Jan. 22, 2011, at A1.
12. Max Weber, *Theory of Social and Economic Organization*, *in* On Charisma and Institution Building: Selected Papers 48 (S. N. Eisentstadt ed., A. K. Henderson & Talcott Parsons trans., 1947) (1968).

13. H. L. A. HART, THE CONCEPT OF LAW 90 (2d ed., 1994).

14. *See* KEN BINMORE, NATURAL JUSTICE 85 (2011):

> If someone deviates and we go to one of the subgames off the equilibrium path, it remains optimal in a perfect equilibrium to stick to your original strategy provided everybody else does. In particular, if your strategy tells you to punish the deviant at some cost to yourself, it will be optimal for you to carry through on the punishment. If you deviate by trying to escape your duty to punish, you will take us to yet another subgame where it is optimal for some other player to punish you for your dereliction of duty. If he fails to discharge his duty, we go to yet another subgame—and so on forever. With only a finite number of players, these chains of responsibility are necessarily closed in the manner that Kant failed to consider.

15. Richard Dawkins would call our following the leader a *meme*. *See* RICHARD DAWKINS, THE SELFISH GENE 189–201 (3rd ed., 2006). *See also* DAVID DEUTSCH, THE BEGINNING OF INFINITY: EXPLANATIONS THAT TRANSFORM THE WORLD 373–74 (2011): "Just as the basic theory of genes was developed long before the discovery of DNA, so today, without knowing *how* ideas are stored in brains, we do know that some ideas can be passed from one person to another and affect people's behaviour. Memes are those ideas." *Id.*, at 376: "[M]emes necessarily become embodied in two different physical forms alternately: as memories in a brain, and as behaviour. . . . Technology can add further stages to a meme's life cycle. For instance, the behaviour may be to write something down—thus embodying the meme in a third physical form, which may later cause a person who reads it to enact other behaviour, which then causes the meme to appear in someone else's brain."

16. *See* 1 FRIEDRICH CARL VON SAVIGNY, SYSTEM OF THE MODERN ROMAN LAW 12 (William Holloway trans., 1867) (1839):

> In the general consciousness of a people lives positive law and hence we have to call it peoples' law. It is by no means to be thought that it was the particular members of the people by whose arbitrary will, law was brought forth; in that case the will of individuals might perhaps have selected the same law, perhaps however and more probably very varied laws. Rather is it the spirit of a people living and working in common in all the individuals, which gives

birth to positive law, which therefore is to the consciousness of each individual not accidently but necessarily one and the same.

17. Niklas Luhmann, Law as a Social System 142–43, 148 (Fatima Kastner, Richard Nobles, David Schiff, & Rosamund Ziegert eds., Klaus A. Ziegert trans., 2004) (1993). Luhmann's celebrated interlocutor, Jürgen Habermas, also acknowledged that law's function is to "stabilize expectations." *See* Jürgen Habermas, Between Facts and Norms: Contributions to a Discourse Theory of Law and Democracy 201 (William H. Rehg trans., 1996) (1992): "A flat revocation of any guarantees of legal certainty leads to the conclusion that the legal system must ultimately give up the idea of satisfying the very function of law, to stabilize expectations. The realists cannot explain how the functionally necessary accomplishments of the legal system are compatible with a radical skepticism on the part of legal experts."
18. Luhmann, *id.*, at 148 (Luhmann uses "society" where this book mostly uses "community" or "group").
19. *Id.*, at 488. For valuable anglophone analysis and critique of Luhmann's work, *see* Hugh Baxter, *Autopoiesis and the "Relative Autonomy" of Law*, 19 Cardozo L. Rev. 1987 (1998).
20. Luhmann, *id.*, at 73–74:

> The mode of operation, which produces and reproduces the social system, is meaningful communication. This statement enables us to say that the legal system is a sub-system of the social system in so far as it uses the mode of operation of communication, that is, that it cannot do anything else but frame forms (sentences) in the medium of meaning with the help of communication. It is an achievement of the social system that this has become possible, and that a long socio-cultural evolution has made this self-evident. This achievement, for instance, provides the legal system with the guarantee that neither paper nor ink, neither people nor other organisms, neither courthouses and their rooms nor telephones or computers are part of the system. The social system has already constituted this frontier. Those who try to communicate with their telephones ("stop ringing, phone!") misunderstand systems; one can communicate not to but only with the help of a telephone.
>
> Consequently, the legal system operates in the form of communication under the protection of boundaries that are drawn by society. This means, however, that the legal system must distinguish

in a special way all that has to be treated as legal communication in the social system.

21. *Id.*, at 93, et seq.
22. H. L. A. Hart, The Concept of Law 26–49 (2d ed., 1994) (ch. 3: "The Variety of Laws").
23. Niklas Luhmann, Law as a Social System 127 (Fatima Kastner, Richard Nobles, David Schiff, & Rosamund Ziegert eds., Klaus A. Ziegert trans., 2004) (1993): "the symbol of validity reacts to the *intrinsic dynamics* of the legal system and is called upon only when the legal system is differentiated to such a degree *that it can change itself.*"
24. *Compare* the famous account in Thomas Hobbes, Leviathan 183–201 (C. B. MacPherson ed., 1968) (1651).
25. What are the customs of the groups to which we belong? What are the expressions of those customs that we call the *law* of our groups? These are distinct and separate questions from "What then should we do?" In this book, we will consider what role our answers about law should and do play in our daily deciding what to do. This book does not try to tell a sweeping story about what moral rights we have or what moral duties we owe in our lives together. In other words, it does not advance a theory of morality that would need to be situated in relation to the great reasoning traditions of moral philosophy. This book just asks what the words we call law distinctively contribute to our thinking about what we should do. This book argues that there is one particular kind of claim about moral rights and corresponding moral duties that is likely never true, and certainly irrelevant to what law is—that is, the claim that some humans have moral rights to be obeyed by other humans. This book contends that whatever else goes into our thinking about what we should do, the contribution that law distinctively makes *as law* is simply to supply us with information about what others in our community are likely to do and to expect. What weight or significance that information deserves in our reasoning about what to do will be affected by all the other reasoning we do and understandings we have about what is good.
26. H. L. A. Hart, The Concept of Law 84 (2d ed., 1994). *Id.*, at 11.

CHAPTER 3

1. J. R. R. Tolkien, The Lord of the Rings Trilogy (1954 and 1955).

2. For an exhaustive account of Mob history up to the change in government structure, *see* David Critchley, The Origin of Organized Crime in America: The New York City Mafia, 1891–1931 (2009).
3. Max Weber, *Theory of Social and Economic Organization*, *in* On Charisma and Institution Building: Selected Papers 48 (S. N. Eisentstadt ed., A. K. Henderson & Talcott Parsons trans., 1947) (1968).
4. Distinctive abilities, whether attributed to the supernatural or to the natural, were facts from which inferences of entitlement might be drawn and claims made. But the need to claim a right to one's role within the group really arose, Max Weber suggested, from self-interested desire to perpetuate incumbency beyond what charisma would naturally have afforded, a sentiment not entirely unfamiliar to tenured academics. (*Id.*, at 54–58.) Weber explained that the self-interest was every bit as much that of those who enjoyed incumbency, including derivative "authority," under the aegis of a charismatic leader. In Rousseau's words: "The strongest is never strong enough to be always the master, unless he transforms strength into right, and obedience into duty." Jean-Jacques Rousseau, The Social Contract and Discourses, Bk. I, Ch. 3 (G. D. H. Cole trans., 1985) (1762). Desire to pass the role to progeny or other favored persons when abilities really receded would have added motivation. Where the divine was once invoked to explain qualities that made others want to follow anyway, now divine will was invoked to explain why those who could see no other reason to follow still should. (Weber, *id.*, at 57.) "[I]n every case, princely power and those groups having interests vested in it—that is, the warlord's following—strive for legitimacy as soon as the rule has become stable. They crave for a characteristic which would define the charismatically qualified ruler." Max Weber, Essays in Sociology 27 (H. H. Gerth & Wright Mills trans., 1946). "Genuine charisma rests upon the legitimation of personal heroism or personal revelation. Yet precisely this quality of charisma as an extraordinary, supernatural, divine power transforms it, after its routinization, into a suitable source for the legitimate acquisition of sovereign power by the successors of the charismatic hero." (*Id.*, at 39.)
5. In his Schweich Lectures, C. J. Gadd described the vision of law and government articulated in the ancient Code of Hammurabi:

   > Its genesis and idea . . . were set forth by the king in a lengthy prologue and epilogue. Anu and Enil, the supreme gods, . . . called the

name of Hammurabi "so that I might cause justice to appear in the land and might destroy naughty and wicked men, so that the strong should not afflict the weak." Later Marduk also delegated him for the same purpose, and thereupon he issued his laws. The epilogue to the Code reiterates these ideas with much emphasis upon the divine commission to secure the happiness of his people and upon his own perfect fulfilment of the charge. The sculptured relief at the head of the stele is a pictorial summary of the leading ideas expressed in the prologue and epilogue—the god extends, and the king piously accepts, the circlet and sceptre expressive of that sovereignty as a function of which the laws were given.

(C. J. GADD, IDEAS OF DIVINE RULE IN THE ANCIENT EAST 43 (1945).)

6. The frequency with which ancient law and government claimed divine endorsement suggests that the articulated idea of a preemptive moral right to be obeyed began as a corollary of those claims to supernatural status. (*See id.*, at 14, concerning Western Asian civilizations: "the principal channel through which the divine purpose flowed into the minds of men was the vicarious will of the king, as the gods' representative upon earth." *See also* JOHN NEVILLE FIGGIS, THE DIVINE RIGHT OF KINGS 17–21 (2d ed., 1922).) "Chiefly leaders were often viewed as ruling because of a sacred charter that recognized them as divine or with structured differential access to divine power." (TIMOTHY EARLE, HOW CHIEFS COME TO POWER: THE POLITICAL ECONOMY IN PREHISTORY 149 (1997), citing Malcolm C. Webb, *The Flag Follows Trade: An Essay on the Necessary Interaction of Military and Commercial Factors in State Formation,* in ANCIENT CIVILIZATION AND TRADE (J. Sabloff & C. C. Lamberg-Karlovsky eds., 1975).) The theoretical details of divine endorsement varied, and not all theories syllogistically entailed the epistemic and moral superiority on which the most plausible claims of preemptive moral duty to follow depend. (*See, e.g.,* GADD, *id.*, at 23: "For the Egyptians transmission of the divine will was not, for a long time, the subject of ideas so definite as those held in Western Asia. The present divinity of the king must have made it seem less important to be in touch with some remoter authority. . . .") But nexus to the supernatural is surely the most likely originating rationale for particular persons' claims of authority and the reason that such claims seemed often to be widely considered credible. Who but the divine could aspire to obtain

authentically preemptive obedience of the kind exemplified in the biblical account of Abraham preparing to sacrifice his son, in disregard of all humanly conceivable moral reason and intuition? (GENESIS 22).

The divine, observed Rousseau, is "an authority of a different order, capable of constraining without violence and persuading without convincing. This is what has, in all ages, compelled the fathers of nations to have recourse to divine intervention and credit the gods with their own wisdom. . . ." (JEAN-JACQUES ROUSSEAU, THE SOCIAL CONTRACT AND DISCOURSES, Bk. II, Ch. 7 (G. D. H. Cole trans., 1985) (1762).) He quoted Macchiavelli: "there has never been, in any country, an extraordinary legislator who has not had recourse to God; for otherwise his laws would not be accepted. . . ." (*Id.*, quoting NICCOLÒ MACCHIAVELLI, DICOURSES ON LIVY, Bk. V, Ch. 11 (1513–17)). In ancient cultures suffused with belief in an engaged divine dimension to their communal lives, leaders' divine-endorsement-driven claims of right to be obeyed had a potential for compelling conceptual coherence that no substitute rationale for authority has ever matched. The divine will was more than just a consistent guide to human goodness. The divine had a moral *right* to rule the creation however the divine pleased, because the creation *belonged* to its creator. Humans were the property of the divine. And the exercise of proprietary rights could be delegated for their more effective use. C. J. Gadd described "a fairly consistent picture of the ideas entertained in Western Asia about the origins of divine rule":

> There was an act of creation, differing greatly in details, but leading to the invention of man as a means of relieving the gods from otherwise unescapable toil, particularly in building their houses. . . . In order that the creatures might be capable of their duties they must be given an ordered life and the skills necessary for sustaining a civilized existence, both for themselves and for the gods. The next stage, then, is for the gods to improve their patrimonies with these essential institutions; order is maintained by the appointment of a king, and skills are dispensed to mankind in a variety of ways.
>
> (GADD, *id.*, at 13.)

The most plausible view of our discoverable history as a species suggests that authority was invented by those atop existing hierarchies of dominance in response to the developing reasoning abilities and communicative skills of the dominated. And the obvious rationale for dominance of some humans over others that could be inferred from perceived origins in a Created Nature was the will of the Creator.

7. Niklas Luhmann described "legal theory's efforts to de-tautologize and de-paradoxicalize the system":

> The operations that serve to de-tautologize and de-paradoxicalize the system will seem to the system to be naturally necessary. An observer, in contrast, can recognize the function of these semantic efforts and speculate about other, functionally equivalent possibilities; to him, every specific semantic solution to this problem appears historically determined and contingent, dependent on the supply of plausibility in the specific sociohistorical circumstances.
>
> Niklas Luhmann, *Law as a Social System*, 83 Nw. U. L. Rev. 136, 145–46 (1989).

8. Disobeying and removing bad government in such circumstances required a conceptual two-step. Bad performance had to be characterized not merely as bad but as cause or evidence of a further fact—the absence or loss of divine endorsement. Max Weber noted that even natural disasters might prompt a Chinese emperor's removal by revealing him not to be "a legitimate 'Son of Heaven.'" (Max Weber, *Theory of Social and Economic Organization, in* On Charisma and Institution Building: Selected Papers 50 (S. N. Eisentstadt ed., A. K. Henderson & Talcott Parsons trans., 1947) (1968). *See also* Frederick W. Mote, Imperial China 900–1800, 8–10, 102, 506–20, 553–59, 861–62 (1999).) Max Gluckman noted a similar story in Africa (Max Gluckman, Custom and Conflict in Africa 39 (1955): "[u]nder the divine kingship, a leader became liable to attack for failures beyond his control . . ."). In medieval Europe, Pope Gregory VII's conflict with the Holy Roman Emperor Henry IV prompted a papal assertion that the Church could declare badly behaved monarchs no longer to be God's Anointed. "He solemnly freed the subjects from their duty of obedience to the king." (Fritz Kern, Kingship and Law in the Middle Ages 108 (S. B. Chrimes trans., 1939) (1914).) And the moral weight of belief in divine endorsement prompted a remarkable artificiality in the characterization by some of the English Parliament's conflict with Charles I. "It was pretended that the Parliament took up arms against the person only of the King but in support of his authority. This shews how loth men were to believe that what was legally wrong will ever be morally

right." (JOHN NEVILLE FIGGIS, THE DIVINE RIGHT OF KINGS 223–24 (2d ed., 1922).)

9. Stephen Perry has argued that Holmes's "basic claim is that the terms 'right' and 'duty' not only do not bear in law the same meaning as in moral contexts, but are, generally speaking, 'empty' terms; there are no such things as legal rights and duties." Stephen R. Perry, *Holmes Versus Hart: The Bad Man in Legal Theory*, *in* THE PATH OF THE LAW AND ITS INFLUENCE 158, 187 (Steven J. Burton ed., 2000). "As Holmes put the point in a letter written to John Chipman Gray in 1914: 'I became convinced that the machinery of rights and duties was a fifth wheel.'" *Id.*, at 184.

10. Locke opened the preface to his *Two Treatises of Government* with an expression of hope that the writings

> are sufficient to establish the Throne of our Great Restorer, Our present King *William*; to make good his Title, in the Consent of the People, which being the only one of all lawful Governments, he has more fully and clearly than any Prince in *Christendom*: And to justifie to the World, the People of *England*, whose love of their Just and Natural Rights, with their Resolution to preserve them, saved the Nation when it was on the very brink of Slavery and Ruine.
>
> JOHN LOCKE, TWO TREATISES OF GOVERNMENT 137 (Peter Laslett ed., 1988) (1690).

11. *See* TIM HARRIS, REVOLUTION: THE GREAT CRISIS OF THE BRITISH MONARCHY 1685–1720 271–96, 433–47 (2006); WOUT TROOST, WILLIAM III, THE STADHOLDER-KING 195–205 (J. C. Grayson trans., 2005); ROGER WOOLHOUSE, LOCKE: A BIOGRAPHY 283 (2007). Locke needed to justify William's kingship in a way that would persuade minds inculcated with the idea of preemptive moral right to rule, reflected in the English monarchy's motto, *dieu et mon droit*. The revolution could not be justified to his audience merely by comparing those personal characteristics of the two contenders that actually affected their prospects of governing well. Locke needed to establish both that James had been morally ousted, and that William *in particular* had a moral right to be obeyed. Locke could not say the truth—that William was just a military strongman with a disciplined army, a set of opinions agreeable to many among the English elite, and a moderate dose of the Weberian charisma that James so conspicuously lacked. (HARRIS, *id.*, at 271–75,

477–86; TROOST, *id.*, at 195–205, 23–24.) Beyond making a breach-of-contract case against James that released the English people from obedience, Locke alleged a new commitment—to William. His argument improbably inferred from the wider population's acquiescence a tacit promise to obey and then made a moral claim that the alleged tacit consent could confer authority in the same sense as divine delegation had hitherto been alleged to do, namely, as a preemptive moral right to be obeyed. (2 JOHN LOCKE, TWO TREATISES OF GOVERNMENT §§ 119, 222 (Peter Laslett ed., 1988) (1690).) Locke's preface hailed the right of William by consent, saying nothing of William's wife Mary, James's daughter. But the collective choice of the English to characterize the new reign as a joint one of William and Mary self-consciously acknowledged the persuasive power of succession principles. Those principles could draw some moral support from their propensity to reduce risks of transitional anarchy. But the apparent strength of the moral case for respecting succession claims and avoiding alternative selection methods came from the old divine-endorsement theory of authority. (HARRIS, *id.*, at 333–34, 478; TROOST, *id.*, at 207–10.)

A frontal attack on the idea of moral right to rule would not have been persuasive, could not safely be made, and would not have sufficiently secured William. Locke's version of right to rule by agreement of the ruled was the best that he could do. David Hume subsequently called "[t]ime and custom" the bases of English monarchs' right to rule. (2 DAVID HUME, A TREATISE OF HUMAN NATURE, Bk. III, Pt. II, Sect. X (1740).) But even if these could amount to a moral reason to follow the leader, and not just a sociological description of the fact of following, that reason would not suffice for Locke's purposes. Locke needed the man who had just shown up with an army at his back to have a moral right to be obeyed. Only a claim of contract could aspire to persuade the English of a moral right to rule acquired in the midst of revolution. Here Locke was in a bind, which he handled by exploiting an ambiguity in the word "tacit." That word could mean "implied," or it could just mean "constructive." In arguing that the people of England tacitly consented by staying around after William arrived, Locke evaded the question whether the choice to stay evidenced a mental state of commitment, or in itself imposed an obligation to obey. The second alternative, if explicitly argued, would have been totally unpersuasive. What moral work could such a fiction hope to do for people worried that perhaps the divine will required them to keep James? Yet had the first alternative been true—had the population silently but actually consented to William's accession and implicitly promised to obey him—then Locke would not have needed to make the argument. When a moral person promises, she implicitly avers a moral right to make the promise. If the potentially persuasive reading of Locke's case for William was accurate, then Locke was seeking to convince the population of a consent theory that they *had already accepted* when they tacitly promised obedience. The reason that Locke published the *Treatises of Government* when he did, though they had in most part been written long before, and though the danger that had precluded past publication might yet reappear, was precisely because so many in the population were skeptical and needed to be won over. (*See* MAURICE CRANSTON, JOHN LOCKE: A BIOGRAPHY 207–08 (1957); Peter Laslett, *Introduction*, JOHN LOCKE, TWO TREATISES OF GOVERNMENT 3, 45–66 (Peter Laslett ed., 1988) (1690); WOOLHOUSE, *id.*, at 275; HARRIS, *id.*, at 433–47; W. A. SPECK, RELUCTANT REVOLUTIONARIES: ENGLISHMEN AND THE REVOLUTION OF 1688, 238–39 (1988).) And there was no behavior in the population beyond ongoing presence to support inferring majority consent of the kind that Locke argued could commit the whole. (2 LOCKE, *id.*, at §§ 95–99.)

Locke needed William to succeed. Had the revolution failed, as had the mid-century one, then Locke's fate would probably have been even worse than his previous expulsion by the Stuarts from a tenured appointment at Oxford. At best it would have meant a return to exile. Locke doubtless remembered the miseries visited on John Milton in the wake of the Stuart Restoration for having, among other things, advanced a consent theory of authority in support of the earlier revolution. Hence Locke's attempts to keep the *Treatises'* authorship anonymous, though he had to know that eventually the secret would become open. (WOOLHOUSE, *id.*, at 207–10, 281–83; Laslett, *id.*, at 66, 4–6; STANLEY FISH, HOW MILTON WORKS 517–18 (2001); BARBARA K. LEWALSKI, THE LIFE OF JOHN MILTON: A CRITICAL BIOGRAPHY 398–407 (2000) ("In Darknes, and with Dangers Compast Round" 1660–65).)

12. The consent criterion for incidence of moral duty to obey had a long pedigree, but a rarefied one. As David Hume observed, it had not figured in the claims of rulers and in the self-understandings of most law-abiding subjects. It could be traced from one of the reasons Socrates gave for obeying the laws of Athens, through Manegold of Lautenbach's reason for denouncing and resisting his monarch, the Holy Roman Emperor Henry IV, during the latter's dispute with the Pope in the eleventh

century, to John Milton's defense of the decision to depose, try, and execute James's father, Charles I, four decades before Locke published. Thomas Hobbes had also made a mid-century case for consent, but, unhelpfully, had called that consent indefeasible. (*See* 2 David Hume, A Treatise of Human Nature, Bk. III, Pt. II, Sect. VIII (1740); Plato, *Crito in* I The Dialogues of Plato 435–36 (Benjamin Jowett trans., 1937); *cf.* Plato, *Apology, id.*, at 412 (suggesting that the contractual duty to obey did not preempt a conflicting duty to the divine); Fritz Kern, Kingship and Law in the Middle Ages 119–21 (S. B. Chrimes trans., 1939) (1914); John Milton, *The Tenure of Kings and Magistrates, in* John Milton, Political Writings 3, 7 n. 21, 8–13 (Martin Dzelzainis ed., Claire Gruzelier trans., 1991) (1650); Thomas Hobbes, Leviathan 228–29 (C. B. MacPherson ed., 1968) (1651). *See also* the Huguenot consent theory advanced in *Vindiciae contra Tyrannes,* discussed in John Neville Figgis, The Divine Right of Kings 113–16 (2d ed., 1922), and James Tyrrell, Patriarcha Non Monarcha (1681) (preface). Late seventeenth-century consent theories owed a significant debt, explicit in Locke's work, to Richard Hooker, of the Lawes of Ecclesiasticall Politie (1593). *See, e.g.,* 2 Locke, *id.*, at § 91.)

13. 2 David Hume, A Treatise of Human Nature, Bk. III, Pt. II, Sect. VIII (1740).
14. Locke's claim that duty to obey might be owed through *tacit* consent shared with Socrates' account a "one could have just left" rationale that may have been personally true for Locke and for Socrates but was certainly not true for most of England in 1688. (2 John Locke, Two Treatises of Government § 121 (Peter Laslett ed., 1988) (1690); Plato, *Crito in* I The Dialogues of Plato 435 (Benjamin Jowett trans., 1937).) And even where departure is physically possible, surely "[c]onsent cannot be binding on people, in the way this argument requires, unless it is given more freely, and with more genuine alternate choice, than just by declining to build a life from nothing under a foreign flag." (Ronald Dworkin, Law's Empire 192–93 (1986).) Even where an alternate is chosen, what promise to the institutions of the chosen community does that *really* imply? Did a Jewish person who fled inquisitorial Spain "consent" to the somewhat softer forms of anti-Semitism that blighted the governance of his potential destination communities?
15. Eddie Izzard, Dress to Kill (Stand-up Comedy Tour, 1998).

16. For the most recent valiant attempt to justify authority through consent despite consent's factual absence, *see* David M. Estlund, Democratic Authority: A Philosophical Framework (2008). For superb critique, *see* William A. Edmundson, *Consent and Its Cousins*, 121 Ethics 335 (2011).
17. One cannot morally promise to do wrong and one cannot morally keep such a promise. Robert Paul Wolff's critique on that score remains as compelling as when he first advanced it. *See* Robert Paul Wolff, In Defense of Anarchism 29, 40–42 (1970).
18. "Men too might as often and as innocently change their Governours, as they do their Physicians, if the Person cannot be known, who has a right to direct me, and whose Prescriptions I am bound to follow. To settle therefore Mens Consciences under an Obligation to Obedience, 'tis necessary that they know not only that there is a Power somewhere in the World, but the Person who by Right is vested with this Power over them." (1 John Locke, Two Treatises of Government § 81 (Peter Laslett ed., 1988) (1690).)
19. Luhmann called law "a social system defined by its own code."

> Legal theory has found it difficult (and perhaps it always will) to grasp this positive quality of the law in the absence of any conception of an external (especially a moral) justification. . . . In this situation the theory of autopoietic systems offers at least the possibility of an adequate description. Whether this description can be introduced into the legal system itself (*i.e.*, used as its self-description) must be left an open question (which means, left to evolution).
>
> Niklas Luhmann, *Law as a Social System*, 83 Nw. U. L. Rev. 136, 148–49 (1989).

20. Charles Darwin, The Origin of Species (1859); Charles Darwin, The Descent of Man (2d ed., 1874).
21. Assertions of divine endorsement supported inferences of preemptive right to be obeyed through implicit variations on an epistemic claim—God or gods, as the creative force, must know what is best for the creation. Even where the gods were characterized as quite selfish, their boundless ability to affect humans adversely made doing what divine will demanded necessarily the best thing for humans to do. The will of the creator defined goodness in the experience of the creation. It did not matter whether one framed the reason for action as doing the good

or as doing the divine will, for these were necessarily synonyms. From divine endorsement of the leader, it logically followed that doing what the leader showed he wanted through his signals of likely action had to be the path to the good, and to think otherwise had to be an epistemic error. Even if the leader seemed a fool or a knave, the fact of divine designation meant that ousting him posed an unacceptable risk of divine retribution. *See* C. J. GADD, IDEAS OF DIVINE RULE IN THE ANCIENT EAST 13–14, 36–37 (1945). *See also* the biblical story of David's refusal to harm the flawed King Saul because "who can stretch forth his hand against the Lord's anointed, and be guiltless?" I SAMUEL 26:9. *See also* I SAMUEL 24.

22. JOSEPH RAZ, BETWEEN AUTHORITY AND INTERPRETATION 136–37 (2009).
23. MAX WEBER, *Theory of Social and Economic Organization, in* ON CHARISMA AND INSTITUTION BUILDING: SELECTED PAPERS 46–62 (S. N. Eisentstadt ed., A. K. Henderson & Talcott Parsons trans., 1947) (1968).
24. *Compare* Stephen R. Perry, *Law and Obligation,* 50 AM. J. JURIS. 263, 279–84 (2005) (arguing that the duty to follow wise guides, if it exists at all, is owed to oneself). For an array of other angles from which Raz's normal justification is susceptible to criticism, *see generally* Kenneth Einar Himma, *Just 'Cause You're Smarter than Me Doesn't Give You a Right to Tell Me What to Do: Legitimate Authority and the Normal Justification Thesis,* 27 OXFORD J. LEGAL STUDIES 121 (2007).
25. JOSEPH RAZ, PRACTICAL REASON AND NORMS 194 (from 1990 Postscript) (1999):

    > The puzzle has always been, how can one avoid the following dilemma? If a rule is justified by certain reasons, then either the action it requires is invariably the action required by the underlying reasons, in which case one might just as well rely on the reason rather than the rule, or else the action the rule requires deviates from that justified by the underlying reasons, in which case following the rule is unjustified. Hence rules are either redundant or unjustified. One escapes from the dilemma in those cases where conformity with the underlying reasons is improved if one does not attempt to comply with them. In such cases conformity with the underlying reasons is secured by complying with the rule, or rather a better degree of conformity than can otherwise

be achieved is so obtained. This can justify complying with the rule even when it requires action which the underlying reasons do not. Such compliance may still be the best strategy to maximise conformity with the underlying reasons. The reason not to comply with another reason is an exclusionary reason. Since rules can only function as rules if one takes them as reasons for action and avoids trying to comply with the underlying reasons, all rules are exclusionary reasons.

Raz's reference to rules functioning as rules seems question-begging; it seems to presuppose that the purpose of rule giving is to preempt receivers' thinking about what to do and to substitute commands to obey for their own decision making. But what if the purpose of rule giving is just to inform, to supplement the knowledge with which people make their own decisions about what to do by supplying predictions of what people in law's community are likely to do and to expect? Rules can function as *vehicles for understanding each other,* and that is in fact how we mostly use them. The understanding we glean may indeed supply us with reasons for action, but those reasons just get weighed with everything else relevant to what we do, they do not *exclude* our thinking about other things that matter. For more on Raz's concept of exclusionary reasons, see the main text of chapter 6.

CHAPTER 4

1. THE MATRIX (Motion Picture, Warner Bros. (distributor), 1999); THE MATRIX RELOADED (Motion Picture, Warner Bros. (distributor), 2003); THE MATRIX REVOLUTIONS (Motion Picture, Warner Bros. (distributor), 2003).
2. LUDWIG WITTGENSTEIN, PHILOSOPHICAL INVESTIGATIONS § 201 (4th ed., P. M. S. Hacker & Joachim Schulte eds., G. E. M. Anscombe, P. M. S. Hacker, & Joachim Schulte trans., 2009) (1953):

   This was our paradox: no course of action could be determined by a rule, because every course of action can be brought into accord with the rule. The answer was: if every course of action can be brought into accord with the rule, then it can also be brought into conflict with it. And so there would be neither accord nor conflict here.

   That there is a misunderstanding here is shown by the mere fact that in this chain of reasoning we place one interpretation behind another, as if each one contented us at least for a moment, until we thought of yet another lying behind it. For what we thereby show is that there is a way of grasping a rule which is *not* an interpretation, but which, from case to case of application, is exhibited in what we call "following the rule" and "going against it."

That's why there is an inclination to say: every action according to a rule is an interpretation. But one should speak of interpretation only when one expression of a rule is substituted for another.

3. *Id.*, § 32:

> Someone coming into a foreign country will sometimes learn the language of the inhabitants from ostensive explanations that they give him; and he will often have to *guess* how to interpret these explanations; and sometimes he will guess right, sometimes wrong.
>
> And now, I think, we can say: Augustine describes the learning of human language as if the child came into a foreign country and did not understand the language of the country; that is, as if the child could already *think*, only not yet speak. And "think" would here mean something like "talk to himself."

4. Helen Keller, The Story of My Life (1903); William Gibson, The Miracle Worker (Three-Act Play, premiered 1959).
5. *See* Dennis Patterson, Law and Truth 126–27 (1996):

> It is not by virtue of interpretation that we have a common world. Rather, we have a world in concert with others because we understand the manifold activities that constitute that world. Catching on to and participating in these activities—knowing *how* to act—is the essence of understanding.
>
> If understanding is primordial, then interpretation is of necessity a secondary endeavor; the very existence of practices of interpretation is dependent upon understanding already in place. As we saw, interpretation cannot begin where there is no understanding, for every interpretation of a sign simply "hangs in the air" with that which it interprets. *By themselves*, interpretations take us nowhere.

6. H. L. A. Hart's early working notes reveal that the problematic nature of an authority assumption was apparent to him: "There is something odd, possibly something mistaken in position which I have taken v. 2 that

the essence/structure of a legal system rests on acceptance of central/certain authority as binding. . . . Perhaps all I need to convey is that the obligation is strictly *obligation*. i.e.: narrower than belief in moral goodness. But? There is a muddle (in me) I suspect here." NICOLA LACEY, A LIFE OF H. L. A. HART: THE NIGHTMARE AND THE NOBLE DREAM 228 (2004).

7. H. L. A. HART, THE CONCEPT OF LAW 110 (2d ed., 1994): "the rule of recognition exists only as a complex, but normally concordant, practice of the courts, officials, and private persons in identifying the law by reference to certain criteria. Its existence is a matter of fact." *Id.*, at 109: "[I]t is important to distinguish 'assuming the validity' from 'presupposing the existence' of such a rule; if only because failure to do this obscures what is meant by the assertion that such a rule *exists*."
8. HANS KELSEN, PURE THEORY OF LAW 201–05 (Max Knight trans., 1967) (1960).
9. Hans Kelsen, *The Function of a Constitution* 117 (Iain Stewart trans., 1964), *in* ESSAYS ON KELSEN, 109, 117 (Richard Tur & William Twining eds., Iain Stewart trans., 1986). *Compare* the perspective of the leading Scandinavian Realist, Alf Ross: "It could be maintained that a certain authority . . . can be established in norms enacted by itself, which amounts to saying that it is possible for a norm to determine the conditions of its own establishment, including the way in which it can be changed. A 'reflexivity' of this kind, however, is a logical impossibility, and is generally recognised as such by logicians." (ALF ROSS, ON LAW AND JUSTICE 81(1958).) "Every system of enacted law is necessarily based on an initial hypothesis which constitutes the supreme authority, but which is not itself created by any authority. It exists only in the form of a political ideology which forms the presupposition for the system." (*Id.*, at 83.) Ross somehow thought that philosophy could illuminate the nature of law without regard to law's social evolution: "Custom is the natural starting point of legal evolution. From the point of view of historical evolution the great problem is rather the growth of a legislative power, how the ideology arose and took hold that certain persons had authority to proclaim new norms which were accepted as 'valid' by the judiciary and the people. This problem turns on the origin of political ideology and is a subject for the sociology of law, not philosophy of law. We accept the growth of a legislative power as a fact." (*Id.*, at 92.)
10. H. L. A. Hart, The Concept of Law 94–99 (2d ed., 1994).

11. "They are, in a sense, officials in virtue of that rule, but they are not officials prior to it (in either the factual or the logical sense). Their behaviour makes the rule possible; but it is the rule that makes them officials." Jules L. Coleman, *Incorporationism, Conventionality, and the Practical Difference Thesis, in* HART'S POSTSCRIPT: ESSAYS ON THE POSTSCRIPT TO THE CONCEPT OF LAW, 99, 121 (Jules L. Coleman ed., 2001).
12. The idea of authority could explain convergent observance of the rule of recognition if there were reason for the observers to believe that the rule came from someone who had a right to be obeyed by them. *See* Julie Dickson, *Is the Rule of Recognition Really a Conventional Rule?*, 27 OXFORD J. LEGAL STUDIES 373 (2007). But when we search for a right to be obeyed underlying a legal system, we find that "it's turtles all the way down." STEPHEN W. HAWKING, A BRIEF HISTORY OF TIME 1 (1988).
13. In his Postscript to *The Concept of Law*, Hart observed: "Rules are conventional social practices if the general conformity of a group to them is part of the reasons which its individual members have for acceptance. . . . [C]onventional social rules . . . include, besides ordinary social customs (which may or may not be recognized as having legal force), certain important legal rules including the rule of recognition, which is in effect a form of judicial customary rule existing only if it is accepted and practised in the law-identifying and law-applying operations of the courts." H. L. A. HART, THE CONCEPT OF LAW 255–56 (2d ed., 1994). Jules Coleman congruently concludes that "the rule of recognition is a coordination convention that creates reasons for acting in the way in which coordination conventions generally do—when they do. This is by creating a system of reciprocal, legitimate expectations." Jules L. Coleman, *Incorporationism, Conventionality, and the Practical Difference Thesis, in* HART'S POSTSCRIPT: ESSAYS ON THE POSTSCRIPT TO THE CONCEPT OF LAW, 99, 119–20 (Jules L. Coleman ed., 2001).
14. On the character of conventions, *see* DAVID K. LEWIS, CONVENTION (1969); ANDREI MARMOR, SOCIAL CONVENTIONS: FROM LANGUAGE TO LAW (2009).
15. 2 DAVID HUME, A TREATISE OF HUMAN NATURE, Bk. III, Pt. II, Sect. VIII (1740).
16. *Id.*, Bk. III, Pt. I, Sect. I.
17. "For the assumption of a basic norm . . . not only contradicts reality, since no such norm exists as the meaning of an actual act of will, but also contains contradiction within itself, since it represents the authorization of

a supreme moral or legal authority, and hence it issues from an authority lying beyond that authority, even though the further authority is merely figmentary." Hans Kelsen, *The Function of a Constitution* 117 (Iain Stewart trans., 1964), *in* ESSAYS ON KELSEN, 109, 117 (Richard Tur & William Twining eds., Iain Stewart trans., 1986).

CHAPTER 5

1. The metaphor of a picture is well deployed in Mark Greenberg, *The Standard Picture and Its Discontents*, in 1 OXFORD STUDIES IN PHILOSOPHY 39 (Leslie Green & Brian Leiter eds., 2011). According to Greenberg's "bindingness hypothesis, whatever ends law has, whatever its functions are, it is supposed to pursue those ends and perform those functions while ensuring bindingness." (*Id.*, at 88.) But lawgiving actions, like all other actions that humans do, are matters for all-things-considered moral judgment, and whether law's recipients will be morally bound to do what law signals is not the only thing for a lawgiver to consider. Imposing a speed limit on a road may be the right thing for a lawgiver to do, all things considered, even though the lawgiver can totally foresee that sometimes the right thing for a driver to do, all things considered, will be to exceed the speed limit. Of course lawgivers should try to avoid telling people to do the wrong thing, but so should we all. All of us should strive to minimize our risk of misleading others into doing less well than they could. That consideration is not distinctively a feature of lawgiving. Where lawgivers signal something that would otherwise be morally discretionary, the good of having a predictively effective legal system will usually help tip recipients' moral scales in favor of doing what law signals. *That* is a consideration distinctive to law. We will examine it further in the next chapter.
2. *See* "Authority" in 1 OXFORD ENGLISH DICTIONARY 798 (2d ed., J. A. Simpson & E. S. C. Weiner eds., 1989).
3. MAX WEBER, *Theory of Social and Economic Organization*, *in* ON CHARISMA AND INSTITUTION BUILDING: SELECTED PAPERS 46–62 (S. N. Eisentstadt ed., A. K. Henderson & Talcott Parsons trans., 1947) (1968).
4. *See, e.g.*, HEIDI M. HURD, MORAL COMBAT 153–56 (1999).
5. *See* "Legitimacy" and "Legitimate" in 8 OXFORD ENGLISH DICTIONARY 811 (2d ed., J. A. Simpson & E. S. C. Weiner eds., 1989).
6. *Id.*, citing, from 1691, amid the controversy surrounding James II's departure from the English throne: "N. Luttrell Diary in Brief Hist.

Relation State Affairs (1857) II. 207 A virulent libell endeavouring to prove the legitimacy of the prince of Wales, is printed."

"[I]n every case, princely power and those groups having interests vested in it—that is, the warlord's following—strive for legitimacy as soon as the rule has become stable. They crave for a characteristic which would define the charismatically qualified ruler." MAX WEBER, ESSAYS IN SOCIOLOGY 27 (H. H. GERTH & Wright Mills trans., 1946). "Genuine charisma rests upon the legitimation of personal heroism or personal revelation. Yet precisely this quality of charisma as an extraordinary, supernatural, divine power transforms it, after its routinization, into a suitable source for the legitimate acquisition of sovereign power by the successors of the charismatic hero." (*Id.*, at 39.) Karl Popper pointed out that we humans have for too much of our history been fixated on the question *"Who should rule?"* at the expense of attention to how to stop our rulers from harming us. The way we long talked about legitimacy was symptomatic of that disease. *See* 1 KARL R. POPPER, THE OPEN SOCIETY AND ITS ENEMIES 121 (4th ed., 1962).

Sometimes perceptions of the supernatural may have been mixed with perceptions of the natural. Elman Service cited his fellow anthropologist Kenneth Read's observation that in the New Guinea Highlands "[p]eople believe that the character of the parent is transmitted to his offspring, and a man of eminence may be likely to seek and to encourage in his son the qualities which inspire confidence and dependence." ELMAN R. SERVICE, ORIGINS OF THE STATE AND CIVILIZATION: THE PROCESS OF CULTURAL EVOLUTION 73(1975), quoting Kenneth E. Read, *Leadership and Consensus in a New Guinea Society*, 61 AMERICAN ANTHROPOLOGIST 425, 427 (1959). Service continued that a "review of the well-known chiefdoms of Polynesia and Micronesia, the southeastern United States, the islands and coasts of the Caribbean, many African societies, and Central Asian pastoralists reveals that inheritance of status by primogeniture must be a nearly universal feature of chiefdoms." *Id.*, at 74.

7. The distinction between revolutionary change in law and resolution of vagueness or ambiguity in law will be further discussed in chapter 9.
8. U.S. CONST. art. III § 3 cl. 1.
9. U.S. CONST. amend. VI.
10. *Compare*, however, Stephen Holmes' account of Chateaubriand's and Talleyrand's pragmatic deployment of "legitimacy" during the Bourbon

Restoration. Stephen Holmes, *Two Concepts of Legitimacy: France after the Revolution*, 10 POLITICAL THEORY 165 (1982). The classic work on the initial revolution is, of course, ALEXIS DE TOCQUEVILLE, THE OLD RÉGIME AND THE FRENCH REVOLUTION (Stuart Gilbert trans., 1955) (1856): "No nation had ever before embarked on so resolute an attempt as that of the French in 1789 to break with the past, to make, as it were, a scission in their life line and to create an unbridgeable gulf between all they had hitherto been and all they now aspired to be." (Foreword by the author, *id.*, at vii.)

11. *Compare* SCOTT J. SHAPIRO, LEGALITY 224 (2011): "it is plausible to suppose that legality itself is not a binary property but also comes in degrees." JOSEPH RAZ, PRACTICAL REASON AND NORMS 150 (1999): "The general traits which mark a system as a legal one are several and each of them admits, in principle, of various degrees. . . . It would be arbitrary and pointless to try and fix a precise borderline between normative systems which are legal systems and those which are not."
12. *See* CHRISTIAN WOLFF, THE LAW OF NATIONS TREATED ACCORDING TO A SCIENTIFIC METHOD Ch. II §§ 255–57 (Joseph Drake trans., 1934) (1764):

    > By nature no nation has the right to any act which belongs to the exercise of the sovereignty of another nation. For sovereignty, as it exists in a people or originally in a nation, is absolute. Since, therefore, the perfection of sovereignty consists in its exercise independently of the will of another, all acts of any nation which belong to the exercise of civil sovereignty are altogether independent of the will of any other nation. . . . [N]o ruler of a state has the right to interfere in the government of another.

13. *See* EUGEN EHRLICH, FUNDAMENTAL PRINCIPLES OF THE SOCIOLOGY OF LAW 26–60 (Walter L. Moll trans., 1936), chs. 2 ("The Inner Order of the Social Associations") and 3 ("The Social Associations and the Social Norms").

CHAPTER 6

1. Erich Fromm, *Disobedience as a Psychological and Moral Problem*, in A MATTER OF LIFE (Clara Urquhart ed., 1963). *Reprinted in* ERICH FROMM, ON DISOBEDIENCE: WHY FREEDOM MEANS SAYING "NO" TO POWER 3 (2010).
2. JOHN RAWLS, A THEORY OF JUSTICE 389 (1971).

3. Footage of the President's speech, and an account of Meyer's repeated requests for permission to attack and of their denial, are available at the *Army Times* website: http://www.armytimes.com/news/2011/09/ap_dakota_meyer_awarded_medal_of_honor_091511/.

   See also C. J. Chivers, *Top Medal for Marine Who Saved Many Lives,* N.Y. Times, Sept. 16, 2011, at A14.
4. Joseph Raz, Between Authority and Interpretation 141–42 (2009):

   > The pre-emptive force of authority is part and parcel of its nature. It cannot succeed as an authority (ie succeed in improving our conformity with reason) if it does not pre-empt the background reasons. The function of authorities is to improve our conformity with those background reasons by making us try to follow their instructions rather than the background reasons. Authorities cannot do so without at least the possibility that their directives will sometimes lead us to act differently than we would have done without them. . . .
   >
   > The pre-emptive standing of authoritative directives shows why the moral question about the law is a serious one. It shows what truth there is in the saying that in accepting authority we surrender our judgement to the authority.

   See also Joseph Raz, The Morality of Freedom 73–75 (1986).
5. *See, e.g.,* David Curtis Wright, The History of China 196–97 (2d ed., 2011): "When I looked in the direction of the gunfire, I found myself staring at a soldier's face. His eyes were popping, bloodshot, and dazed, as if he were on drugs." (Eyewitness account of Shen Tong.) *Compare* Orville Schell, Mandate of Heaven, 142 (1995): "The slaughter was so merciless that rumors began circulating that the soldiers had been administered some kind of drug as a stimulant. A more likely explanation was that all the frustration, embarrassment, humiliation, and anger that had been building within the military during the preceding two weeks was now finally finding its awful release."
6. Genesis 22.
7. Oliver Wendell Holmes, Jr., *The Path of the Law,* 10 Harv. L. Rev. 457, 458 (1897) (laying "down some first principles for the study of this body of dogma or systematized prediction which we call the law").
8. Tom R. Tyler, Why People Obey the Law, 45–46 (2d ed., 2006).
9. *Id.,* at 40.

10. Stu Woo, *Amazon Takes Action in Illinois as War on Sales Taxes Continues*, Wall Street Journal, Mar. 11, 2011, Business Section; Verne G. Kopytoff, *Amazon Pressured on Sales Tax*, N.Y. Times, Mar. 14, 2011, at B1.
11. *See* Quill Corp. v. North Dakota, 504 U.S. 298 (1992).
12. Public Act 96–1388 (Illinois, 2010).
13. Tyler found that where people felt their interactions with government had been procedurally fair, they perceived more moral justification for lawgiving (framed by Tyler as the perceived legitimacy of legal authorities) and were consequently more likely to conform their behavior to law. *See* Tom R. Tyler, Why People Obey the Law, 100, 103, 107, 270, 284 (2d ed., 2006). The significance of procedural fairness in Tyler's conclusions followed naturally from the experiences with government on which his study focused, namely, interacting with police and going to court. Thinking about the goodness of law and government based on experiences with police and judges builds in a focus on how the law is applied rather than on the merits of the law that is being applied and the way the lawgivers became lawgivers, because at the level of policing and trial adjudication, the content of the law that is applied and how it came to be law are out of everyone's hands.
14. Gonzales v. Raich, 545 U.S. 1 (2005).
15. *See* Erik Eckholm, *California Dispensaries Moving to Block U.S. Marijuana Crackdown*, N.Y. Times, Nov. 8, 2011, at A17 ("A thriving industry of growers and storefront dispensaries has emerged in California that pays substantial sums in state and local taxes, but that federal drug officials see as largely illegal."). *See also* William Fisher, Technology, Law, and the Future of Entertainment 3 (2004) (reporting on a survey showing most responders thought that online music downloading in defiance of intellectual property law was not immoral, an attitude at least as old as that popular gift from one teenager to another in the 1980s, the mixed tape). *See also id.*, at 243, 298.
16. Some state lawgivers who do not repeal their laws may frankly be disagreeing with the Supreme Court's unanimous conclusion that the elaborative words through which the Court resolves disputes arising under the Constitution become part of the law of the Constitution, higher in hierarchy than state law. *See* Cooper v. Aaron, 358 U.S. 1 (1958). *Compare* Edwin Meese, III, *The Law of the Constitution*, 61 Tul. L. Rev. 979 (1987). As we will see in chapter 9, vagueness or ambiguity in law's words effectively confers elaborative discretion on dispute resolvers

about what law requires and the dispute resolvers' elaborations add to the words that count as law. In a legal system where later courts look to the words added by earlier courts, those earlier courts succeed in supplementing the law, not just for the parties in dispute, but for all to whom law applies.

17. *See* John Milton, *The Tenure of Kings and Magistrates*, *in* John Milton, Political Writings 3, 7 n. 21, 8–13 (Martin Dzelzainis ed., Claire Gruzelier trans., 1991) (1650); 2 John Locke, Two Treatises of Government §§ 119, 222 (Peter Laslett ed., 1988) (1690). *See also* the Huguenot consent theory advanced in *Vindiciae contra Tyrannes*, discussed in John Neville Figgis, The Divine Right of Kings 113–16 (2d ed., 1922), and James Tyrrell, Patriarcha Non Monarcha (1681) (preface). Late seventeenth-century consent theories owed a significant debt, explicit in Locke's work, to Richard Hooker, of the Lawes of Ecclesiasticall Politie (1593). *See, e.g.*, 2 Locke, *id.*, at § 91.

18. Charles Louis de Secondat, Baron de Montesquieu, The Spirit of the Laws, Bk. 24, Ch. 5 (Thomas Nugent trans., 4th ed., 1766) (1748):

> When the Christian religion, two centuries ago, became unhappily divided into Catholic and Protestant, the people of the North embraced the Protestant, and those of the South adhered still to the Catholic.
>
> The reason is plain: the people of the North have, and will for ever have, a spirit of liberty and independence, which the people of the South have not; and therefore a religion, which has no visible head, is more agreeable to the independency of the climate, than that which has one.

19. Alexis de Tocqueville, Democracy in America 187 (Arthur Goldhammer trans., 2004) (1835):

> The inhabitants of Mexico, wishing to establish a federal system, took the federal constitution of their neighbors the Anglo-Americans as their model and copied it almost entirely. In borrowing the letter of the law, however, they were unable to borrow as well the spirit that animated it. Again and again we therefore find them ensnaring themselves in the machinery of their divided government. With sovereignty no longer circumscribed

by the constitution, the states trespass upon that of the union and the union upon that of the states. Even today Mexico is still lurching from anarchy to military despotism and back again.

Compare MAX WEBER, THE PROTESTANT ETHIC AND THE SPIRIT OF CAPITALISM, 165 (Talcott Parsons trans., 1958) (1905) (discussing the Puritans' "sober legality").

20. *Compare* Montesquieu's speculations on the relation of climate to character: CHARLES LOUIS DE SECONDAT, BARON DE MONTESQUIEU, THE SPIRIT OF THE LAWS, Bk. 14 (1748).
21. STANLEY MILGRAM, OBEDIENCE TO AUTHORITY 19 (1974).
22. *Id.*, at 21.
23. *Id.*, at 35.
24. *Id.*, at 1–2.
25. *Id.*, at 7–8.
26. TOM R. TYLER, WHY PEOPLE OBEY THE LAW 282 (2d ed., 2006). *See also id.*, at 65, and the work of social psychologists since Milgram on the dangers of deference, notably HERBERT C. KELMAN & V. LEE HAMILTON, CRIMES OF OBEDIENCE: TOWARD A SOCIAL PSYCHOLOGY OF AUTHORITY AND RESPONSIBILITY 278–306 (1989) (exploring the implications for deference and for perceptions of personal responsibility of what the authors characterize as individuals' rule, role, or value orientations).
27. *See* ROBERT J. SHILLER, IRRATIONAL EXUBERANCE 159 (2d ed., 2005), observing that the Milgram "results were widely interpreted as demonstrating the enormous power of authority over the human mind. Indeed the results may be understood partly on those terms. But there is another interpretation: that people have learned that when experts tell them that something is all right, it probably is, even if it does not seem so."

    To address this concern at least partially, Milgram repeated the experiment off campus. "As it turned out, the level of obedience in Bridgeport, although somewhat reduced, was not significantly lower than that obtained at Yale. A large proportion of the Bridgeport subjects were fully obedient to the experimenter's commands (48 percent of the Bridgeport subjects delivered the maximum shock versus 65 percent in the corresponding condition at Yale). . . ." STANLEY MILGRAM, OBEDIENCE TO AUTHORITY 69 (1974).
28. *See* H. L. A. Hart, *Are There Any Natural Rights?*, 64 PHIL. REV. 175, 178, 182–91 (1955); John Rawls, *Legal Obligation and the Duty of Fair Play, in* LAW AND PHILOSOPHY 3–4, 8–11 (Sidney Hook ed., 1964). *Compare*

A. JOHN SIMMONS, MORAL PRINCIPLES AND POLITICAL OBLIGATIONS 138–39 (1979) (arguing that the "open benefits" of governance cannot morally make the case for duty to obey). "Fair play" arguments for authority do not support authority in the essential sense of moral duty to obey lawgivers, because the duties to preserve the efficacy of the system and to help law achieve particular substantively good things—such as coordination for good purposes—are not owed to law*givers*, but to one's fellow law receivers as co-beneficiaries of the shared signaling system that serves the shared human community. "It's not about you" would be a perfectly accurate response to anyone relying on fair play to support his claim of right to be obeyed. To allege that an otherwise contestable belief in lawgivers' weighty or even preemptive moral right to be obeyed must be artificially maintained and acted upon in the interest of fair play is to beg the question, for if the delusion that there is such a right were dispelled through the visible disregard of disbelievers, then no ostensible issue of fairness would exist. The true moral culprits are those who help to perpetuate the delusion by paying lip service to the idea of authority while quietly choosing their own actions in knowing disregard of that idea. For example, if on balance the moral weight of reasons relevant to action does not support doing what a compulsory vaccination law predicts that I will do, then I may morally choose not to be vaccinated. But it would be immoral for me to avoid vaccination while citing the law as a conclusive reason for others to be vaccinated.

29. JOHN RAWLS, A THEORY OF JUSTICE 354 (1971); *compare* JOSEPH RAZ, THE MORALITY OF FREEDOM 102 (1986).
30. RONALD DWORKIN, LAW'S EMPIRE 195–216 (1986).
31. Youngstown Sheet and Tube Co. v. Sawyer, 343 U.S. 579 (1952).
32. Isabel Wilkerson, *Growing Peril on South African Roads: Wave of Carjackings*, N.Y. TIMES, Sept., 27, 1994: "The threat of a carjacking figures into people's everyday routines now. Some people no longer stop at traffic lights, especially at night. They just pause and move on."
33. *See* SCOTT J. SHAPIRO, LEGALITY (2011). "Not all laws are plans, however: customary rules, we have seen, are merely planlike." (*Id.*, at 386.) We could equally say that plans are custom-like. One way to coordinate our actions is to talk with each other and make a plan. But we have to be personally in touch to do that. Another way to coordinate our actions is to belong to a community that has customs, including customs of treating particular people as leaders. Treating people as leaders means treating people as lawgivers. Treating people as lawgivers means treating

people as effective predictors of what is likely to be done and expected in the group. All of us, lawgivers included, have reason to put plenty of thought into those of our actions that are likely to have big consequences. We surely hope that the laws we get from lawgivers reflect lots of the kind of thinking we may call planning. But our most foundational laws, the expressions of custom that sustain the systems that set people up as lawgivers, owe nothing to planning at all. "Evolution is not a planning scheme." Niklas Luhmann, Law as a Social System 252 (Fatima Kastner, Richard Nobles, David Schiff, & Rosamund Ziegert eds., Klaus A. Ziegert trans., 2004) (1993).

34. I am grateful to my colleague Steven Smith for putting the point this way. *See also* Steven D. Smith, *Hart's Onion: The Peeling Away of Legal Authority*, 16 S. Cal. Interdisc. L.J. 97, 123 (2006) (identifying the inadequacy to establish authority of various much-cited reasons for conforming to instructions).
35. *Compare* Brian Leiter, *The Demarcation Problem in Jurisprudence: A New Case for Scepticism*, 31 Oxford J. Legal Studies 663 (2011) (considering the failure in philosophy of science to identify the essential properties of science).
36. Joseph Raz, Practical Reason and Norms 183 (from 1990 Postscript) (1999).
37. *Id.*, at 37–39, 186.
38. For critique of the idea of exclusionary reasons from an array of angles, *see* Larry Alexander & Emily Sherwin, The Rule of Rules: Morality, Rules, and the Dilemmas of Law 73–77 (2001); Larry Alexander, *Law and Exclusionary Reasons*, 18 Philosophical Topics 5 (1990); William A. Edmundson, *Rethinking Exclusionary Reasons*, 12 Law and Philosophy, 329 (1993); Michael Moore, *Authority, Law, and Razian Reasons*, 62 So. Cal. L. Rev. 829 (1989); Stephen Perry, *Second-Order Reasons, Uncertainty and Legal Theory*, 62 So. Cal. L. Rev. 913 (1989); Donald Regan, *Authority and Value: Reflections on Raz's Morality of Freedom*, 62 So. Cal. L. Rev. 995 (1989).
39. *See* Ronald Dworkin, Law's Empire (1986).
40. Malcolm Gladwell, Blink: The Power of Thinking Without Thinking (2005).
41. Star Wars (Motion Picture, 20th Century Fox, 1977).
42. *See*, however, Herbert C. Kelman & V. Lee Hamilton, Crimes of Obedience: Toward a Social Psychology of Authority and Responsibility 191 (1989): "When asked to put themselves in the shoes

of Calley or his men [at My Lai], a majority of our respondents predicted that they would follow orders and shoot. Nearly all of these respondents assumed that most people would do the same. . . . Clearly, however, not everyone considered obedience inevitable in the hypothetical situation we described. Just as many of the men under Calley's command found ways of refusing or evading his orders, so many—a third—of our respondents predicted that they would refuse to shoot. . . . The strongest predictor of the 'refuse' response was educational attainment. . . ."

43. 2 DAVID HUME, A TREATISE OF HUMAN NATURE, Bk. III, Pt. II, Sect. X (1740).
44. *Id.*, at Sect. IX.
45. NIKLAS LUHMANN, LAW AS A SOCIAL SYSTEM 142–3, 148 (Fatima Kastner, Richard Nobles, David Schiff, & Rosamund Ziegert eds., Klaus A. Ziegert trans., 2004) (1993).
46. 2 DAVID HUME, A TREATISE OF HUMAN NATURE, Bk. III, Pt. II, Sect. X (1740).
47. *Id.*, at Bk. III, Pt. I, Sect. I.
48. *Id.*, at Bk. III, Pt. II, Sect. VIII. *See also* Leslie Green, *"Because Everyone Thinks So": Hume on Authority and Common Opinion* (59/2010, Oxford Legal Research Paper Series, 2010).
49. HUME, *id.*, at Sect. X.

CHAPTER 7

1. MAGNA CARTA Ch. 39 (1215): "No freeman shall be taken or imprisoned or disseised or exiled or in any way destroyed, nor will we go upon him nor send upon him, except by the lawful judgment of his peers or by the law of the land." *See* 1 WINSTON CHURCHILL, A HISTORY OF THE ENGLISH SPEAKING PEOPLES: THE BIRTH OF BRITAIN 256 (1956): "Throughout the document it is implied that here is a law which is above the King and which even he must not break. This reaffirmation of a supreme law and its expression in a general charter is the great work of Magna Carta; and this alone justifies the respect in which men have held it."
2. John Austin's awkward attempt to invest customary law with authority through tacit endorsement by a sovereign was famously demolished by Hart. *See* H. L. A. HART, THE CONCEPT OF LAW 44–48 (2d ed., 1994); JOHN AUSTIN, THE PROVINCE OF JURISPRUDENCE DETERMINED 31–32 (Prometheus 2000) (1832). The tacit endorsement argument went back to Hobbes, who saw the threat that visible custom posed to the idea of authority. *See* THOMAS HOBBES, LEVIATHAN 315–17

(Ch. 26) (C. B. MacPherson ed., 1968) (1651): "... we are not to understand that such Customes have their force, onely from Length of Time; but that they were antiently Lawes written, or otherwise made known, for the Constitutions, and Statutes of their Soveraigns; and are now Lawes, not by vertue of the Præscription of time, but by the Constitutions of their present Soveraigns. . . . it is not that *Juris prudentia,* or wisdome of subordinate Judges; but the Reason of this our Artificiall Man the Common-wealth, and his Command, that maketh Law."

3. *See, e.g.,* KATHERINE FISCHER DREW, MAGNA CARTA 100 (2004).
4. "And it appeareth in our Books, that in many Cases, the Common Law doth controll Acts of Parliament, and somtimes shall adjudge them to be void: for when an Act of Parliament is against Common right and reason, or repugnant, or impossible to be performed, the Common Law will controll it, and adjudge such Act to be void. . . ." 8 Co. Rep. 113b, 118a; 77 Eng. Rep. 646, 652 (1610).
5. SIR OWEN DIXON, JESTING PILATE 203–13 (2d ed., 1997) (1965) (Dixon's remarks were focused on the Australian story, but in fact may be applied more generally).
6. The most prominent theory of law that is in apparent tension with the "only words" claim is Ronald Dworkin's famous account in *Law's Empire.* (RONALD DWORKIN, LAW'S EMPIRE (1986).) But the practices and principles of a legal system are indescribable except in language, and so for Dworkin too, law must ultimately be words, for otherwise his Hercules is wholly ineffectual. The effectiveness of Hercules' decisions depends on what Hercules' words convey to others in Hercules' community. If Hercules' communicative efforts fail to *mean* for us through a shared language, then his expository syntheses of our community's moral commitments are lost to us; they are not, for us, anything to do with *law.* This will be discussed further in chapter 9.
7. *Compare* ROBERT C. ELLICKSON, THE HOUSEHOLD: INFORMAL ORDER AROUND THE HEARTH 135 (2008): "When household participants are intimates enmeshed in a long-lived relationship, however, formalization usually is a mistake."
8. On the contribution that legal arrangements may make to inspiring and justifying trust, *see* KARL R. POPPER, THE OPEN SOCIETY AND ITS ENEMIES (4th ed., 1962); JOHN HART ELY, DEMOCRACY AND DISTRUST (1980); SCOTT J. SHAPIRO, LEGALITY (2011).
9. *See, e.g.,* Oliver Wendell Holmes, Jr., *The Path of the Law,* 10 HARV. L. REV. 457, 461 (1897); Felix S. Cohen, *Transcendental Nonsense and the*

Functional Approach, 35 COLUM. L. REV. 809, 839(1935); WALTER WHEELER COOK, THE LOGICAL AND LEGAL BASES OF THE CONFLICT OF LAWS 33 (1942). The extent to which various realists entertained "prediction" theories of law is valuably discussed in BRIAN LEITER, NATURALIZING JURISPRUDENCE: ESSAYS ON AMERICAN LEGAL REALISM AND NATURALISM IN LEGAL PHILOSOPHY 15–118 (2007) and Michael Steven Green, *Leiter on the Legal Realists*, 30 LAW & PHILOSOPHY 381–418 (2011).

10. H. L. A. HART, THE CONCEPT OF LAW 84 (2d ed., 1994).
11. Hart thought that the concept of obligation did not necessarily entail moral reason for action. Here is Raz's response:

> [R]ules telling other people what they ought to do can only be justified by their self-interest or by moral considerations. My self-interest cannot explain why they ought to do one thing or another except if one assumes that they have a moral duty to protect my interest, or that it is in their interest to do so. While a person's self-interest can justify saying that he ought to act in a certain way, it cannot justify a duty to act in any way except if one assumes that he has a moral reason to protect this interest of his. Therefore, it seems to follow that I cannot accept rules imposing duties on other people except, if I am sincere, for moral reasons.

Joseph Raz, *Hart on Moral Rights and Legal Duties*, 4 OXFORD J. LEGAL STUDIES 123, 130 (1984). *See also* Stephen R. Perry, *Holmes Versus Hart: The Bad Man in Legal Theory*, *in* THE PATH OF THE LAW AND ITS INFLUENCE 158, 187 (Steven J. Burton ed., 2000), arguing that Oliver Wendell Holmes's "basic claim is that the terms 'right' and 'duty' not only do not bear in law the same meaning as in moral contexts, but are, generally speaking, 'empty' terms; there are no such things as legal rights and duties."

12. JOHN FINNIS, NATURAL LAW AND NATURAL RIGHTS 282 (1980):

> legislative draftsmen do *not* ordinarily draft laws in the form imagined by Aquinas: "There is not to be killing"—nor even "Do not kill," or "Killing is forbidden," or "A person shall not [may not] kill." Rather, they will say "It shall be [or: is] an offence to . . ." or "Any person who kills . . . shall be guilty of an offence." Indeed it is quite possible to draft an entire legal system without using normative vocabulary at all.

Finnis attributes these drafting choices to the importance of distinguishing the consequences respectively signaled by separate bodies of law—crime, torts, property, administrative law, among others. In contrast to many criminal statutes, the common law of contract and tort remains heavily embroidered with "duty talk," notwithstanding the case made by the law and economics movement that most of those legal "obligations" should be understood as offering choices between courses of action (for example, between keeping a promise or breaking it and paying money) that may often be morally made in whichever ways achieve the most efficient allocation of resources. The real reason that we think the "It shall be an offense to kill" statute refers to something *truly* non-optional while the common law opinion expressing a "duty to perform" contracts refers to something actually quite optional, is that we do *not* regard law as directly determining moral obligation. We do not really believe in a general moral duty to obey lawgivers. We recognize ourselves to have an obvious moral duty not to kill that would exist regardless of what the law said. We do not recognize ourselves to have an obvious moral duty to perform all contracts, especially after we have attended some law and economics workshops at the University of Chicago. For us, the true substance of law lies not in moral instruction, one way or the other, but in prediction. That is the distinctive value *as law* that human communications have to their recipients in the human communities to which they pertain.

13. *See* Richard A. Posner, Economic Analysis of Law 50–53 (6th ed., 2003); Ronald H. Coase, *The Problem of Social Cost*, 3 J.L. & Econ. 1, 1–2 (1960); Oliver Wendell Holmes, Jr., *The Path of the Law*, 10 Harv. L. Rev. 457, 462 (1897) ("[t]he duty to keep a contract at common law means a prediction that you must pay damages if you do not keep it,—and nothing else").
14. H. L. A. Hart, The Concept of Law 187 (2d ed., 1994). *See* John Stuart Mill, Nature, the Utility of Religion, and Theism 3–65 (2d ed., 1874).
15. John Finnis argues that customs in international law "derive their authoritativeness directly from the fact that, if treated as authoritative, they enable states to solve their co-ordination problems." John Finnis, Natural Law and Natural Rights 244 (1980). But "treated as authoritative" here just means "treated as law"—"authority" is here used as a synonym for legality—and the critical mental state, transparent in the case of international law, is an expectation concerning the likely actions and expectations of others.

the internal advantages of a republican, together with the external force of a monarchical, government. I mean a confederate republic." That understanding of federalism was to persist in scholarly circles well into the following century. Describing the polity established by the U.S. Constitution as "an incomplete national government," Tocqueville contrasted it with federal government on the basis that the American union government regulated and taxed the inhabitants directly, rather than only addressing its commands to the states. "Here the term Federal Government is clearly no longer applicable . . . : a form of government has been found out which is neither exactly national nor federal; but no further progress has been made, and the new word which will one day designate this novel invention does not yet exist." 1 ALEXIS DE TOCQUEVILLE, DEMOCRACY IN AMERICA 186 (Henry Reeve trans., 3rd ed., 1838).

26. CHARLES-LOUIS DE SECONDAT, BARON DE MONTESQUIEU, THE SPIRIT OF THE LAWS Bk. XI, Ch. 4, 172–73 and Ch. 6, 181–84 (Thomas Nugent trans., rev'd ed., 1873) (1748).

27. To the extent that power sharing prevents individual lawgivers from conclusively determining the reach of their own powers, we see an unambiguously good consequence coming from applying a "many minds" principle. *Compare* Adrian Vermeule, *Many-Minds Arguments in Legal Theory*, 1 J. LEGAL ANALYSIS 1 (2009) (elaborating a range of reasons why more is not always better).

28. Hamilton summarized their case in THE FEDERALIST, No. 81:

> The authority of the proposed Supreme Court of the United States, which is to be a separate and independent body, will be superior to that of the legislature. The power of construing the laws according to the *spirit* of the Constitution, will enable that court to mould them into whatever shape it may think proper; especially as its decisions will not be in any manner subject to the revision or correction of the legislative body. This is as unprecedented as it is dangerous. In Britain, the judicial power, in the last resort, resides in the House of Lords, which is a branch of the legislature; and this part of the British government has been imitated in the State constitutions in general. The Parliament of Great Britain, and the legislatures of the several States, can at any time rectify, by law, the exceptionable decisions of their respective courts. But the errors and usurpations of the Supreme Court of the United States will be uncontrollable and remediless.

See also Brutus, Nos. 12 and 15, in 2 HERBERT J. STORING, THE COMPLETE ANTIFEDERALIST 423–26, 437–42 (1981).

29. "[T]he important constitutional check which the power of instituting impeachments in one part of the legislative body, and of determining upon them in the other, would give to that body upon the members of the judicial department" was "a complete security," said Hamilton, against "judiciary encroachments on the legislative authority." THE FEDERALIST, No. 81.
30. THE FEDERALIST, No. 78, n. 1. CHARLES-LOUIS DE SECONDAT, BARON DE MONTESQUIEU, THE SPIRIT OF THE LAWS Bk. XI, Ch. 6, 178 (Thomas Nugent trans., rev'd ed., 1873) (1748): "Of the three powers above-mentioned, the judiciary is in some measure next to nothing: there remain, therefore, only two. . . ."
31. *See* Laurence Claus, *Montesquieu's Mistakes and the True Meaning of Separation*, 25 OXFORD J. LEGAL STUDIES 419, 422–31 (2005).
32. *See, e.g.,* Garcia v. SAMTA, 469 US 528, 545–47 (1985) (Blackmun, J., majority Opinion of the Court):

> Neither the governmental/proprietary distinction nor any other that purports to separate out important governmental functions can be faithful to the role of federalism in a democratic society. The essence of our federal system is that within the realm of authority left to them under the Constitution, the States must be equally free to engage in any activity that their citizens choose for the common weal, no matter how unorthodox or unnecessary anyone else—including the judiciary—deems state involvement to be. Any rule of state immunity that looks to the "traditional," "integral," or "necessary" nature of governmental functions inevitably invites an unelected federal judiciary to make decisions about which state policies it favors and which ones it dislikes. . . . [T]he States cannot serve as laboratories for social and economic experiment . . . if they must pay an added price when they meet the changing needs of their citizenry by taking up functions that an earlier day and a different society left in private hands. . . . We therefore now reject, as unsound in principle and unworkable in practice, a rule of state immunity from federal regulation that turns on a judicial appraisal of whether a particular governmental function is "integral" or "traditional."

33. *See* THOMAS HOBBES, LEVIATHAN (C. B. MacPherson ed., 1968) (1651).

34. LUDWIG WITTGENSTEIN, PHILOSOPHICAL INVESTIGATIONS § 69 (4th ed., P. M. S. Hacker & Joachim Schulte eds., G. E. M. Anscombe, P. M. S. Hacker, & Joachim Schulte trans., 2009) (1953).
35. RONALD DWORKIN, LAW'S EMPIRE 190 (1986).
36. LON L. FULLER, THE MORALITY OF LAW 53 (1964).
37. "It is the judges (as we have seen) that make the common law. Do you know how they make it? Just as a man makes laws for his dog. When your dog does anything you want to break him of, you wait till he does it, and then beat him for it. This is the way you make laws for a dog: and this is the way the judges make law for you and me. They won't tell a man beforehand what it is he *should not do*—they won't so much as allow of his being told: they lie by till he has done something which they say he should not *have done*, and then they hang him for it. What way, then, has any man of coming at this dog-law? Only by watching their proceedings: by observing in what *cases* they have hanged a man. . . ." 5 JEREMY BENTHAM, THE WORKS OF JEREMY BENTHAM 235 (John Bowring ed., 1843).
38. Donoghue v. Stevenson, [1932] A.C. 562 (House of Lords).
39. LON L. FULLER, THE MORALITY OF LAW 53 (1964).
40. U.S. CONST. Art. I § 9 cl. 3 and § 10 cl. 1.
41. *See* Calder v. Bull, 3 U.S. (3 Dall.) 386 (1798). In Smith v. Doe, 538 U.S. 84 (2003), the Supreme Court by majority upheld applying a sex offender registration law to those who had offended before the law was enacted.
42. LON L. FULLER, THE MORALITY OF LAW 54 (1964).
43. *See* H. L. A. HART, THE CONCEPT OF LAW 203 (2d ed., 1994); H. L. A. HART, ESSAYS ON BENTHAM 265–68 (1982).
44. H. L. A. HART, THE CONCEPT OF LAW 98 (2d ed., 1994).
45. JOHN FINNIS, NATURAL LAW AND NATURAL RIGHTS 12–15 (1980).
46. ALL THE PRESIDENT'S MEN (Motion Picture, Warner Bros., 1976), based on CARL BERNSTEIN & BOB WOODWARD, ALL THE PRESIDENT'S MEN (1974). Todd S. Purdum, *F.B.I. Official Revealed He Was Watergate Source in Interview*, N.Y. TIMES, May 31, 2005.

CHAPTER 8

1. GAME OF THRONES (Television Series, HBO, 2011), based on GEORGE R. R. MARTIN, A GAME OF THRONES (1996).
2. Kareem Fahim & Mark Mazzetti, *Rebels' Assault on Tripoli Began with Careful Work Inside Capital*, N.Y. TIMES, Aug. 23, 2011, at A11, quoting Yusuf Muhammed.

3. *See* JEAN-JACQUES ROUSSEAU, THE SOCIAL CONTRACT AND DISCOURSES, Bk. I, Ch. 6 (G. D. H. Cole trans., 1985) (1762): "*Each of us puts his person and all his power in common under the supreme direction of the general will, and, in our corporate capacity, we receive each member as an indivisible part of the whole.* . . . This public person, so formed by the union of all other persons, formerly took the name of *city*, and now takes that of *Republic* or *body politic*; it is called by its members *State* when passive, *Sovereign* when active, and *Power* when compared with others like itself. Those who are associated in it take collectively the name of *people*, and severally are called *citizens*, as sharing in the sovereign power, and *subjects*, as being under the laws of the State."
4. ÉTIENNE DE LA BOÉTIE, DISCOURSE ON VOLUNTARY SERVITUDE (Harry Kurtz trans., 1975) (written approximately 1552; posthumously first published 1576).
5. "The people were in fact, the fountain of all power, and by resorting to them, all difficulties were got over. They could alter constitutions as they pleased. It was a principle in the Bills of rights, that first principles might be resorted to." 2 RECORDS OF THE FEDERAL CONVENTION 476 (Max Farrand ed., 2d ed., 1937). (Madison's notes recording proceedings of the Convention on August 31, 1787.)
6. *See, e.g.*, Steven Erlanger, *Yeltsin Is Seeking New Constitution to Scrap Congress*, N.Y. TIMES, Apr. 30, 1993: "Making his first political move since his triumph in Sunday's referendum, President Boris N. Yeltsin of Russia summoned regional leaders to Moscow today to receive a new draft constitution that would strengthen the presidency and eliminate the Congress of People's Deputies, which had led the attacks on him."
7. 1 KARL R. POPPER, THE OPEN SOCIETY AND ITS ENEMIES 121(4th ed., 1962). As we discussed further in chapter 7, the other part of the answer is *power sharing*.
8. JOHN HART ELY, DEMOCRACY AND DISTRUST 88 (1980).
9. *See* Laurence Claus, *Constitutional Guarantees of the Judiciary: Jurisdiction, Tenure, and Beyond*, 54 AM. J. COMP. L. 459, 482–83 (2006); Barry Friedman & Erin F. Delaney, *Becoming Supreme: The Federal Foundation of Judicial Supremacy*, 111 COLUM. L. REV.1137 (2011).
10. *See* Steven G. Calabresi & Gary Lawson, *The Unitary Executive, Jurisdiction Stripping, and the Hamdan Opinions: A Textualist Response to Justice Scalia*, 107 Colum. L. Rev. 1002 (2007); Laurence Claus, *Constitutional Guarantees of the Judiciary: Jurisdiction, Tenure, and*

Beyond, 54 AM. J. COMP. L. 459 (2006); Laurence Claus, *The One Court that Congress Cannot Take Away: Singularity, Supremacy, and Article III*, 96 GEO. L.J. 59 (2007).

11. Laurence Claus, *The One Court that Congress Cannot Take Away: Singularity, Supremacy, and Article III*, 96 GEO. L.J. 59, 62 (2007).
12. United States v. Carolene Prod., 304 U.S. 144, 152 n.4 (1938).
13. *See* Detainee Treatment Act of 2005 § 1005 (e) and (h); Hamdan v. Rumsfeld, 548 U.S. 557 (2006); Military Commissions Act of 2006 § 7; Boumediene v. Bush, 553 U.S. 723 (2008).
14. For other recent initiatives that did not become law, *see* Pledge Protection Bill of 2004 § 2 (passed by the House of Representatives as H.R. 2028 on September 23, 2004) and Pledge Protection Bill of 2005 § 2 (introduced to the House of Representatives and Senate, respectively, as H.R. 2389 and S.1046 on May 17, 2005) (purporting to eliminate the Supreme Court's jurisdiction to determine the constitutionality of the Pledge of Allegiance as defined in 4 U.S.C. § 4 or of that pledge's recitation). *See also* Constitution Restoration Bill of 2005 § 101 (introduced to the House of Representatives and Senate, respectively, as H.R. 1070 and S. 520 on March 3, 2005) (purporting to eliminate the Supreme Court's jurisdiction to determine the constitutionality of government actors' "acknowledgment of God as the sovereign source of law, liberty, or government"); Marriage Protection Bill of 2004 § 2 (passed by the House of Representatives as H.R. 3313 on July 22, 2004) and Marriage Protection Bill of 2005 § 2 (introduced to the House of Representatives as H.R. 1100 on March 3, 2005) (purporting to eliminate the Supreme Court's jurisdiction to determine the constitutionality of the Defense of Marriage Act (28 U.S.C. § 1738C)).
15. When we see how pervasive power sharing among institutions of government contributes to courts' success at keeping everyone else in line, we see that Friedrich Hayek was wrong to treat the separation that Montesquieu noticed and the accomplishments of the common law courts as alternative explanations of English "political liberty." *See* 1 FRIEDRICH A. HAYEK, LAW, LEGISLATION AND LIBERTY 85 (1973): "The freedom of the British which in the eighteenth century the rest of Europe came so much to admire was thus not, as the British themselves were among the first to believe and as Montesquieu later taught the world, originally a product of the separation of powers between legislature and executive, but rather a result of the fact that the law that governed the decisions of the courts was the common law, a law

existing independently of anyone's will and at the same time binding upon and developed by the independent courts. . . ." There was a *reason* that the eighteenth century was the time when people began to notice a distinctive quality to English life that Montesquieu called "political liberty." Courts and common law had long existed, but it was the settlement reached through the Glorious Revolution of 1688–89 that secured and increased power sharing within the system. The Act of Settlement's provision for judicial job security was just part of that picture. (*See* Act of Settlement of 1701, 13 W. III c. 2 § 3 cl. 11: "That after the said limitation shall take effect as aforesaid, judges commissions be made quamdiu se bene gesserint [tr.: as long as they shall conduct themselves properly], and their salaries ascertained and established; but upon the address of both Houses of Parliament it may be lawful to remove them.")

16. *See* 1 Derek Parfit, On What Matters (2011), particularly chs. 8, 15, and 17; Thomas M. Scanlon, Jr., What We Owe to Each Other (1998); John Rawls, A Theory of Justice (1971).
17. John Austin's awkward attempt to invest customary law with authority through tacit endorsement by a sovereign was famously demolished by Hart. *See* H. L. A. Hart, The Concept of Law 44–48 (2d ed., 1994); John Austin, The Province of Jurisprudence Determined 31–32 (Prometheus 2000) (1832). The tacit endorsement argument went back to Hobbes, who saw the threat that visible custom posed to the idea of authority. *See* Thomas Hobbes, Leviathan 315–17 (Ch. 26) (C. B. MacPherson ed., 1968) (1651).
18. British North America Act of 1867 (United Kingdom, 30 & 31 Victoria, Ch. 3). (Renamed the Constitution Act of 1867 in the Schedule to the Constitution Act of 1982, which was enacted by the British Parliament in the Canada Act of 1982 (United Kingdom, 1982, Ch. 11).)
19. *See* Peter Stein, Roman Law in European History (1999).
20. *See* Peter W. Hogg, Constitutional Law of Canada 60 (4th ed., 2001). "If the United Kingdom Parliament were to do the unthinkable after 1982 and pass a law purporting to extend to Canada, and if such a law were challenged in the courts in Canada (as it obviously would be), the courts in Canada would ask whether such a law was authorized by the rules of the Canadian legal system. The only conceivable answer to that question would be no: Canada's legal system does not recognize the right of the United Kingdom (or Portugal or any other foreign country) to enact laws binding in Canada."

21. *See* Canada Act of 1982 (United Kingdom, 1982, Ch. 11):

    1 Constitution Act, 1982 enacted
    The Constitution Act, 1982 set out in Schedule B to this Act is hereby enacted for and shall have the force of law in Canada and shall come into force as provided in that Act.
    2 Termination of power to legislate for Canada
    No Act of the Parliament of the United Kingdom passed after the Constitution Act, 1982 comes into force shall extend to Canada as part of its law.

22. "These then are the three traits of Parliamentary sovereignty as it exists in England: first, the power of the legislature to alter any law, fundamental or otherwise, as freely and in the same manner as other laws; secondly, the absence of any legal distinction between constitutional and other laws; thirdly, the non-existence of any judicial or other authority having the right to nullify an Act of Parliament, or to treat it as void or unconstitutional." ALBERT VENN DICEY, INTRODUCTION TO THE STUDY OF THE LAW OF THE CONSTITUTION 91 (10th ed., 1965) (1885).
23. "The people were in fact, the fountain of all power, and by resorting to them, all difficulties were got over. They could alter constitutions as they pleased. It was a principle in the Bills of rights, that first principles might be resorted to." 2 RECORDS OF THE FEDERAL CONVENTION 476 (Max Farrand ed., 2d ed., 1937). (Madison's notes recording proceedings of the Convention on August 31, 1787.) *Compare* Luther Martin, "Genuine Information," delivered to the Maryland legislature, November 29, 1787, in 3 Farrand, *id.*, at 189: "The same reasons which you *now* urge for destroying our *present* federal government, may be urged for *abolishing the system*, which you now propose to adopt; and as the *method prescribed* by the *articles* of confederation is *now totally disregarded* by you, as *little regard* may be shown by you to the *rules prescribed* for the amendment of the *new system*." *See* ARTICLES OF CONFEDERATION OF 1781, Art. XIII.
24. U.S. CONST. Art. III § 3 cl. 1: "Treason against the United States, shall consist only in levying War against them, or in adhering to their Enemies, giving them Aid and Comfort."
25. 1 W. & M., sess. 2, c. 2 (Eng); *see* LOIS G. SCHWOERER, THE DECLARATION OF RIGHTS, 1689, *passim* (1981).
26. *See* 2 JOHN LOCKE, TWO TREATISES OF GOVERNMENT §§ 95–99, 119, 222 (Peter Laslett ed., 1988) (1690); TIM HARRIS, REVOLUTION: THE GREAT CRISIS OF THE BRITISH MONARCHY 1685–1720,

at 271–96, 333–34, 433–47, 478 (2006); Wout Troost, William III, The Stadholder-King 195–205, 207–10 (J. C. Grayson trans., 2005); Roger Woolhouse, Locke: A Biography 275, 283 (2007); Maurice Cranston, John Locke: A Biography 207–08 (1957); Peter Laslett, *Introduction*, John Locke, Two Treatises of Government 3, 45–66 (Peter Laslett ed., 1988) (1690); W. A. Speck, Reluctant Revolutionaries: Englishmen and the Revolution of 1688, at 238–39 (1988). Parliament's approval of the Declaration of Rights did not suffice to show majority support even on a representative basis, because the proportion of the population who were eligible to vote in parliamentary elections was small and malapportioned. *See* Edmund S. Morgan, Inventing the People: The Rise of Popular Sovereignty in England and America 42 (1988) (estimating the reach of the franchise in counties at approximately one-fifth of the adult male population); J. H. Plumb, *The Elections to the Convention Parliament of 1689*, 5 Cambridge Hist. J. 235 (1937) (elaborating electoral circumstances that rendered even the 40-shilling freehold property qualification for male voting in counties an overstatement of popular participation).

27. Roger Woolhouse, Locke: A Biography 181, 207–10, 214 (2007).
28. 2 John Locke, Two Treatises of Government § 93 (Peter Laslett ed., 1988) (1690).
29. 12 T. B. Howell, State Trials 508–11 (1816) (asterisked footnote).
30. *See, e.g.*, 1 The Diary of Samuel Pepys: Introduction and 1660, 265 (Robert Latham & William Matthews eds., 1970) (entry for October 13, 1660, describing Pepys' witnessing of a hanging, drawing, and quartering for regicide). *Id.*, at 269–70 (entries for October 20 and 21, describing aftermath of quarterings).
31. Roger Woolhouse, Locke: A Biography 181, 283–84 (2007).
32. 2 Records of the Federal Convention 93, 476, 665 (Max Farrand ed., 2d ed., 1937) (Madison's notes); *compare* Articles of Confederation of 1781, Art. XIII.
33. *Compare* John Milton, *The Tenure of Kings and Magistrates*, *in* John Milton, Political Writings 11 (Martin Dzelzainis ed., Claire Gruzelier trans., 1991) (1650): "[T]he Titles of Sov'ran Lord, natural Lord, and the like, are either arrogancies, or flatteries, not admitted by Emperours and Kings of best note, and dislikt by the Church both of Jews, *Isai.* 26.13. and ancient Christians, as appears by *Tertullian.* . . ."
34. 2 John Locke, Two Treatises of Government §§ 95, 100–04 (Peter Laslett ed., 1988) (1690).

35. *See* Tim Harris, Revolution: The Great Crisis of the British Monarchy 1685–1720, at 239–348 (2006); Wout Troost, William III, The Stadholder-King 173–94 (Ch. 8: "James II, William III and Louis XIV (1685–88)") (J. C. Grayson trans., 2005).
36. *See* Douglass C. North, John Joseph Wallis, & Barry R. Weingast, Violence and Social Orders: A Conceptual Framework for Interpreting Recorded Human History (2009).
37. *Compare* John Rawls, A Theory of Justice 136–42 (1971) (hypothesizing an "original position" for the purpose of conceiving principles of justice in human community).
38. *See* Jane Goodall, The Chimpanzees of Gombe: Patterns of Behavior (1986). *See* Ch. 12 ("Aggression"), 313–56 (especially 318–19, "Coalitions and Snowballing"), and Ch. 15 ("Dominance"), 409–42 (especially 418–24, "Coalitions," 424–29, "Motivation and Alpha Status," and 429–36, "Loss of Rank").
39. *See* Albert Venn Dicey, Introduction to the Study of the Law of the Constitution 39–40 (10th ed., 1965) (1885).
40. *See*, most famously, the Representation of the People Act of 1832 (2 & 3 Will. IV, Ch. 45) (known as the Reform Act of 1832), and the Parliament Act of 1911 (1 & 2 Geo. V, Ch. 13).
41. Regina (Jackson and others) v. Attorney General, [2006] 1 A.C. 262, 302–03 ¶ 102 (House of Lords, decided October 13, 2005). *See also* the speech of Lord Hope of Craighead, *id.*, at 304 ¶ 107:

> Owen Dixon, "The Law and Constitution" (1935) 51 LQR 590, 596 was making the same point when he said that it is of the essence of supremacy of the law that the courts shall disregard as unauthorised and void the acts of any organ of government, whether legislative or administrative, which exceed the limits of the power that organ derives from the law. In its modern form, now reinforced by the European Convention on Human Rights and the enactment by Parliament of the Human Rights Act 1998, this principle protects the individual from arbitrary government. The rule of law enforced by the courts is the ultimate controlling factor on which our constitution is based. The fact that your Lordships have been willing to hear this appeal and to give judgment upon it is another indication that the courts have a part to play in defining the limits of Parliament's legislative sovereignty.

42. Pierre Legrand observes:

> [L]aw's being is such that any attempt to transport it "above" or "beyond" singularity rapidly loses itself in artificial if not arbitrary acts of separation. Whether one is talking about a municipal ordinance, a European directive, or an international convention, whether one is addressing security issuance, syndicated loans, or Incoterms, each manifestation of law is an event, that is, it occurs or deploys itself as "something" that is never the repetition of anything else and that will never be repeated either—it occurs as something operating within a specific historical situation and within a historical situation which, because time is what it is, is inevitably specific. (There is, I hasten to add, nothing mystical about this account.) Indeed, this singularity is such that it necessarily exceeds the limits of any rational or analytical accounting if only because it exceeds conscious experience. Incoterms—yes, Incoterms!—as they are implemented by merchants, lawyers, arbitrators, and judges, generate, on each and every occasion, an original configuration. The originality may be slight, but it is present even in what seems most familiar. Every purported replication of the "legal" in fact produces singularity—that is, generates "something" that differs from what has come before and from what will come after. It can be a matter of cognitive inclinations, predispositions, or associations. It can be a matter of legal reasoning. Whatever "there is," there is not unalloyed sameness. . . . The ever-present "fact" of the facticity of law is, if you will, the only repetition—put another way, *global* means *several local places at once.*
>
> Pierre Legrand, *On the Singularity of Law*, 47 HARV. INT'L. L. J. 517, 527 (2006).

43. Contrast Giorgio Agamben's claim that "[w]hatever singularity, which wants to appropriate belonging itself, its own being-in-language, and thus rejects all identity and every condition of belonging, is the principal enemy of the State. Wherever these singularities peacefully demonstrate their being in common there will be a Tiananmen, and sooner or later the tanks will appear." GIORGIO AGAMBEN, THE COMING COMMUNITY 87 (Michael Hardt trans., 1993) (1990). We might agree with Agamben about how "the State" is likely to react to experiencing the presence of even unspecific protests, should those protests persist for any time. But we might suspect that those in power who move against the protestors worry less about being displaced by no law than they worry about being

displaced by law of someone else's making. However enticing a sense of living singularly in parallel may be, in even the simplest camp-out we swiftly generate trash that needs taking away. We humans cannot live together long without the behavior-shaping expressions of identity we call "what we do," and ultimately, what is law for us.

44. Roscoe Pound, *Law in Books and Law in Action*, 44 AMER. L. REV. 12 (1910).

CHAPTER 9

1. *Compare* SCOTT J. SHAPIRO, LEGALITY 188 (2011): "I hope it is clear at this point how the Planning Theory will rebut Hume's Challenge. For on the perspectival interpretation of the word "legal," statements of legal authority, legal rights, and legal obligations are *descriptive*, not normative. They describe the normative point of view of the law. . . . The Planning Theory, in other words, conforms to Hume's Law because legal reasoning does not involve the derivation of an ought from an is, but rather an is from an is." *Id.*, at 192: "And once a legal reasoner recognizes the existence and content of the master plan, he can begin to make descriptive assessments about the law's perspective on moral rights, obligations, and validity, even if he judges the law's perspective mistaken from the moral point of view."
2. MONTY PYTHON'S LIFE OF BRIAN (Motion Picture, HandMade Films, 1979).
3. Discovering the intention of lawgivers is not our real reason for paying attention to law, whereas discovering intention *is* the real reason that we listen to words in conversations of the kind memorably described by Stanley Fish in STANLEY FISH, IS THERE A TEXT IN THIS CLASS? THE AUTHORITY OF INTERPRETIVE COMMUNITIES (1980): "She tells him that he has mistaken her meaning, but this is not to say that he has made a mistake in combining her words and syntax into a meaningful unit; it is rather that the meaningful unit he immediately discerns is a function of a mistaken identification (made before she speaks) of her intention." *Id.*, at 311.
4. LEWIS CARROLL, ALICE'S ADVENTURES IN WONDERLAND (1865).
5. HANS CHRISTIAN ANDERSEN, ANDERSEN'S FAIRY TALES 263–68 (E. V. Lucas & H. B. Paull trans., 1945) (1837).
6. "Interpreting is the act of determining, or trying to determine, what is meant *by* an utterance or a gesture, that is, of what it is intended to be the expression." STANLEY FISH, THERE'S NO SUCH THING AS FREE

SPEECH: AND IT'S A GOOD THING TOO, 185 (1994). *See also* Stanley Fish, *The Intentionalist Thesis Once More, in* THE CHALLENGE OF ORIGINALISM 99 (Grant Huscroft & Bradley W. Miller eds., 2011).

7. The contemporary literature has taken to using the word *construction* for the extent to which judicial adding to the words that are law slides beyond supplying semantic synonyms and resolves vagueness in application by introducing new content. Using "construction" in this way plays on an ambiguity in *that* word, putting to work both prongs of *construal* and *creation*. The first place to go when approaching this literature is the work of Lawrence Solum. *See* Lawrence B. Solum, Semantic Originalism (November 22, 2008) (available at http://ssrn.com/abstract=1120244); Lawrence B. Solum, *The Interpretation-Construction Distinction*, 27 CONST. COMMENT. 95 (2010); Lawrence B. Solum, *What Is Originalism? The Evolution of Contemporary Originalist Theory, in* THE CHALLENGE OF ORIGINALISM 12 (Grant Huscroft & Bradley W. Miller eds., 2011). For a range of "originalist" positions adopted by contemporary scholars, *see* JACK M. BALKIN, LIVING ORIGINALISM (2011), Jack M. Balkin, *Abortion and Original Meaning*, 24 CONST. COMMENT. 291 (2007), and Jack M. Balkin, *Original Meaning and Constitutional Redemption*, 24 CONST. COMMENT. 427 (2007); RANDY E. BARNETT, RESTORING THE LOST CONSTITUTION: THE PRESUMPTION OF LIBERTY (2004) and Randy E. Barnett, *An Originalism for Nonoriginalists*, 45 LOY. L. REV. 611 (1999); Jeffrey Goldsworthy, *Originalism in Constitutional Interpretation*, 25 FED. L. REV. 1 (1997); John O. McGinnis & Michael B. Rappaport, *Original Interpretive Principles as the Core of Originalism*, 24 CONST. COMMENT. 371 (2007) and John O. McGinnis & Michael B. Rappaport, *Original Methods Originalism: A New Theory of Interpretation and the Case Against Construction*, 103 NW. U. L. REV. 751 (2009); KEITH E. WHITTINGTON, CONSTITUTIONAL INTERPRETATION (1999) and KEITH E. WHITTINGTON, CONSTITUTIONAL CONSTRUCTION (1999).
8. LUDWIG WITTGENSTEIN, PHILOSOPHICAL INVESTIGATIONS Boxed Remark after § 35 (4th ed., P. M. S. Hacker & Joachim Schulte eds., G. E. M. Anscombe, P. M. S. Hacker, & Joachim Schulte trans., 2009) (1953): "Can I say 'bububu' and mean 'If it doesn't rain, I shall go for a walk?'—It is only in a language that I can mean something by something."
9. For a very helpful account of the debate's evolution, *see* Lawrence B. Solum, Semantic Originalism 13–25 (November 22, 2008) (available at http://ssrn.com/abstract=1120244).

10. *See, e.g.*, Henry P. Monaghan, *Our Perfect Constitution*, 56 N.Y.U. L. Rev. 353, 375 n. 130 (1981): "Although the intention of the ratifiers, not the Framers, is in principle decisive, the difficulties of ascertaining the intent of the ratifiers leaves little choice but to accept the intent of the Framers as a fair reflection of it."
11. For a recent expression of this position, *see* Richard S. Kay, *Original Intention and Public Meaning in Constitutional Interpretation*, 103 Nw. U. L. Rev. 703 (2009).
12. *See* Gary Lawson, *Proving the Law*, 86 Nw. U. L. Rev. 859, 875 (1992).
13. *See* Pepper v. Hart [1992] A.C. 593 (H.L.) (U.K.).
14. Antonin Scalia, A Matter of Interpretation: Federal Courts and the Law (1997).
15. *See* Frank H. Easterbrook, *Statutes' Domains*, 50 U. Chi. L. Rev. 533, 544, 545, 547 (1983):

> My suggestion is that unless the statute plainly hands courts the power to create and revise a form of common law, the domain of the statute should be restricted to cases anticipated by its framers and expressly resolved in the legislative process....
>
> The meta-rule I have suggested above is a "clear statement" approach revised to turn on the method the legislature has adopted. If it enacts some sort of code of rules, the code will be taken as complete (until amended); gaps will go unfilled. If instead it charges the court with a common law function, the court will resolve new problems as they arise, but using today's wisdom rather than conjuring up the solutions of a legislature long prorogued....
>
> Because legislatures comprise many members, they do not have "intents" or "designs," hidden yet discoverable. Each member may or may not have a design. The body as a whole, however, has only outcomes.

16. *See* U.S. Const. Art. III § 3 cl. 2.
17. *See* U.S. Const. Amend. II.
18. *See*, relatedly, Vasan Kesavan & Michael Stokes Paulsen, *The Interpretive Force of the Constitution's Secret Drafting History*, 91 Geo. L.J. 1113, 1118 (2003). Like information about actual lawgivers' understandings, information about drafters' understandings has evidential value in the search for public meaning.
19. *See* Bradley W. Miller, *Origin Myth: The Persons Case, the Living Tree, and the New Originalism*, *in* The Challenge of Originalism 120 (Grant

Huscroft & Bradley W. Miller eds., 2011); Bradley W. Miller, *Beguiled by Metaphors: The "Living Tree" and Originalist Constitutional Interpretation in Canada*, 22 CAN. J. L. & JUR. 331 (2009).

20. *See*, in the decision of the Constitutional Court of South Africa abolishing the death penalty, S.v. Makwanyane [1995] ZACC 3, ¶ 156, per Ackermann, J.:

> We have moved from a past characterised by much which was arbitrary and unequal in the operation of the law to a present and a future in a constitutional state where state action must be such that it is capable of being analysed and justified rationally. The idea of the constitutional state presupposes a system whose operation can be rationally tested against or in terms of the law. Arbitrariness, by its very nature, is dissonant with these core concepts of our new constitutional order. Neither arbitrary action nor laws or rules which are inherently arbitrary or must lead to arbitrary application can, in any real sense, be tested against the precepts or principles of the Constitution.

21. *See, e.g.*, Ian Binnie, *Constitutional Interpretation and Original Intent, in* CONSTITUTIONALISM IN THE CHARTER ERA 345 (Grant Huscroft & Ian Brodie eds., 2004), discussed in Bradley W. Miller, *Origin Myth: The Persons Case, the Living Tree, and the New Originalism, in* THE CHALLENGE OF ORIGINALISM 120 (Grant Huscroft & Bradley W. Miller eds., 2011).
22. 115 N.Y. 506 (1889).
23. *See* H. L. A. Hart, *Positivism and the Separation of Law and Morals*, 71 HARV. L. REV. 593, 606–15 (1958), discussed in Frederick Schauer, *A Critical Guide to Vehicles in the Park*, 83 N.Y.U. L. REV. 1109 (2008).
24. LUDWIG WITTGENSTEIN, PHILOSOPHICAL INVESTIGATIONS § 201 (4th ed., P. M. S. Hacker & Joachim Schulte eds., G. E. M. Anscombe, P. M. S. Hacker, & Joachim Schulte trans., 2009) (1953).
25. *See, e.g.*, Frederick Schauer, *Easy Cases*, 58 SO. CAL. L. REV. 399 (1985).
26. U.S. CONST. Amend. XIV § 1: "All persons born or naturalized in the United States, and subject to the jurisdiction thereof, are citizens of the United States and of the State wherein they reside. No State shall make or enforce any law which shall abridge the privileges or immunities of citizens of the United States; nor shall any State deprive any person of life, liberty, or property, without due process of law; nor deny to any person within its jurisdiction the equal protection of the laws."

27. Hoh Ah Kow v. Nunan, 12 F. Cas. 252, 255, 257 (C.C.Cal. 1879).

28. U.S. CONST. Amend. II: "A well regulated Militia, being necessary to the security of a free State, the right of the people to keep and bear Arms, shall not be infringed."

29. *Compare* JACK M. BALKIN, LIVING ORIGINALISM (2011).

30. *See* John O. McGinnis & Michael B. Rappaport, *The Abstract Meaning Fallacy*, U. ILLINOIS L. REV. (forthcoming, 2012).

31. *See*, however, THOMAS WOODCOCK & JOHN MARTIN ROBINSON, THE OXFORD GUIDE TO HERALDRY 1–3 (1988), suggesting that "the identification with any certainty of arms on a shield on a battlefield would have been so difficult that it must be assumed that such was not the practical purpose of arms." *Id.*, at 3.

32. *See* Yick Wo v. Hopkins, 118 U.S. 356, 369 (1886) (unanimous Opinion of the Court, per Miller, J.): ". . . the equal protection of the laws is a pledge of the protection of equal laws." *Compare* Christopher R. Green, *The Original Sense of the (Equal) Protection Clause: Pre-Enactment History*, 19 GEO MASON U.C.R.L.J. 1 (2008); Christopher R. Green, *The Original Sense of the (Equal) Protection Clause: Subsequent Interpretation and Application*, 19 GEO. MASON U.C.R.L.J. 197 (2009).

33. *See* Peter Westen, *The Empty Idea of Equality*, 95 HARV. L. REV. 537 (1982).

34. *See* LAWRENCE KOHLBERG, THE PHILOSOPHY OF MORAL DEVELOPMENT: MORAL STAGES AND THE IDEA OF JUSTICE 17–19 (1981). *See also* LAWRENCE KOHLBERG, THE PSYCHOLOGY OF MORAL DEVELOPMENT: THE NATURE AND VALIDITY OF MORAL STAGES (1984); LAWRENCE KOHLBERG, CHARLES LEVINE, & ALEXANDRA HEWER, MORAL STAGES: A CURRENT FORMULATION AND A RESPONSE TO CRITICS (1983).

35. DECLARATION OF INDEPENDENCE (GENERAL CONGRESS, UNITED STATES OF AMERICA, July 4, 1776).

36. *See* OFFICIAL RECORD OF THE DEBATES OF THE AUSTRALASIAN FEDERAL CONVENTION, 3rd Session, 686 (Melbourne, 1898).

37. *See* U.S.S.R. CONST. Ch. X, especially Arts. 125, 127, 128 (1936).

38. *See* Laurence Claus, *Montesquieu's Mistakes and the True Meaning of Separation*, 25 OXFORD J. LEGAL STUDIES 419, 445–51 (2005).

39. *Compare* the cases made for a wider expository enterprise in MARK TUSHNET, TAKING THE CONSTITUTION AWAY FROM THE COURTS (1999) and LARRY D. KRAMER, THE PEOPLE THEMSELVES: POPULAR CONSTITUTIONALISM AND JUDICIAL REVIEW (2004).

40. U.S. Const. Amend. V: "No person shall be held to answer for a capital, or otherwise infamous crime, unless on a presentment or indictment of a Grand Jury, except in cases arising in the land or naval forces, or in the Militia, when in actual service in time of War or public danger; nor shall any person be subject for the same offense to be twice put in jeopardy of life or limb; nor shall be compelled in any criminal case to be a witness against himself, nor be deprived of life, liberty, or property, without due process of law; nor shall private property be taken for public use, without just compensation." There is current debate about whether the Fourteenth Amendment's Due Process Clause has a significantly different original public meaning. *See* Ryan C. Williams, *The One and Only Substantive Due Process Clause*, 120 Yale L.J. 408 (2010); Nathan S. Chapman & Michael W. McConnell, *Due Process as Separation of Powers*, 121 Yale L. J. 1672 (2012).
41. Magna Carta Ch. 39 (1215): "No freeman shall be taken or imprisoned or disseised or exiled or in any way destroyed, nor will we go upon him nor send upon him, except by the lawful judgment of his peers or by the law of the land."
42. Virginia Bill of Rights, June 12, 1776, § 8: "That in all capital or criminal prosecutions a man hath a right to demand the cause and nature of his accusation, to be confronted with the accusers and witnesses, to call for evidence in his favor, and to a speedy trial by an impartial jury of twelve men of his vicinage, without whose unanimous consent he cannot be found guilty; nor can he be compelled to give evidence against himself; that no man be deprived of his liberty, except by the law of the land or the judgment of his peers."
43. See U.S. Const. Amends. VI & VII.
44. *See* Planned Parenthood of Southeastern Pennsylvania v. Casey, 505 U.S. 833, 846–47 (1992) (Opinion of the Court, per O'Connor, Kennedy, and Souter, JJ.):

> Although a literal reading of the Clause might suggest that it governs only the procedures by which a State may deprive persons of liberty, for at least 105 years, since *Mugler v. Kansas*, 123 U.S. 623, 660–661, 8 S.Ct. 273, 291, 31 L.Ed. 205 (1887), the Clause has been understood to contain a substantive component as well, one "barring certain government actions regardless of the fairness of the procedures used to implement them." *Daniels v. Williams*, 474 U.S. 327, 331, 106 S.Ct. 662, 665, 88 L.Ed.2d 662 (1986). As Justice Brandeis

> (joined by Justice Holmes) observed, "[d]espite arguments to the contrary which had seemed to me persuasive, it is settled that the due process clause of the Fourteenth Amendment applies to matters of substantive law as well as to matters of procedure. Thus all fundamental rights comprised within the term liberty are protected by the Federal Constitution from invasion by the States." *Whitney v. California,* 274 U.S. 357, 373, 47 S.Ct. 641, 647, 71 L.Ed. 1095 (1927) (concurring opinion). "[T]he guaranties of due process, though having their roots in Magna Carta's *'per legem terrae'* and considered as procedural safeguards 'against executive usurpation and tyranny,' have in this country 'become bulwarks also against arbitrary legislation.'" *Poe v. Ullman,* 367 U.S. 497, 541, 81 S.Ct. 1752, 1776, 6 L.Ed.2d 989 (1961) (Harlan, J., dissenting from dismissal on jurisdictional grounds) (quoting *Hurtado v. California,* 110 U.S. 516, 532, 4 S.Ct. 111, 119, 28 L.Ed. 232 (1884)).

Casey concerned the Due Process Clause of the *Fourteenth* Amendment. Whether the original public meaning of the Fourteenth Amendment clause differs significantly from that of its precursor in the Fifth Amendment is a matter of current scholarly debate. *See* Ryan C. Williams, *The One and Only Substantive Due Process Clause,* 120 YALE L.J. 408 (2010); Nathan S. Chapman & Michael W. McConnell, *Due Process as Separation of Powers,* 121 YALE L. J. 1672 (2012). The Court's current jurisprudence does not relevantly distinguish between the two guarantees.

45. Bolling v. Sharpe, 347 U.S. 497, 500 (1954) (unanimous Opinion of the Court, per Warren, C.J.):

> Segregation in public education is not reasonably related to any proper governmental objective, and thus it imposes on Negro children of the District of Columbia a burden that constitutes an arbitrary deprivation of their liberty in violation of the Due Process Clause.
>
> In view of our decision that the Constitution prohibits the states from maintaining racially segregated public schools, it would be unthinkable that the same Constitution would impose a lesser duty on the Federal Government. We hold that racial segregation in the public schools of the District of Columbia is a denial of the due process of law guaranteed by the Fifth Amendment to the Constitution.

46. John Hart Ely, Democracy and Distrust 32 (1980) (characterizing the *Bolling* Court's claim to get equal protection out of due process as "gibberish, both syntactically and historically"). Jack Balkin disagrees (Jack M. Balkin, Living Originalism 244–55 (2011)), relying on early nineteenth-century case law that condemned as violations of due process various statutes targeting individuals for adverse treatment. But those cases concerned statutes that took away things explicitly covered by the Due Process Clause—"life, liberty, or property." The courts in those cases were straightforwardly applying a guarantee that the government could not kill people, lock them up, or take away their property without due process. Just passing a statute was not in itself due process. The principle of Magna Carta required more than that. Daniel Webster famously said as much in his *Dartmouth College* address. (Trustees of Dartmouth College v. Woodward, 17 U.S. (4 Wheat.) 518, 581 (1819).) Balkin advances from those cases to a conclusion that the Fifth Amendment's Due Process Clause limits how Congress can hand out benefits, like education. Balkin reads the Due Process Clause as if it is an open-ended promise of due process, just as the Equal Protection Clause is an open-ended promise of equal protection. But the Due Process Clause is explicitly *only* about the terms on which government *deprives* people of life, liberty, or property. The clause has nothing to say about the terms on which government *gives*. There are real reasons why a document apportioning roles among lawgiving institutions might draw that distinction. The further courts move beyond protecting people from government, and into policing more pervasively how governments are governing, the more pervasively the courts *become* the government. The U.S. Constitution does give the courts quite a lot of governing to do, and would give them more if it included so-called "positive" rights to have government do things for us. But nothing in the Fifth Amendment's due process language does that.
47. Griswold v. Connecticut, 381 U.S. 479, 484 (1965) (Opinion of the Court, per Douglas, J.).
48. *See* Laurence Claus, *Implication and the Concept of a Constitution*, 69 Aust. L. J. 887, 896–904 (1995).
49. On the inaptitude of attempts to draw support for illustrative reasoning from the Ninth Amendment ("[t]he enumeration in the Constitution of certain rights shall not be construed to deny or disparage others retained by the people"), *see* Laurence Claus, *Protecting Rights from Rights: Enumeration, Disparagement, and the Ninth Amendment*, 79 Notre Dame L. Rev. 585 (2004). *Compare* Ryan C. Williams, *The Ninth Amendment*

as a Rule of Construction, 111 COLUM. L. REV. 498 (2011), addressing the voluminous literature since 2004.

50. Calder v. Bull, 3 U.S. (3 Dall.) 386, 399 (1798) (Iredell, J.). Chase's overtly illustrative reasoning appears, *id.*, at 387–89. In 1787, Iredell wrote the following in private correspondence: "Without an express Constitution the powers of the Legislature would undoubtedly have been absolute (as the Parliament in Great Britain is held to be), and any act passed not inconsistent with natural justice (for that curb is avowed by the judges even in England), would have been binding on the people." II GRIFFITH JOHN MCREE, LIFE AND CORRESPONDENCE OF JAMES IREDELL, ONE OF THE ASSOCIATE JUSTICES OF THE SUPREME COURT 172 (1858).
51. *See* RONALD DWORKIN, LAW'S EMPIRE (1986). We humans argue all the time. What makes the outcomes of some arguments *lawgiving* is that we have a custom of letting the say-so of some humans *settle* some arguments and signal what our likely behaviors and expectations will be. Hercules' words distinctively matter to us in a way that causes us to call them law and similar sounds coming from an eccentric on a soapbox *not* law. The focus of enquiry into the nature of law therefore needs to be on what Hercules' communicative actions distinctively succeed in doing and how they succeed in doing it. Hercules' deciding what to do, like all of our individual decisions about what to do each day, is of course a matter for all-things-considered moral judgment. In making those moral judgments each day, we of course reflect on "the people we want to be and the community we aim to have." (*Id.*, at 413.) What *existing law* contributes to those judgments are the reasons for action that we get from learning about the people we already are and the community we already have.
52. Cooper v. Aaron, 358 U.S. 1 (1958). The Court's holding "that the federal judiciary is supreme in the exposition of the law of the Constitution, and . . . that the interpretation of the Fourteenth Amendment enunciated by this Court in the Brown case is the supreme law of the land, and Art. VI of the Constitution makes it of binding effect on the States," *id.*, at 18, necessarily implied that other government actors are not free to interpret the Court's words according to those other actors' own perceptions of political perfection.

CHAPTER 10

1. OLIVER WENDELL HOLMES, JR., THE COMMON LAW 1 (1881).
2. HANS CHRISTIAN ANDERSEN, ANDERSEN'S FAIRY TALES 263–68 (E. V. Lucas & H. B. Paull trans., 1945) (1837).

3. *See* LOUIS MENAND, THE METAPHYSICAL CLUB 205–10, 216–17 (2001).
4. Charles Sanders Peirce, *How to Make Our Ideas Clear,* 12 POPULAR SCIENCE MONTHLY, 286, 293 (1878).
5. Oliver Wendell Holmes, Jr., *The Path of the Law,* 10 HARV. L. REV. 457, 458 (1897) (laying "down some first principles for the study of this body of dogma or systematized prediction which we call the law").
6. THE WIZARD OF OZ (Motion Picture, Metro-Goldwyn-Mayer, 1939), based on L. FRANK BAUM, THE WONDERFUL WIZARD OF OZ (1900).

ACKNOWLEDGMENTS

This book expands for a wider audience an account of law that first appeared on the Social Science Research Network in 2008 and in the pages of the *University of Illinois Law Review* in 2009 as *The Empty Idea of Authority*. I am grateful to those who have helped me along the way to a place where this could be written. First, my thanks go to the three distinguished jurists who mentored me in clerkships—the great Australians John M. Macrossan and Sir Ronald Wilson, and the great American Frank H. Easterbrook. Next, to Oxford—to my doctoral supervisor, the brilliant John Finnis, and to the splendid and supportive law dons of Christ Church, Edward Burn, John Cartwright, and Edwin Simpson. To the University of Queensland faculty who shepherded me onward, in particular Darrell Lumb and C. John F. Kidd, and to Queensland Supreme Court Librarian Aladin Rahemtula for igniting my imagination about what might await in America. To the faculty past and present and those from elsewhere who have visited us at the University of San Diego, for guidance and friendship—in particular, Larry Alexander, Carl Auerbach, Jordan Barry, Laura Berend, Roy Brooks, Lynne Dallas, Michael Devitt, Donald Dripps, Robert Fellmeth, Stanley Fish, Gail Heriot, Yale Kamisar, Michael Kelly, Adam Kolber, Edward Larson, Bert Lazerow, Pierre Legrand, Orly Lobel, Lesley McAllister, David McGowan, Miranda McGowan, Leslie Oster, Kris Panikowski, Frank Partnoy, Teresa Player, Saikrishna Prakash, Jack Rakove, Michael Ramsey, Lisa Ramsey, Michael Rappaport, Maimon Schwarzschild, Ted Sichelman, Steven Smith, Allen Snyder, Lawrence Solum, Mary Jo Wiggins, Christopher Wonnell, and Fred Zacharias. And to Deans Daniel Rodriguez and Kevin Cole for providing encouragement and summer research support and now Dean Stephen Ferruolo, who arrived in the homestretch semester and let me stay off the appointments committee! Also invaluable have been USD student research assistants Husam Atari, Matthew Ichinose, and Ryan Scott, USD staff Brigid Bennett, Miriam Deberry, and Arlene Penticoff, and reference librarians Ruth Levor, Melissa Fung, and Jane Larrington.

My thanks also go to my editors, and to those others who played pivotal roles in the production process, in particular, Michelle Lipinski, Gwen Colvin, Mary Rosewood, Ninell Silberberg, Bhuvaneswari H. Nagarajan, and Jennifer Gong. I am also grateful to the insightful anonymous reviewers of the book proposal for Oxford University Press and Cambridge University Press. Friends who have valuably commented and encouraged include, in particular, Beth Noveck, who afforded me far more of her valuable time than even close friendship warrants, and Jorge Barrera, Bobby Bartlett, Justin Bois, Stephen Brien, Megan Callan, Edward Jocson, David Johnson, Jefferey Lin, David Linden, Donald Markwell, Elizabeth Pierce, Jeff Pojanowski, Michael Prentiss, Nicholas Quinn Rosenkranz, and Paul Waldau. My thanks also go to John Knight for introducing me to systems theory. And finally, I am deeply grateful to my parents, Paul and Gloria, and to my siblings, Andrew and Fiona, for their love and support.

INDEX

CPSIA information can be obtained
at www.ICGtesting.com
Printed in the USA
BVHW052006230719
554168BV00011B/479/P

9 780199 735099